COLLEGE READING & STUDY STRATEGY PROGRAMS

RONA F. FLIPPO
Fitchburg State College

DAVID C. CAVERLY
Southwest Texas State University

Editors

International Reading Association
Newark, Delaware 19714

The International Reading Association attempts, through its publications, to provide a forum for a wide spectrum of opinions on reading. This policy permits divergent viewpoints without assuming the endorsement of the Association.

Copyright 1991 by the
International Reading Association, Inc.

Library of Congress Cataloging in Publication Data

College reading and study strategy programs [edited by]
    Rona F. Flippo, David C. Caverly.
        p.   cm.
    Includes bibliographical references and index.
    1. Reading (Higher education). 2. Study, Method of.
3. Educational evaluation. I. Flippo, Rona F. II. Caverly,
David C. III. International Reading Association.
LB2395.3C64   1991   90-24780
428.4'071'1 – dc20   CIP
ISBN 0-87207-362-9

Cover design: Larry Husfelt

Contents

Foreword   *v*

Introduction   *vii*

1
Reading, Writing, and Academic Literacy   1
Sharon L. Pugh and Faridah Pawan

2
Program Organization   28
Kathy Carpenter and Linda L. Johnson

3
Program Evaluation   70
Hunter R. Boylan, Anita P. George, and Barbara S. Bonham

4
Reading Tests   118
*Rona F. Flippo, Madlyn L. Hanes, and
Carol J. Cashen*
Appendix to Chapter 4: Commercially
Available Tests Reviewed   173
Rona F. Flippo and Carol J. Cashen

Author Index   211

Subject Index   214

Foreword

College reading, a.k.a. developmental reading, study skills, and developmental studies, has been the unheralded workhorse of the field of reading for nearly six decades.

College reading classrooms have served as experimental laboratories for many generations of literacy researchers. College reading kept interest alive in study skills areas such as memory training, writing, notetaking, text anxiety, high-order literacy, and personal/social adjustment when no one else was paying them much mind. College reading has been a dependable source of graduate assistantships for advanced degree students. College reading also has been one of the hidden resources in helping minorities find their way through college when other, higher priced programs have flashed and waned.

Now, after some 60 years of evolution and silent service, college reading comes of age through the voices of the authors and editors of this book. Having read it with relish, I can assure you that it is a valuable contribution to the substance of the field, as well as an important historical marker.

With this publication, neither college reading nor the larger field of literacy education will ever be the same.

Anthony V. Manzo
University of Missouri-Kansas City

Introduction

Developing and organizing a college-level reading and study strategy program can be a monumental task for those new to the field. Keeping an existing program vibrant and dynamic enough to meet the literacy challenges of the 1990s can be difficult even for seasoned veterans. Until now, no comprehensive collection of knowledge about managing reading and study strategy programs has been available for practitioners, administrators, and researchers. This book— along with its companion volume, *Teaching Reading and Study Strategies at the College Level*—provides a review of the theoretical, empirical, and programmatic issues in this field for both the new and the veteran professional.

Chapter 1 sets the stage with a review of current thinking about the development of literacy at the college level. Through an insightful and provocative discussion, Pugh and Pawan present three views of how functional literacy at this level should be defined.

In Chapter 2, Carpenter and Johnson look at the various organizational schemes of reading and study strategy programs at the college level. After reviewing historical trends in the growth of college reading programs, they present four perspectives on the organization of current programs and the research support for each perspective.

Boylan, George, and Bonham review the literature surrounding the evaluation of college reading and study strategy programs in Chapter 3. Based on an overview of the changing role of education evaluation during the latter half of this century, they present current theoretical models for evaluation. Next, they examine the applications of these models within a variety of existing reading and study strategy programs, as well as the implications of such applications. Finally, they explore trends and issues in program evaluation.

In Chapter 4, Flippo, Hanes, and Cashen discuss the issues and problems surrounding the assessment of reading at the college level. Using the origins of college reading tests as a foundation, they explore the various types of tests currently available. They follow this review with a thorough discussion of the issues involved in selecting an appropriate reading test. Finally, Flippo and Cashen selectively review many of the commercial reading tests available for use with the college population. This evaluation is based on a point-by-point critique of each test, summarized in a handy appendix at the end of the chapter.

In the interest of covering our topic in the depth it merits, we chose to limit our scope to reading and study strategy programs. Although many college-level remedial and developmental programs include components in adult basic education, English as a second language, writing, mathematics, tutoring, and counseling, we chose not to include these related but somewhat separate areas.

To provide comprehensiveness and organizational consistency, we asked the authors to include four general components in their chapters: (1) an introduction and rationale for the topic; (2) a review of the relevant literature; (3) a synthesis of this literature, including a discussion of implications, recommendations, and future avenues of research; and (4) a bibliography of references and suggested readings. The authors have indicated the most relevant works on this list by noting them with an asterisk.

We chose not to force conformity on our authors in terms of the terminology they used. The college programs included here, and the personnel teaching or directing them, go by many labels. We let the authors of each chapter decide on the terms that seemed to fit most appropriately with their orientation and experience.

We believe you will find this book the most comprehensive and up-to-date source available on college reading and study strategy programs. While several excellent books address similar topics for elementary or secondary populations, this is one of the first to thoroughly examine college-level programs. It is intended to provide specific and necessary information to a diverse audience, including practitioners looking for ready answers, administrators interested in developing relevant and beneficial programs, and university professors training personnel for roles in college reading and study strategy programs without the benefit of a textbook or compilation of readings. This volume also should be of interest to reading educators, educational researchers, and librarians who want to add a comprehensive review of the literature in this area to their collections.

RFF
DCC

Acknowledgments

We wish to thank the International Reading Association for recognizing the need for this book. We are indebted to the individuals in IRA who encouraged and assisted us throughout the various stages of the manuscript's preparation.

The field of reading owes a great debt to those who have devoted so much of their talents, careers, research, and writing to enriching our knowledge base in reading and study strategy instruction at postsecondary levels. We wish to acknowledge their critical contributions. We also wish to thank the professional organizations that have played an important role in advancing knowledge in this field.

We owe our greatest thanks to the excellent researchers and writers who authored the chapters included in this book. They were invited to contribute because of their expertise in both the specific area covered in their chapter and the field of college reading in general. Thank you for making this book possible.

This book is dedicated to Al Raygor, who provided his inspiration, and to Ron Mitchell, who supported our project.

RFF
DCC

Contributors

Barbara S. Bonham
National Center for
  Developmental Education
Appalachian State University
Boone, North Carolina

Hunter R. Boylan
National Center for
  Developmental Education
Appalachian State University
Boone, North Carolina

Kathy Carpenter
University of Nebraska-Kearney
Kearney, Nebraska

Carol J. Cashen
University of Wisconsin-Parkside
Kenosha, Wisconsin

David C. Caverly
Southwest Texas State University
San Marcos, Texas

Rona F. Flippo
Fitchburg State College
Fitchburg, Massachusetts

Anita P. George
The Learning Center
Mississippi State, Mississippi

Madlyn L. Hanes
Penn State University-Delaware
  County Campus
Media, Pennsylvania

Linda L. Johnson
University of Iowa
Iowa City, Iowa

Faridah Pawan
Universiti Malaya
Kuala Lumpur, Malaysia

Sharon L. Pugh
Indiana University
Bloomington, Indiana

1

Reading, Writing, and Academic Literacy

Sharon L. Pugh
Faridah Pawan

The news is out, only it isn't really news. "The Conditions of the Professoriate: Attitudes and Trends, 1989," a report by the Carnegie Foundation for the Advancement of Teaching, finds that college and university faculty are overwhelmingly critical of the preparation of undergraduates for higher education. We are not surprised by this finding; we have been listening to similar judgments for years. Arons (1979) warned college professors not to expect all students to possess cognitive skills such as the ability to understand variables, perform propositional thinking, recognize knowledge gaps, distinguish between observations and inferences, reason hypothetically, and attain metacognitive awareness. When we subtract these processes, a basic kind of literacy is left that at best would prepare students for the absorption of information in the lowest dualistic concept of knowledge and learning (Perry, 1970).

Others have documented a lack of classroom experiences that would foster higher order thought processes. Applebee (1984), reporting case studies of writing across the curriculum and across grade levels in 200 schools, found that students spend only 3 percent of their school and homework time writing compositions of one paragraph or more. The emphasis in school writing, he notes, is on demonstrating previous learning rather than on building new knowledge; this emphasis focuses attention on information rather than on discourse. Topics assigned often elicited a superficial survey response rather than deep engagement with personally important subject matter. In an intensive study of 1,016 classrooms across the nation, Goodlad (1985) found that high school students spend about 16 percent of class time writing, but this includes nondiscourse activities such as fill-in exercises and short answers. Over 50 percent of class time is spent listening to teachers talk, while only 5 percent is spent on student-centered discussion, which suggests a lack of experience in dialectics and argument.

To these reports Hirsch (1989) adds the evidence of cross-national comparisons, which invariably place American students in the lowest strata of achievement. Hirsch concludes that in many institutions "the educational level of incoming students is so low that the first and second years of college work must be largely devoted to remedial work" (p. 29).

These reports clearly indicate a need for improvement. But while it is easy to reiterate the need for new and intensified school reform efforts, talk is not enough. College educators have yet to define their own role in bringing about improvements in student learning at all levels—a role that must include formulating and communicating a concept of academic literacy that is truly functional in postsecondary learning.

Views of Literacy

To begin, we must acknowledge that our concept is a complex one requiring definition from at least three angles.

One angle is the relationship of literacy to its traditional components—reading and writing—and how this relationship relates to the print cultures that have dominated Western thought for the past few centuries. The second angle is the mind-set that has grown out of these print cultures—ways of thinking and valuing that have become so familiar that we may find them difficult to examine. Literacy is more than proficiency with written language; it is a state of mind. The third angle (which we cannot explore in the present discussion but which will be increasingly important in the future) involves the relationship between print and computer literacies, again going beyond technical proficiency and looking at the mind-sets that each medium fosters and exploits.

Eisenstein (1979) points out that Western society lives, breathes, and thrives on printed matter. As print technologies have advanced, the availability of printed material has progressed from abundant to overwhelming. Kozol (1985) argues that we need a literacy that enables us to bring order and meaning not only to this superabundance of print but also to life amid the information explosion. In any case, this print overload has led to a renewed focus on reading in the development of academic skills.

With regard to reading, works from Bloom's taxonomy to Adler and van Doren's (1972) *How to Read a Book* have emphasized higher order thinking. Clifford (1984) reports that Western academic institutions define literate individuals as those who are able to synthesize, organize, and interpret ideas as well as to apply information gained from reading to new situations. Adler and van Doren, Culler (1975), and Fish (1980) would add that literate individuals also are familiar with cultural and conventional "vraisemblance" (de Beaugrande, 1984)—the various genres of thought embedded in texts. Such high-level literacy abilities are the means by which individuals become "informed readers" (Fish), or those guided by awareness of their own prior knowledge and its contribution to the new meanings they construct from texts. Such readers attend not only to what texts say to them but also to what they say to texts—an interaction rather than a one-way transmission, with the goal of discovering new meanings and insight.

In a similar vein, Freire and Macedo's (1987) concept of literacy includes the ability to read oneself. In fact, they believe that this ability should precede more conventional aspects of literacy. They claim that "the very act of learning to read and write has to start from a very comprehensive act of reading the world, something which humans do before reading the words" (xiii). Reading the world includes taking a conscious approach toward learning and the acquisition of knowledge. Readers of the world (and therefore of themselves) focus on knowledge relevant to their future needs as well as those of the present. This "power of envisagement," as Freire terms it, results in hypothetical thinking and experimentation to test the truth and usefulness of theoretically conceived ideas.

Christiansen (1988) expresses a similar view of literacy, but with emphasis on writing rather than reading. She describes how a group of innercity high school seniors used their literacy to gain the knowledge they needed to challenge the reasons for their low SAT scores. They did this by historically analyzing the tests, the organization that markets them, and the relationship of both to racial and class issues. Their written critiques, in the form of both journal entries and essays, enabled the students to realize and assess their literacy abilities far more accurately than did the test (which, ironically, is considered a measure of academic preparedness). The test scores still stood, but the students were intellectually empowered by the experience of discovering the roots of the problem and articulating an informed stance about it.

The Critical Thinking Movement

From the previous discussion, and particularly the last example, we can see that academic literacy surpasses a language-based concept. While language plays its usual vital role, we assert that literacy is a state of mind that grows out of a particular communication culture. Illych (1987) contends that the mind-set that grows out of a print culture is shared by all members of that culture, even those who do not read and write. This interesting argument is an example of the view that by themselves, particular behaviors such as reading and writing define literacy only in a weak sense. To define literacy in a strong sense, we can look at statements by those in the critical thinking movement.

Paul (1987) made a distinction between weak (micrological) and strong (macrological) critical thinking skills that can provide a parallel for defining micro- and macrological senses of literacy. This distinction centers on the concept of dialectical or dialogical reasoning—an approach to knowledge building that makes use of multiple perspectives, and an open-minded search for the best truth given the current state of knowledge.

Problem solving in the macrological sense involves the gathering and critical evaluation of information. People's primary tendency, however, is to be egocentric and "strongly prone to irrational belief formation"; their secondary nature, which must be deliberately developed, is their "implicit capacity to function as rational persons" (Paul, p. 131).

Paul advocates instruction that leads students to be relativistic and open-minded in their thinking, to explore anomalies, and to face information that confronts their own beliefs. He regards dialogical thinking as being related to character, and strong critical thinking as being integral to the individual's ethical position in life. In this, Paul seems to agree with Perry (1970), who argues that intellectual and ethical development proceed in tandem along a continuum from dualism (a finite view of knowledge) to multiplicity (acceptance of diversity) to relativism (an infinite view of knowledge in which one stakes out a reasonable turf with flexible boundaries). At the most advanced stages of this development, students commit themselves to an intellectual stance to govern their identities and lifestyles as well as the types of knowledge and information they select to process. This highest form of literacy is achieved only with the understanding that such commitment is not a rigid stance but an unfolding activity to be subjected to the ongoing test of new information.

Belenky et al. (1986) take Perry's notions a step farther, arguing for the social nature of knowledge and against the notion that individuals can take a stand unrelated to the positions of others within a community. They believe that the ultimate objective of literacy should not be the ability to justify one's own way of believing, understanding, or knowing but to connect with those of others. The goal of connected knowers, in contrast to that of separate knowers, is to achieve intellectual and personal collaboration. Such language seems to harmonize with Paul's views and suggests that the unself-centered rationality he advocates is not so secondary in some segments of the population.

The theme of connection between intellectual and ethical growth is also strong in Kozol's (1985) endorsement of Charles Muscatine's concept of humane literacy (from a conversation with Muscatine cited by Kozol, p. 174). This concept includes attributes that could be considered elements of character: informed irreverence (a questioning stance arising from a broad array of knowledge), tolerance for ambiguity, political sophistication, respect for history, wise anger (as a logical response to exploitation), arrogance of taste (confidence in one's unique views), and global literacy. Unlike other views of critical literacy, Kozol's concept has content as well as process implications. To respect the lessons of history one must know history, to be politically sophisticated requires a certain kind of experience, and to be globally literate requires some attention to geography.

In support of his view of cultural literacy, Hirsch (1987) argues that school curricula have overemphasized processes and denigrated information. To redress this imbalance, he advocates the return of information to the center of education, in the form of a national curriculum. He sees facts as the capital learners invest, and further learning as the interest their investments earn (Hirsch, 1989). Thus, Hirsch considers literacy an accumulative commodity—a view that contrasts with those of writers such as Paul and Kozol.

Comparing Hirsch's and Kozol's positions on literacy—one called *cultural,* the other *humane*—provides one basis for distinguishing between micro- and macrological concepts. Micrological concepts focus on particular operations and accumulations, whether of language skills, particular content knowledge, or any other separable elements of the construct. Along with Hirsch's cultural literacy, we would place in this category studies focusing on reading and writing per se and their interrelationships. We are not arguing that these aspects of literacy are inferior or unimportant. We *are* arguing that a micrological view is inoperable without the context of a macrological perspective.

In the macrological view, literacy is a state of mind—a world view that encompasses beliefs, values, expectations, discriminations, and styles as well as particular competencies. It might be best described in the framework of Kuhn's (1970) notion of paradigm shifts; the development of knowledge is an ongoing, cyclical process in which each level of discovery is a plateau from which to launch new explorations. According to this view, the technology of exploration—whether it be stone tools, printing presses, or computers—is relevant only within the context of the vision that employs it. In that sense, a single literacy is developing through particular disciplines and media, and we are traveling in its orbit at the threshold of the twenty-first century.

Citing Schwartz and Olgivy (1979), Marzano et al. (1988) summarize characteristics of the shift in prevailing views of knowledge at the end of the twentieth century. They identify seven major areas of change from earlier eras:

1. *From simple to complex.* Instead of trying to reduce areas to their simplest terms, we now look at how open systems interact.

2. *From hierarchical to heterarchical.* The more recent view rejects the idea of increasing powers of know-

ing with an ultimate explanation at the top and looks for lateral more than hierarchical connections.

3. *From mechanical to holographic.* Paralleling a move from machines composed of moving parts to machines with hidden circuits, we have moved from a view of cause-effect sequences to the idea of total and simultaneous interconnectedness.

4. *From determinate to indeterminate.* We no longer believe that reality is "knowable" enough that with diligent effort we can accumulate enough knowledge to make precise predictions. We now aim for possibility and probability.

5. *From linear to mutual causality.* Having dispensed with a unidirectional view of cause and effect, we have adopted a notion of recursive feedback among interacting systems, again eliminating simple predictability.

6. *From assembly to morphogenesis.* A building block concept has given way to an organic concept in which new forms can arise from interactions among systems.

7. *From objective to perspective.* We have given up the myth that the observer can operate separately and neutrally with regard to the observed. The knower is inextricably involved with the knowledge, which is itself fluid and changing.

In summary, if literacy is a state of mind—as we contend it is—contemporary literacy must accommodate contemporary views of knowledge.

In the following sections of this chapter, we will look at academic literacy in terms of the distinction between micrological and macrological perspectives. Micrological studies focus on particular competencies, most often reading, writing, and their interconnections. Macrological studies attempt to work within a broader framework for conceptualizing the mind-set of academic literacy.

Micrological Studies of Literacy

When we look at the existing literature, we find two main purposes being pursued: to explain or conceptualize the case for linking reading and writing, and to make suggestions for linking the two processes. Most studies conclude that reading and writing are connected, mutually supportive, and fundamentally involved in thinking. Terminology for discussing a cognitive view of literacy is becoming established. Common terms include *intentionality,* referring to the driving force of purpose; *transaction,* meaning the contracts that readers and writers enter into with one another; and *intertextuality,* which draws our attention to the fact that texts exist everywhere, in print as well as in other forms, and that these texts constantly mingle in the individual's mind to produce novel concepts.

The Reading/Writing Connection

A number of studies focus on the role of writing instruction in improving reading. Stotsky (1982) discusses a number of writing activities that have been linked to reading improvement, including dictation, reproduction (the paragraph paraphrasing common in foreign language instruction), other paraphrasing exercises, precis writing, sentence combining, and sentence pattern practice. She acknowledges that these activities stick to a literal level of understanding, but considers them useful for that reason because they "give students structures, active practice in grappling literally with the language, and ideas of [the] forms of discourse" that are characteristic of informational and argumentative material (p. 339).

Marshall (1987) looks at the effects of writing tasks on short story reading, concluding that analytic writing improved literature test scores. But experimental studies that look at results in terms of test scores are not as common as more conceptual approaches that explain and apply assumed connections. Sanacore (1983) emphasizes both prior knowledge and writing as means of improving reading. To help students apply prior knowledge, he cites methods using guided prereading, structured overviews, graphic organizers, or study systems. Instruction in writing based on types of forms, patterns, and purposes in various texts provides tools for understanding written discourse. Sanacore also recommends that teachers participate in the class's reading and writing activities to encourage students' awareness of text comprehension as an act of composition and vice versa.

Gebhard (1983) stresses four principles that should underpin a program to teach writing in reading and content area courses: 1) expanding the audience by having students work in pairs or small groups; 2) ensuring that writing develops out of a broad context of interests; 3) varying material and assignments to provide experience in both analysis and production of a range of logical patterns; and 4) assigning writing (including journal writing) that will help students integrate new into known material. All four of these principles can provide some means of integrating reading and writing. Supporting this view, Browning (1986) describes a strategy of writing journal reactions to reading assignments that improves student involvement in reading.

Other studies emphasize the application of reading instruction to writing improvement on the basis of the same principles as those that apply writing instruction to reading. Pitts (1986) concludes that reading a text while hearing it read aloud improves the writing of basic skills freshmen. Kennedy (1980) mentions four effects on writing of instruction in reading. Students 1) develop a sense of the sound of a written text; 2) become more precise with words; 3) become aware of the writer's planning and communication strategies; and 4) gain competence as readers, and therefore revisers, of their own texts.

Kennedy also notes that many college students demonstrate insufficient experience with written discourse. She asserts that this inexperience is evident even in mental/motor behaviors such as handwriting, spelling, and oral reading. It is even more evident in comprehension problems, including the inability to draw inferences and shape inner thoughts. Kennedy describes this inability as "an articulatory rather than a conceptual disorder" (p. 139), and asserts that the cure is plenty of practice writing about what has been read. The active analysis of the reading material that the writing process requires will help students form schemata for further comprehension.

Broderick and Caverly (1987), in their review of the uses of microcomputers in the teaching of writing, describe how the computer can promote interactive learning in the prewriting, writing, editing, and publishing stages of composition. When judiciously managed, this interaction enhances students' use of reading during the writing process by making them critical readers of their own texts.

Stotsky (1983) considers both the theoretical and the applied studies of the relationships between reading and writing to be diffuse and incomplete. She reviews a large number of empirical studies, organized into three categories: correlational studies, those examining the effects of writing on reading, and those exploring the effects of reading on writing. Subjects in these studies ranged from young children to college students. The conclusion Stotsky draws from the correlational studies is that better writers tend to be better readers and vice versa. The experimental studies show that writing instruction can improve reading when the instruction is specifically designed to do so, but not when reading improvement is sought as a casual byproduct. Increased reading experience, Stotsky concludes, has a globally positive effect on writng, but reading instruction per se has not been found to improve writing. She points out that these empirical studies were concerned almost exclusively with academic texts and writing and were therefore dependent on mastery of what she calls "the language of formal schooling" (p. 637). They focused on ways in which instruction could help students acquire this special language rather than on deeper levels of reading/writing relationships.

Stotsky's recommendations for future directions in research emphasize descriptive studies rather than examinations of instructional effects. She suggests that researchers find out more about particular groups, such as poor writers who are also poor readers and poor writers who are good readers. She also recommends more case study investigations of the amount and kind of reading done by good and poor writers to help clarify effects. Another recommendation is that better measures of the various processes involved be developed. Stotsky calls for more research on reading and writing in second language learning.

In their review of the research, Tierney and Lays (1986) summarize the conclusions as follows:

- There is a moderate and fluctuating correlation among measures of reading and writing achievement and attitude.
- Selected experiences demonstrate positive mutual effects between reading and writing.
- Certain values and behaviors are drawn from reading into writing and vice versa.
- Successful writers use reading and vice versa.

Tierney and Lays attribute any failure among practitioners to appreciate the interrelationships between reading and writing to a simplistic view of how these relationships should be defined and assessed.

Birnbaum (1986) reports observations at various grade and college levels demonstrating the relationship between reflective thinking and the use of written language. She quotes at length from the statement of a college senior who "exemplifies much that we strive for in literacy" because he is "at home in the world of written language. As he shuttles between reading and writing, he extrapolates from one process and uses that knowledge in the other" (pp. 40-41). Birnbaum suggests the need for additional case studies of older, exemplary readers/writers, longitudinal studies of forms of discourse at various age levels, and studies of the characteristics of reflective behavior.

Linking Language Processes

It should be observed that some writers warn against oversimplifying the parallels between reading and writing. Goodman and Goodman (1983) point out that certain pragmatic considerations must be taken into account—such as the fact that normally the demand for reading is much greater than it is for writing, and that while people need not write while reading, they must read while writing.

Langer (1986b) similarly cautions against taking an overly simplistic view that may obscure differences between reading and writing processes. She concludes that although reading and writing share important characteristics as meaning-construction activities, as processes they differ markedly in terms of intent and emphasis on particular operations.

While some writers caution against exaggerating the similarities between reading and writing, a number of studies present conceptual frameworks for viewing the two as integrated processes. Tierney and Pearson (1983), for example, propose a composing model of reading applicable to both reading and writing, consisting of five steps: (1) planning, which involves goal setting and knowledge mobilization; (2) drafting, which entails schema selection and instantiation; (3) aligning, which includes collaboration and role immersion; (4) revising, which involves reexamination and redevelopment; and (5) monitoring, or the conscious supervision of these processes.

Trosky and Wood (1982) offer another model that equates reading and writing processes. With this three-step model, different aspects of writing are linked to aspects of reading. In the first step, the composing aspect of writing is related to assembling elements and identifying sequences in reading; in the second step, transcription (putting the composition on paper) is related to reflection; and in the third step, editing is related to reaction.

Other writers point out similar relationships. Crafton (1983) emphasizes the common development of both processes of literacy in early learning. Atwell (1983) presents the sociolin-guistic basis for the interrelatedness of all four language systems (speaking, listening, reading, and writing). Aulls (1983) com-pares skill, psycholinguistic, and discourse models of reading, concluding that the last most clearly integrates reading and writing. Moxley (1984) discusses the central role of meaning construction in reading and writing. Rubin and Hansen (1986) identify several kinds of knowledge critical to both reading and writing, including informational, structural (discourse forms and writing formulas), transactional (reader/author relation-ships), aesthetic, and process knowledge. This perspective views both composing and comprehending as crucial to thought processes: composing because it actively engages the learner in constructing, developing, and expressing meaning, and comprehending because it requires the reconstruction of meaning expressed by another writer.

A number of recent studies have provided a close-up view of reader/writers at work, giving us new insights into the implications of the relationship. In a study of a small class of students enrolled in a freshman basic skills course combining reading and writing, Reagan (1985) found that as the course progressed students changed from a paragraph approach to writing to a more schematic planning approach. They also moved from viewing revision as a separate process to seeing it as part of the overall composing process. Case studies of two students illustrated the strong influence of personality and cul-tural factors on any performance in school, suggesting the shortcomings of quantitative data in efforts to understand intel-lectual processes. This study underscores the value of qualita-tive data in understanding changes in students' composing processes.

Dahl (1984) investigated reading/writing transactions from the learner's perspective in a special section of her fresh-man-level learning skills course. By examining schema maps, compositions, journal entries, and interview reports, as well as her own observation notes, she identified many ways in which reading and writing interact in students' learning and problem-solving efforts. In both reading and writing, students were primarily concerned with building and revising meaning. When they read unfamiliar materials, they patterned summaries more closely on the original text than they did when reading more familiar materials. Also, writing they produced shortly after reading tended to reflect the syntax and language of the text. These findings suggest that students were actively trying to model the kind of literacy they identified in their academic texts. They also suggest that students use language associated with unfamiliar knowledge as a kind of prop in the constructive process of building their own schemas for this knowledge. Smith (1985) observed the same kind of phenomenon in written summaries by graduate students dealing with subjects in which they had no background.

Dahl (1984) also found that mapping information and switching back and forth between the reader's and writer's roles helped students conceptualize meaning and perceive new relationships. Based on these and other findings, she proposed a transaction model of reading and writing delineating four shared processes and four transactive relationships, or ways in which reading and writing affect one another. This model provides a useful structure for the practitioner seeking ways to relate reading and writing.

Studies such as those described above help us understand not only how students construct meaning from their texts but also how they guide their own development as readers, writers, and learners. Sternglass and Pugh (1986) have collected extensive data of this kind from a seminar in which 16 graduate students kept retrospective journals on their reading and writing processes over a full semester. The researchers found that each student developed a narrative of him or herself in which both the retrospective journals and the seminar's required papers played a role in the plot. We need to replicate this inquiry in other settings to find out how college students develop their learning personas as academic literates.

Kucer (1983), studying a group of freshmen enrolled in the basic skills section of a required freshman writing course, compared the characteristics of texts rated high and low in coherence by independent raters. He found that while writers of less coherent texts provided as many propositions for readers to use in building a macrostructure, the role of these propositions in the macrostructure often was unclear. These writers also were less able to provide sufficient cues for text processing. Their texts contained more disputed propositions, and readers were less sure whether their interpretations matched those of the authors. Finally, Kucer found evidence that a writing instruction curriculum based on reading helped students attain better control over text by teaching them to provide cues from which to build a coherent reading.

In her dissertation and subsequent monograph, Shanklin (1982) synthesizes the major theories relating to reading and writing integration, and proposes a reading-theory-based model of the writing process. The relationships she notes between reading and writing include the following:

- Both are constructive processes.
- Both call for use of world knowledge and interpretive procedures in the construction of meaning.
- Both are based on making new transactions in establishing meaning.
- Both make use of self-provided feedback.
- Both are developmental processes, occurring naturally in a literate society.
- In both, errors are likely to be evidence of challenges in processing or efforts to explore unfamiliar meanings.

Moving Toward a Macrological Perspective

A number of writers advocate instructional approaches that encourage students to develop strategies for relating reading and writing in terms of their thinking processes. Hunt (1984) recommends using a whole language perspective at the college level, contending that the purpose for using language must transcend the study of language. He describes a research approach to reading and writing instruction with an emphasis on peer sharing, critiquing, and editing.

Salvatori (1983) argues that reading complex or literary texts fosters a sensitive and reflective frame of mind, which is important in writing. He describes the reading process as an "extremely complicated activity in which the mind is at one and the same time relaxed and alert, expanding meanings as it selects and modifies them, confronting the blanks and filling them with modifiable projections produced by intertextual and intratextual connections" (p. 661). Dealing with complexity and ambiguity in reading helps students handle the same elements of uncertainty in their writing.

Squire (1983) emphasizes the lack of experience in expressing ideas in writing as a main cause of thinking deficiencies among high school students. He blames this inexperience on teachers' failure to understand that composing and comprehending are interrelated. Asserting that comprehending and composing reflect the same cognitive process, Squire calls for the development of these functions through such activities as summarizing, retelling, rephrasing, reprocessing, elaborating, and translating among communication media. He advocates this approach in all disciplines in which comprehension of material is viewed as the construction and reconstruction of whole ideas.

Studies examining the uses of reading and writing in content learning often emphasize the value of the analysis and synthesis required in writing as means of developing thought. Hull and Bartholomae (1986) cite recent advances in knowledge about how students learn to write, noting that these advances have made possible the process approach to instruction. They discuss two perspectives: writing as complex behavior and writing as a complex intellectual process. They also distinguish between technically competent writing that reflects no intellectual growth or learning and writing that embodies efforts to increase understanding. They advocate the latter, which they call "speculative" writing, as a powerful aid to learning in subject areas.

Beyer (1982), reviewing research supporting the use of writing to enhance social studies learning, cites inventing hypotheses, generating new knowledge, developing concepts and generalizations, reinforcing or extending previous learning, and developing empathy as particularly useful activities. He concludes that teaching writing in social studies may be more effective than giving separate writing instruction. Koeller (1982) makes a similar point regarding the use of writing as an aid to learning in science. She recommends teaching such concepts as mapping, clustering, writing formats, and frames of reference for tools to help students understand science content.

Evans (1984) applied Worting and Tierney's (1982) principles from the Bay Area Writing Project (concerning the use of writing to enhance content learning) to elementary mathematics. She and a colleague had students do three kinds of writing: "how to " explanations, definitions, and troubleshooting, or explanations of errors made. Students made significant gains between pre- and posttest scores, leading Evans to conclude that writing can help students learn math.

Marton (1979) proposes that cognitive skills, or students' ability to use principles, are an aspect of knowledge. Using an introspective interview technique to examine college students' processing of text materials, he identifies two groups of processors: (1) students who assume the text has a meaning to convey and manipulate their reading to find it, and (2) students who attend to the text itself and try to remember the exact wording. He concludes that conducting a constructive meaning search is integral to content learning. On a pragmatic level, he affirms that content learning involves not just the acquisition of information but, more significantly, the use and extension of information.

Macrological Studies of Literacy

In this era of decline in absolutes (Langer & Applebee, 1988), all scholarly fields have moved from a belief in the accumulation of knowledge toward a belief in the tentative nature of truth, inquiry, and interpretation as ongoing processes in understanding. In this context, reading and writing are seen as basic tools to use in judging and negotiating knowledge rather than in discovering it (Bleich, 1987).

McGinley and Tierney (1988) label the type of literacy needed in such a context critical literacy—that is, one that enables individuals to use reading and writing in a multiperspective approach to knowing. Students who engage in different types of reading and writing learn new ways of thinking and learning, which these researchers call "traversing the topical landscape" (p. 11). Such a view specifies roles for readers and writers. Readers undertake the mental tasks of forming schemata (Anderson & Pearson, 1984), developing images and momentary understandings of texts (Langer 1986a, 1986b), and determining relationships between text arguments and their own experiences (Wittrock, 1984). Writers separate themselves from what they know (Havelock, 1963)—a separation that makes possible increasingly articulate introspectivity (Ong, 1986). Writing holds thought still long enough for writers to examine its sources, its destinations, its strengths, and its flaws.

Writing also requires writers to sharpen their communication. To make themselves clear without gesture, facial expression, intonation, or feedback from a hearer, they have to be aware of the possible ambiguities of their statements and make their language work with no existential context (Ong). They need to anticipate readers' reactions in order to support a dialogue between reader and text. Writing also gives rise to intertextuality (Hawkers, 1977); that is, a text is created out of other texts, borrowing, adapting, and sharing common formulas and themes (Ong). Writers find their sources in both lived and literate experiences.

In like vein, Siegel (1988) sees literacy as a process of inquiry that requires making selections involving the inquirer's values and experiences. If individuals conduct research from only an external, observational perspective, restrained by others' meanings, learning also will be restrained. As an illustration, John-Stein (1985) notes that many successful scientists say their real learning began when they were able to work by themselves in the laboratory, engaging in the inquiry process on their own terms. The same holds true for students. If they acquire information from an external viewpoint, they never get into the "laboratory" of their own experiences and ideas, so their real inquiry does not begin.

Langer and Applebee (1988) describe an inquiry approach to literacy in the context of history instruction. Instead of being asked to read for facts and events, students were told to strive for historical-mindedness. This approach encouraged the students to examine their own biases as well as those of the participants in and recorders of historical events. As readers, the students scrutinized texts for biases within social, political, and economic contexts; focused on meanings and implications; looked for corroboration among witnesses' accounts; and strove for reasoned interpretations, recognizing that historical certainty is impossible.

Literacy as inquiry, in its truest form, consists of a three-way dialogue among the reader, the text, and the context, including other readers of the text (Harste, Woodward, & Burke, 1984). Mitchell (1989) describes how Douglas Hofstadter, author of *Godel, Escher, Bach: An Eternal Golden Braid,* adopts such a dialogic approach in his classroom. Hofstadter assigns students to write dialogues to describe or propose a theory. A good dialogue involves students with the thoughts of their characters, encouraging them to draw these thoughts into their own reasoning systems and to include them in the internal search for resolutions and understanding.

Reading and writing, in the macrological sense of literacy, should go beyond communication in academic or social interactions. They should lead to self-exploration, self-awareness, and self-direction (Jackson, 1988). With reference to the study of literature, Bleich (1987) asserts that literacy should enable each individual to pose the question, "What do this text and my reactions to it tell me about myself, about feelings, wishes, and desires that previously may have been unknown to me?" This is where real inquiry, and therefore real literacy, begins— with an assessment of where one is before one moves forward.

The notion that literacy involves particular ways of using knowledge within both personal and social contexts is compatible with current sociolinguistic theory. We might then look at studies establishing a broad framework for understanding how knowledge is constructed as a way of approaching a practical concept of literacy, especially for postsecondary learning. A number of such studies establish the basic principle that learning is a complex, constructive, and relativistic activity that is creative on the part of every learner and that requires the organization and structuring of fluid information as knowledge is built and formed, not acquired. It is in this organizing and structuring process that the essence of literacy may be found.

Riegel (1973, 1979) has proposed a stage of dialectical operations—superseding Piaget's stage of formal operations—as the highest level of mature development. While the term formal operations encompasses the development of logical and structural thinking, a further stage is required to describe how adults operate in life when faced with situations in which logic and structure can assist in discovering problems but not in solving them. Like Perry's (1970) higher reaches of relativism, dialectical thinking is a process in which characteristics of a given situation, as well as principles or rules, are taken into account; this process is guided by hypotheses, not axioms. The development of this capacity requires opportunities to handle information in novel ways.

Gibbs, Morgan, and Taylor (1982) describe a set of studies that investigate the content (as opposed to the quantity) of students' learning from texts. They asked their students to verbalize their understanding of texts while reading. Analyzing these open-ended protocols, the researchers identified five ways of conceptualizing learning: (1) learning as a quantitative increase in knowledge; (2) learning as memorizing; (3) learning as the acquisition of facts and procedures that can be retained or utilized in practice; (4) learning as the abstraction of meaning; and (5) learning as an interpretive process aimed at the understanding of reality.

The first three concepts view knowledge as external to the student, something to be acquired; the last two view knowledge as internal, requiring the student to draw out meaning from text and relate it to a larger reality, implying tolerance for self-change. These concepts of knowledge can be compared to Belenky et al.'s (1986) identification of five types of knowers: silent, received, intuitive, procedural, and constructive. The procedural and constructive knowers are those who can control their knowledge in a social context and thereby achieve effective communication with others.

It might be reasoned that internally controlled ways of knowing cannot be externally induced. Gibbs, Morgan, and Taylor (1982) report studies showing that interventions intended to enhance student learning, such as inserted text questions and study skills taught as techniques, may actually distort learning and promote surface rather than deep processing. These approaches may remove deep processing from the control of the student and "technify" the process of learning. These researchers believe that letting the students have uninterrupted interplay with texts on their own terms has the best chance of inducing deep processing. Learning should be assessed vertically by analyzing how students think about content (as reflected in their written or oral texts), rather than horizontally through conventional measures of retention.

Conclusions

Referring to philosopher John Austin, Bruner (1984) discusses the nature of language as a social instrument for creating or stipulating a shared world and for getting things done in that world. All social psychology, he argues, must now deal with these uses of language. Bruner also makes a distinction between paradigmatic (or manipulative) and syntagmatic (or narrative) modes of language, the latter being the mode in which humans negotiate among themselves in their continuous endeavor to make the implicit knowledge of culture explicit. The pragmatic mode of language is the vehicle for this work, the goal of which is to increase the sharing of perspectives.

One common characteristic of the language of academia is the gap between the complexity of an idea and the capability of language users to stretch the language to fit the meaning. Waterhouse, Fischer, and Ryan (1980) have called this need for ingenious extension of language the semiotic extension; this, we may presume, is what is happening during deep processing. Laurillard (1979) points out that the processing level for a given learner varies with the context and expectations of the task. Thus, the sharing of perspectives that Bruner views as the main work of literacy is a matter of constant negotiation.

The literature reviewed in this chapter shows that students need to be able to read language and synthesize it in writing, but it shows even more strongly that they need to be able to assess meaning in personal and social contexts, pose questions, communicate negotiations of material with other members of the learning community, and develop a fluid concept of knowledge. Newcomers to the society of academia may have difficulty at first entering into such negotiations with one another and especially with faculty, and they will continue to have difficulty as long as they lack opportunities to participate in that society's communications.

A strong, macrological sense of academic literacy, therefore, calls for more than attention to reading and writing, although these certainly are not to be neglected. It calls for involving the students in the learning processes of whatever disciplines they are studying and inviting them to participate in the communications of these disciplines. For this reason, the best developmental instruction will take place within the context of content learning, guided by those who represent the community of thought into which the student is being inducted.

In our less than ideal world, however, content instructors may not assume responsibility for developing students' literacy within their disciplines. Often it is teachers of developmental and process courses who are called on to help students acquire the mind-set of academia without losing the view that learning is the critical comprehension of reality (Freire & Macedo, 1987). Process teachers therefore need a strong macrological view of what learning means in the various disciplines and how it is supported by language. At the same time, as

Hamilton-Wieler (1989) notes, they must deal with the interfering effects of institutional requirements such as examinations and grades, understanding that students are often caught in a bind between surviving and pursuing their own meaningful goals. The developmental instructor helps students manage the intricate negotiations between personal and institutional purposes as they make their way through college.

The instructor is not the only one who guides in this venture. At least as important is the guidance students receive from one another and from themselves as they undertake what Shor and Freire (1987, p. 147) call the "conceptual ballet we learn in a university." Conceptual language and thinking must be mastered, but connections with the learners' own experiences, and with the experiences learners have in communicating with one another, are necessary for macrological literacy to develop. Helping students make these connections is what process teachers do well, and often do alone. They provide settings for personal reflection within social contexts, encourage dialogical reading and discussion, incorporate writing into the collaborative learning of the group, explore the nature of knowledge in general and within particular disciplines, and help students articulate their own identities as critical learners. This is the literacy that empowers. This is the literacy that succeeds.

References and Suggested Readings

Adler, M.J., & van Doren, C. (1972). *How to read a book*. (revised and updated). New York: Simon & Schuster.

Anderson, R.C., & Pearson, P.D. (1984). A schema-theoretic view of basic processes in reading comprehension. In P.D. Pearson (Ed.), *Handbook of reading research*. White Plains, NY: Longman.

Applebee, A.N. (1984). *Contexts for learning to write: Studies of secondary school instruction*. Norwood, NJ: Ablex.

*Arons, A.B. (1979). Some thoughts on reasoning capacities implicitly expected of college students. In J. Lochead & J. Clement (Eds.), *Cognitive process instructions: Research on teaching thinking skills*. Philadelphia, PA: The Franklin Institute Press.

Atwell, M. (1983). Reading, writing, listening: Language in response to context. In U. Hardt (Ed.), *Teaching reading with the other language arts* (pp. 21-30). Newark, DE: International Reading Association.

Aulls, M. (1983). Relating reading and other language arts: A need for reasoned directions. In U. Hardt (Ed.), *Teaching reading with the other language arts* (pp. 1-20). Newark, DE: International Reading Association.

*Belenky, M.F., Clinchy, B.M. Goldberger, N.R., & Tarule, J.M. (1986). *Women's ways of knowing*. New York: Basic Books.

Beyer, B. (1982). Using writing to learn social studies. *The Social Studies, 73*(3), 100-105.

Birnbaum, J.C. (1986). Reflective thought: The connection between reading and writing. In B.T. Petersen (Ed.), *Convergences: Transactions in reading and writing* (pp. 30-43). Urbana, IL: National Council of Teachers of English.

Bleich, D. (1987). *Subjective criticism*. Baltimore, MD: Johns Hopkins University Press.

Broderick, B., & Caverly, D.C. (1987). Computerized writing instruction in developmental writing programs. *Review of Research in Developmental Education, 5*(2), 1-4.

Browning, N.F. (1986). Journal writing: One assignment does more than improve reading, writing, and thinking. *Journal of Reading, 30,* 39-44.

*Bruner, J. (1984). Pragmatics of language and language of pragmatics. *Social Research, 51,* 969-984.

*Christiansen, L. (1988). Writing the word and the world. *English Journal, 75*(2), 14-18.

Clifford G.J. (1984). Buch und Lesen: Historical perspectives on literacy and schooling. *Review of Educational Research, 54,* 472-500.

Crafton, L. (1983). Oral and written language related processes of a sociopsycholinguistic nature. In U. Hardt (Ed.), *Teaching reading with the other language arts* (pp. 31-46). Newark, DE: International Reading Association.

Culler, J. (1975). *Structuralist poetics: Structuralism linguistics and the study of literature*. Ithaca: Cornell University Press.

Dahl, K. (1984). *Reading and writing as transacting processes*. Unpublished doctoral dissertation, Indiana University, Bloomington, IN.

de Beaugrande, R. (1984). Writer, reader, critic: Comparing critical theories as discourse. *College English, 46,* 533-559.

Eisenstein, E. (1979). *The printing process as an agent of change: Communications and cultural transformation in early modern Europe* (2 vols.). New York: Cambridge University Press.

Evans, C.S. (1984). Writing to learn math. *Language Arts, 61,* 828-835.

Fish, S. (1980). *Is there a text in this class?* Cambridge, MA: Harvard University Press.

*Freire, P. (1970). *Pedagogy of the oppressed*. New York: Seabury.

*Freire, P. (1973). *Education for critical consciousness*. New York: Seabury.

*Freire, P., & Macedo, D. (1987). *Literacy: Reading the word and the world*. Granby, MA: Bergin & Garvey.

Gebhard, A. (1983). Teaching writing in reading and content areas. *Journal of Reading, 27,* 207-211.

*Gibbs, G., Morgan, A., & Taylor, L. (1982). A review of the research of Ference Marton and the Goteborg group: A phenomenological research perspective on learning. *Higher Education, 11,* 123-145.

Goodlad, J. (1985). *A place called school*. New York: McGraw-Hill.

Goodman, K., & Goodman, Y. (1983). Reading and writing relationships: Pragmatic functions. *Language Arts, 60,* 590-599.

Hamilton-Wieler, S. (1989, October). Awkward compromises and eloquent achievements. *English Education, 21*(3), 152-169.

Harste, J. Woodward, V., & Burke, C. (1984). Examining our assumptions of literacy and learning. *Research in the Teaching of English, 18*(1), 257-277.

Havelock, E.A. (1963). *Preface to Plato*. Cambridge, MA: Belknap.

Hawkers, T. (1977). *Structuralism and semiotics*. Berkeley, CA: University of California Press.

Hirsch, E.D., Jr. (1987). *Cultural literacy: What every American needs to know*. Boston, MA: Houghton Mifflin.

Reading, Writing, and Academic Literacy

Hirsch, E.D., Jr. (1989). The primal scene of education. *New York Review of Books, 36*(3), 29-34.

Hull, G., & Bartholomae, D. (1986). Teaching writing. *Educational Leadership, 2,* 44-53.

Hunt, R. (1984). *Whole language, whole literature: Avoiding the classroom truncation of language development.* Paper presented at Center for Expansion of Language Training Rejuvenation Conference, Bloomington, IN.

*Illych, I. (1987). A plea for research on lay literacy. *North American Review, 272*(3), 10-17.

Jackson, J. (1988). Improving literacy by developing self-understanding. *Journal of Reading, 32*(2), 132-139.

John-Stein, V. (1985). *Notebooks of the mind.* Albuquerque, NM: University of New Mexico Press.

Kennedy, M.L. (1980). Reading and writing: Interrelated skills of literacy at the college level. *Reading World, 20,* 131-141.

Koeller, S. (1982). Expository writing: A vital skill in science. *Science and Children, 20,* 12-13.

*Kozol, J. (1985). *Illiterate America.* New York: New American Library.

Kucer, S.B. (1983). *Using text comprehension as a metaphor for understanding text production: Building bridges between reading and writing.* Unpublished doctoral dissertation, Indiana University, Bloomington, IN.

Kuhn, T.S. (1970). *The structure of scientific revolutions* (2nd ed.). Chicago, IL: University of Chicago Press.

*Langer, J.A. (1986a). *Children reading and writing: Structures and strategies.* Norwood, NJ: Ablex.

Langer, J.A. (1986b). Reading and writing and understanding: An analysis of the construction of meaning. *Written Communication, 3,* 219-267.

*Langer, J., & Applebee, A. (1988). Speaking of knowing: Conceptions of learning in academic subjects. In J. Langer & A. Applebee (Eds.), *Academic learning in high school subjects.* (ED 297 336)

*Laurillard, D. (1979). The process of student learning. *Higher Education, 8,* 395-409.

Marshall, J.D. (1987). The effects of writing on students' understanding of literary texts. *Research in the Teaching of English, 21,* 602-614.

Marton, F. (1979). Skill as an aspect of knowledge. *Higher Education, 50,* 602-614.

Marzano, R., Brandt, R., Hughes, C.; Jones, B.F., Presseisen, B., Rankin, S., & Suhor, C. (1988). *Dimensions of thinking: A framework for curriculum and instruction.* Alexandria, VA: Association for Supervision and Curriculum Development.

McGinley, W., & Tierney, R. (1988). *Reading and writing as ways of knowing and learning* (Technical Report No. 423). Cambridge, MA: Bolt, Beranek, & Newman.

Mitchell, K. (1989). Superman, Socrates, and me: The tale of a classroom. *Indiana Alumni Magazine, 52*(2), 30-35.

Moxley, R. (1984). The compositional approach to reading in practice and theory. *Journal of Reading, 27,* 636-643.

Ong, W.J. (1986). *Orality and literacy.* London: Methuen.

*Paul, R. (1987). Dialogical thinking: Critical thought essential to the acquisition of rational knowledge and passions. In J.B. Baron & R. Sternberg (Eds.), *Teaching thinking skills: Theory and practice.* New York: W.H. Freeman.

*Perry, W. (1970). *Forms of intellectual and ethical development in the college years.* Orlando, FL: Holt, Rinehart & Winston.

Pitts, S.K. (1986). Read aloud to adult learners? Of course! *Reading Psychology, 7,* 35-42.

Reagan, S. (1985). *The effects of reading and writing instruction on the composing processes of college freshman basic skills writers.* Unpublished doctoral dissertation, Indiana University, Bloomington, IN.

Riegel, K. (1973). Dialectic operations: The final period of cognitive development. *Human Development, 16,* 346-370.

Riegel, K. (1979). *The relational basis of language: Foundations of dialectical psychology.* New York: Academic.

Rubin, A., & Hansen, J. (1986). Reading and writing: How are the first two "R's" related? In J. Orasanu (Ed.), *Reading comprehension: From research to practice* (p. 163-170). Hillsdale, NJ: Erlbaum.

Salvatori, M. (1983). Reading and writing a text: Correlations between reading and writing patterns. *College English, 45,* 657-666.

Sanacore, J. (1983). Improving reading through prior knowledge and writing. *Journal of Reading, 26,* 714-720.

Schwartz, P., & Olgivy, J. (1979). *The emergent paradigm: Changing patterns of thought and belief.* Menlo Park, CA: Values and Lifestyles Program.

Shanklin, N. (1982). *Relating reading and writing: Developing a transactional theory of the writing process.* Unpublished doctoral dissertation, Indiana University, Bloomington, IN.

Shor, I., & Freire, P. (1987). *A pedagogy for liberation: Dialogues on transforming education.* Granby, MA: Bergin & Garvey.

Siegel, M. (1988). *Semiotics: New insights on new jargon for language educators.* Paper presented at the Annual Meeting of the American Educational Research Association, New Orleans, LA.

Smith, S. (1985). Comprehension monitoring in experienced readers. *Journal of Reading, 28,* 292-300.

Squire, J. (1983). Composing and comprehending: Two sides of the same basic process. *Language Arts, 60,* 81-88.

Sternglass M., & Pugh, S. (1986, July). Retrospective accounts of language and learning processes. *Written Communications, 3* (3).

Stotsky, S. (1983). Research in reading/writing relationships: A synthesis and suggested directions. *Language Arts, 60,* 627-642.

Stotsky, S. (1982). The role of writing in developmental reading. *Journal of Reading, 25,* 330-339.

*Tierney, R., & Lays, M. (1986). What is the value of connecting reading and writing? In B.T. Petersen (Ed.), *Convergences: Transactions in reading and writing.* (pp. 15-29). Urbana, IL: National Council of Teachers of English.

Tierney, R., & Pearson, P.D. (1983). Toward a composing model of reading. *Language Arts, 60,* 68-80.

Trosky, O., & Wood, C. (1982). Using a writing model to teach reading. *Journal of Reading, 26,* 34-40.

*Waterhouse, L.H., Fischer, K.M., & Ryan, E.B. (1980). *Language awareness and reading.* Newark, DE.: International Reading Association.

Wittrock, M.C. (1984). Writing and the teaching of reading. In J.M. Jensen (Ed.), *Composing and comprehending.* Urbana, IL: National Council of Teachers of English.

Worting, A., & Tierney, R. (1982). Two studies of writing in high school science. San Francisco, CA: Bay Area Writing Project.

2

Program Organization

Kathy Carpenter
Linda L. Johnson

S ince their beginnings, colleges and universities in the United States have provided reading and study skills programs for their students. These programs have served both students who requested assistance and those identified by admissions officers as likely to have difficulty with college studies. On the whole, these programs have proved marginally successful in helping students who might otherwise have left college (Kulik, Kulik, & Shwalb, 1983). In this chapter we discuss the organizational and programmatic factors that affect the success of college-level reading and study skills programs.

To understand how reading and study skills programs fit into the organizational hierarchy of an institution of higher learning, we must discuss them in connection with the broader range of learning assistance programs. Learning assistance programs include any remedial or developmental program intended to help students succeed academically in college. They range in scope from a single reading course offered through the English department to comprehensive programs housed in their own department.

Institutions refer to their learning assistance programs by a variety of names (e.g., learning center, reading lab, study skills center, academic skills center, reading and study skills program). We use the term *learning center* or *learning assistance program* to refer to all of these programs.

In this chapter, we first review the need for learning assistance programs by examining historical trends in their development and the distribution of programs in colleges and universities across the country. Then we examine the organizational features of current programs and the factors that influence them. Next, we analyze types of programs now in existence with reference to research findings. Finally, we draw conclusions based on our analysis and the research.

Recognizing the Need for Learning Assistance Programs

The existence of college learning assistance programs indicates that high schools are not in a position to prepare all their graduates for the intense independent learning required in college. The need for learning assistance extends from the earliest colleges in the country to the newest, from open admission junior colleges to highly selective universities, and from high-risk students to straight A students.

Historical Trends

Since colonial days, colleges and universities in America have recognized, however reluctantly, the need for some form of learning assistance. In the seventeenth century, Harvard University—acknowledging that some of its students were ill prepared to meet the demands of its curriculum—provided a remedial program in Latin, a language in which many classes were conducted (Boylan & White, 1987). Remedial programs in basic skills have been present on college campuses in one form or another since the middle of the nineteenth century. Programs specifically for reading and study skills have existed since the early twentieth century.

Boylan and White (1987) note that the impetus for establishing remedial college programs in the nineteenth century was the development of land grant colleges. These colleges opened their doors to underprepared students because they could not find enough qualified students to attend them. To help such students, colleges frequently instituted preparatory departments, which resembled secondary schools within the college. These departments offered courses in mathematics, reading, and writing to students who might take 6 years to complete a 4-year college program. After cooperation between high schools and colleges began and the College Boards were established, greater numbers of qualified students enrolled in colleges and universities (Brier, 1984). However, changing college admission standards made it difficult for students to meet requirements. In 1907, for instance, half the students at Harvard, Princeton, and Yale had failed to meet entrance requirements (Maxwell, 1979).

In the first decades of the twentieth century, many college preparatory programs were redesigned to accommodate students at all levels who were experiencing academic difficulty. By then, the courses included training in study skills as well as in basic skills such as reading. Students in these courses studied the same topics students study today—time management, concentration, notetaking, and test taking (Enright & Kerstiens, 1980).

In the 1930s, colleges and universities established remedial reading clinics to help students cope with the lengthy reading assignments required in their general survey courses. According to Maxwell (1979), reading laboratories owe their existence to Stella Center, who founded the Reading Laboratory in the extension department of New York University. Pioneer reading programs at Minnesota and Harvard started 2 years later. After 1941, when Robert Bear of Dartmouth published a pamphlet called *How to Read Rapidly and Well,* many developmental reading programs began to appear.

The focus of reading instruction in the 1940s was similar to that of many programs today. Instructors used a diagnostic-prescriptive approach, with individualized practice. Triggs (1942) noted a lack of commercial materials, diagnostic tools, and trained instructors. Although his ideal was to work with students individually, his compromise solution was to use small groups in combination with clinical work.

The machines that gave the name "laboratory" to the new centralized reading programs were brought over from psychology laboratories, where researchers were experimenting with eye movements. By 1946, such machines as tachistoscopes, the Keystone Ophthalmic Telebinocular, the Ophthalm-O-Graph, and the Metronoscope were in fairly common use (Enright & Kerstiens, 1980). Today we sometimes find the descendants of these machines in reading laboratories.

After World War II, government funding enabled colleges to establish learning centers for veterans. These centers offered reading, writing, and study skills programs, as well as tutoring services. During the 1950s, these centers became institutionalized and expanded their services (Maxwell, 1979).

The greatest growth in learning assistance occurred during the 1960s and 1970s, when many 2-year colleges and some universities implemented open admissions policies. These policies forced many postsecondary institutions to expand their learning assistance and tutoring programs to cope with underprepared students. Federal funding became available to promote education for disadvantaged students. This federal commitment to affirmative action and equal educational opportunity stimulated the rapid expansion of developmental programs.

The 1970s became the era of the adult learner when large numbers of older students, particularly women, enrolled as undergraduates. Many students were underprepared for academic studying, and soon the open doors became revolving doors. In response, institutions established more remedial programs that offered innovative services such as academic counseling, individualized programs, and self-paced courses. Many institutions established these programs—by then called learning assistance programs—primarily to assist the nontraditional student population.

Unfortunately, many of these programs failed to improve the retention rate of high-risk students (Roueche & Snow, 1977). Gradually programs have begun to come under closer evaluation, and some improvements have been made (Smith & Smith, 1988).

Meeting Students' Needs

Students' need for and interest in learning assistance are apparent from both questionnaire data and anecdotal evidence. Today, programs are frequently geared to all students, not just the underprepared—with good reason. Evidence of the need for assistance is easy to find even in highly selective colleges and universities.

Perry (1959) describes the need for reading improvement at Harvard University in the 1940s. In 1946 all entering freshmen took a reading test, and the bottom scorers were assigned remedial reading—even though the lowest scoring students still scored above the 85th percentile according to national norms. When these results were revealed, the course was made more difficult, and 800 students enrolled. Perry discovered that these students did not lack the mechanics of reading, but they needed to improve their ability to set purposes for reading as well as their flexibility in achieving their purposes.

In a study of 1,029 Western Michigan University freshmen (Carter, 1959), 66 percent reported that they had not been taught to read a textbook chapter in high school, and 62 percent said they had received no reading instruction from their high school teachers at all. Most said they would have benefited from a high school developmental reading course. Shaw (1961) estimated that 95 percent of entering students lacked study skills.

The situation has not changed. Simpson (1983) surveyed 395 freshmen at a midwestern university and found that they could report using only a few study strategies, frequently could not explain why a strategy might be effective, used the same study strategy regardless of the subject, and were unable to explain how they knew whether they were prepared for an upcoming test. She concluded that the general college student population would benefit from study skills instruction.

Clearly, reading and study skills instruction is needed by many average and even high-achieving students. While most students figure out how to study by themselves, some otherwise well-prepared students may find themselves on academic probation because of insufficient study skills. Most learning assistance programs were established to increase the retention rate of underprepared students. Despite this stated goal, however, many colleges and universities have been able to serve both populations with independent or coordinated programs. Stanford University's learning assistance center is a good example. At one point at least, the center served more than half the freshmen each year (Roueche & Snow, 1977). Even straight A students, many of whom were found to have inefficient study methods, benefited from the program.

Prevalence of Learning Assistance Programs

According to several nationwide surveys, most degree-granting institutions now have some kind of program that provides learning assistance. In 1974, Smith, Enright, & Devirian (1975) mailed surveys to 3,389 U.S. colleges and universities, 38 percent of which (1,258) returned a completed form. Of these, 759 (60 percent) reported that they operated a learning assistance center, while an additional 115 planned to establish one within the next 2 years. Only 10 percent of these learning centers existed before 1960. Although the authors did not report how many centers offered reading instruction, they did report that 79 percent offered study skills courses.

The number of college learning assistance programs has grown steadily since the time of that report. Sullivan (1980) surveyed 2,872 U.S. and Canadian postsecondary institutions that offered at least an associate's degree. Of the 2,713 U.S. institutions, 50.6 percent operated at least one learning assistance program. More than 75 percent of the surveyed 4-year public institutions in the United States operated learning centers.

Roueche (1983) surveyed 2,508 U.S. colleges and universities. Of the 58 percent responding, only 160 (11 percent) lacked programs, courses, or other alternatives for responding to the needs of low-achieving students.

Boylan (1986) estimated that 30,000 instructors and other staff members worked in learning assistance centers across the country, and that about 1.5 million students were enrolled in basic skills programs. According to the National Center for Education Statistics (Wright, 1985), 16 percent of college freshmen took remedial reading in the 1983-1984 academic year; 66 percent of all colleges and universities offered remedial reading courses. Cranney (1987) postulates that the peak has been reached, and that budget cutbacks will force learning assistance professionals to struggle to maintain the gains they have made. He notes that while community colleges may be able to hold their own, university programs will be more subject to cuts.

The need for reading and learning assistance programs on college campuses will continue indefinitely, regardless of whether programs for students are fully funded. Inevitably, some students will lack effective study skills or adequate background in a subject, no matter how outstanding their schooling has been. Other students will simply wish to improve their already adequate study skills.

Organizational Influences and Features

The nature of a learning assistance program is dependent on a number of philosophical and practical influences. These influences determine both the diversity of a program and the direction it takes.

Influences on Program Nature

The way learning assistance programs are created, revised, and expanded are subject to a number of influences. The most telling of these are school philosophy, the academic background of the program's staff, funding issues, government policies, and the type of institution involved.

School philosophy. Both the services a learning assistance program provides and the activities it sponsors are influenced by the philosophical orientation of the postsecondary institution. If the institution has a liberal, humanistic orientation, it seeks to offer a variety of services to help all students reach their academic goals. If the orientation is academically conservative, departmental faculty and administrators may believe that students should rely on their own resources. Under these conditions, learning assistance may be limited.

Academic background. The training, experience, and educational beliefs of learning assistance personnel determine in part how resources are allocated. The theoretical perspective of those responsible for the program may determine the nature and range of activities they undertake. For example, if instructors are trained through a guidance and counseling department, they are likely to include individual and small group academic counseling in the program.

Funding. Funding for a learning assistance program may be linked to the emphasis placed on certain programs or activities. Funding agency stipulations may determine the scope and direction of the program. If funding is available from only one source, the programs goals may reflect the requirements of the funding agency; other concerns may be neglected until additional funds are found.

Policies and statutes. Government or administrative policies may place restrictions on a learning assistance program. Conversely, they may establish objectives that are difficult, if not impossible, to meet. Most often such restrictions and externally established objectives hinder efforts to assist all students desiring help. For example, a learning assistance program may be restricted to serving only minority students or those admitted with less adequate educational preparation. Usually, such programs adhere to the mandates placed on them, even though this may mean refusing to help students who do not fall under the guidelines.

Type of institution. Tax-supported institutions may require a different orientation than private colleges, and universities may desire a completely different format from what a community college would prefer.

In order to meet the varying needs and expectations of students, faculty, and administrators on their individual campuses, learning assistance educators build customized programs and centers. Program administrators must address a variety of issues, including how students are directed toward developmental activities, whether they receive individualized or group instruction, where and when they will receive tutoring, whether they are enrolled in regular classes, how extensive the drop-in and outreach services are, and how services are evaluated. The goal is to try to provide students with the best possible learning assistance, based on the available resources and professional expertise.

Philosophical Perspectives on Organization

Those working in learning assistance settings have evolved various philosophical perspectives that heavily influence the structure of their programs. Practitioners identified with specific philosophies in the following pages may argue that they are not limited to one perspective, and certainly most developmental educators create a blend of activities from many perspectives. However, the writings of these practitioners often suggest a particular orientation or preference. We intend the following discussion only to identify and clarify trends in theoretical orientation, not to rigidly classify the beliefs of any individuals.

Counseling perspective. Many learning assistance programs, particularly those associated with student services, operate under the belief that learning emerges through a heavy emphasis on personal counseling. Counseling proponents regard individual counseling and regular conferences with professional staff members as a way to help students break emotional barriers and negative attitudes toward learning, which traditional classroom and familiar lecture/drill/homework programs often fail to remedy. Students often approach learning with a background of negative experiences, fear of failure, and self-dissatisfaction. A counseling approach combines work on improving learning attitudes and self-image with instruction in reading and study skills.

Raygor (1977) identified emotional problems that manifest themselves in reading and study behaviors and listed 10 characteristics that he felt an ideal learning center program should include to address those problems. The emotional problems he noted were distortion of reality, unwillingness to take risks, compulsive reading, nervousness and tenseness during instruction, refusal to read, lack of concentration, fear of discovery, transference symptoms, giving up, escapism, blame-placing, and examination panic. He concluded that the ideal learning center program should include individualized instruction, diagnosis and treatment models, counseling, flexible schedules, self-paced instruction, flexible grades and credits, competency-based objectives, appropriate program evaluation, services that reflect the academic goals of the institution, and a trained staff.

Robyak and Patton (1977) cite research suggesting that poor academic performance results from emotional factors as well as from skill deficits. Thus, they argue, students should receive academic advice and counseling—preferably on a one-to-one basis—as well as assistance in developing reading, writing, and study skills. Forums and workshops should be offered on specific topics throughout each semester, and students should be encouraged to participate. For instance, small groups might focus on stress, test taking, test anxiety, time management, or effective listening.

In the literature, we found several articles describing learning assistance programs that either had counseling components or were administered by counselors. At the University of

South Carolina, Schmelzer and Brozo (1982) employed "skills therapy" in their learning center. They advocated that instructors be as knowledgeable about counseling techniques as they are about reading and study skills. The skills therapist interviews the student, makes a diagnosis on the basis of the interview, develops a mutually agreed upon treatment plan, and provides regular and continuing support.

Frequently study skills programs also include a counseling component. Pollock and Wilkinson (1988) describe a program at Brock University in which, when necessary, study skills were taught through individual counseling.

Another program with a counseling orientation emphasized academic enrichment for entering high-risk students. Academic counselors with master's degrees in educational psychology taught a course involving both group discussions and individual counseling (Landward & Hepworth, 1984).

Administrative perspective. An administrative perspective emphasizes a more structured atmosphere than do other perspectives, and is usually adapted from theories developed for business management. Programs with this orientation pretest students and use the results to develop an individualized plan with specific learning objectives. A learning contract establishes what the educator expects and elicits a commitment from the student. Materials and center facilities are usually provided to assist in the completion of each learning objective, and student progress is monitored periodically. Developmental educators who would argue that effective learning comes from a well-organized, administratively sound program include Roueche and Snow (1977) and Boylan (1982).

According to proponents, an administrative perspective not only enhances learning but also facilitates the administration of the program as a whole, particularly the data collection and program evaluation aspects. Program administrators write objectives and goals for each section of the program and gather data. Through periodic evaluations, they decide which objectives are being met as well as which ones need further effort. Thus, their approach to improving the program is the same as their approach to helping students improve their learning skills.

Castelli and Johnson (1983), working at two different kinds of universities, took an administrative perspective when they developed the idea that the learning center should take a leadership role in predicting and responding to change. They recommended that learning center directors "cultivate and use the channels of power" (p. 31) and develop an understanding of how universities work in order to avoid being subject to the whims and trends of college decision making.

Within this perspective, different programs take different approaches. According to Hartsough (1983-1984), the learning assistance program at West Virginia State University took a contractual approach. Specialists in basic skills and developmental studies used contracts to help undermotivated students set goals and plan careers. Educators at Morehead State University in Kentucky used an information systems approach to increase retention (White, 1984). The university implemented a diagnostic-prescriptive model comprising advisement and counseling, learning laboratories, professional development for faculty, and an honors program. The information systems component kept track of and evaluated each freshman student. Developmental reading classes were individualized and self-paced.

Mechanistic perspective. Content tutoring and appropriate material selection to ameliorate specific skill deficiencies are the major components of the mechanistic perspective. Christ (1971) stressed that the materials do the teaching; "learning facilitators" identify weaknesses and assign students to materials. Students also might be assigned to specific learning center classes and subject-specific tutoring groups, or assistance might be provided on an individual basis through self-instructional packets.

Proponents of the mechanistic perspective maintain that the use of technology can improve the work of learning facilitators through the systematic identification, development, organization, and utilization of a full range of learning resources. Using the learning options made available through technology can help students learn more in less time.

Mechanistic programs using self-instruction with program materials were abundant in the early 1970s (Reedy, 1973);

more recently, however, programs that combine a mechanistic approach with tutoring or direct instruction appear to be more common (McMurtrie, 1982). Townsend (1983) described a self-instructional program for underprepared Pennsylvania college students in which students were given competency-based pre- and posttests in 11 skill areas. Students studied from individualized reading programs determined by test results. Because students had problems setting personal as well as academic goals, Townsend planned to include counseling techniques in the future.

Basic skills perspective. The basic skills perspective presupposes that deficiencies in the basic skills of reading, writing, and mathematics are the major contributions to academic difficulties. Proponents believe that if students improve their basic skills, they will be more likely to succeed in college. Materials and instruction in programs with this focus may or may not be closely related to the reading and writing required in the college curriculum.

Maxwell (1979) is one author who suggests that underprepared college students can upgrade their skills and attain their educational goals in a learning program with a basic skills orientation. Pugh (1985) and Fairbanks (1974), both developmental educators with a strong reading background, share Maxwell's philosophy.

A voluntary program for high-risk students at the City University of New York typifies successful basic skills programs (Bengis, 1986). In this program, established in 1982, students with low scores on skills assessments of reading, writing, and mathematics enroll in a 6-week summer session. They receive basic skills instruction as well as tutoring and counseling. Instructors work together to plan instruction and share effective teaching methods.

As the above program illustrates, most learning assistance programs that stress one theoretical perspective recognize the need for additional services that may be more congruent with a different perspective.

Trends in Administrative Organization

Because of the numerous influences on learning assistance programs, it is unlikely that any two programs are identical. Goals, structure, and activities are institution-specific, and each program exploits whatever resources and expertise are available to provide needed services. However, we can classify programs in a general sort of way according to their location in the college hierarchy.

Colleges have many options in organizing learning assistance programs. An institution might create a large-scale program directed specifically at improving the retention of high-risk students. It might offer programs for students on academic probation. It might provide a learning center or coursework for students who want to improve their already adequate reading and study skills. These programs may be housed in several different departments or in one department under a single administrator. They may be controlled by an office of academic affairs or by the student affairs office. The internal structure may comprise any or all of a number of elements, including a lab, a series of courses, peer tutoring, drop-in services, small group instruction, individualized self-instruction, or counseling services.

Often, the responsibility for providing learning assistance is divided among several schools or departments within a university. The school of education may provide study skills training, peer counseling, remedial reading instruction, and tutoring; the English department may teach developmental reading and writing; the linguistics department may teach writing courses for foreign students; the law school may sponsor reading and writing courses for law students; administrative personnel may offer writing and time management courses for faculty and staff; the dean of graduate studies may provide tutoring for graduate students; and the office of student affairs may offer counseling and tutoring.

One of the most comprehensive recent surveys of learning assistance programs was conducted in 1983-1984 by the

U.S. Department of Education (Cahalan & Farris, 1986; Wright, 1985). The investigators found that most colleges (90 percent) offered remedial support services such as diagnosis, learning assistance labs, tutoring, and counseling. Pre-enrollment summer programs were available at 25 percent of the colleges, most frequently at 4-year selective colleges. Overall, 33 percent had a separate department or division for support services. Programs often contained courses in reading, writing, or mathematics, and 21 percent had remedial course offerings in academic subjects such as science or social science. Courses in study skills were not differentiated from courses in career planning and decision making, but such developmental courses were available in 58 percent of the institutions.

In another study, Roueche and his colleagues (Roueche, Baker, & Roueche, 1984) found that more than half of the postsecondary institutions provided orientation programs specifically for high-risk students. Most institutions favored structured courses over drop-in facilities for these students, although drop-in sites were frequently available.

According to a survey by Smith, Enright, and Devirian (1975), learning centers in the early 1970s tended to be administered by English departments in 2-year colleges and by counseling or education departments in universities. By the early 1980s, nearly half the respondents to a Gordon and Flippo (1983) survey were located in their own department; another 33 percent were in the English department, and 22 percent were in the college of education.

Administrative Structure: Centralized or Dispersed?

If learning assistance programs are to meet the demands of today's postsecondary students, where should they be placed in the institution's organizational structure? The national trend has been to form a central service unit for the entire institution (Walker, 1980; Wright, 1985). A single center provides credibility and continuity for programs and promotes cooperation among staff members. Colleges and universities are best served by a central unit for several other reasons as well:

- Developmental activities are closely related, and each service—reading, writing, study skills, tutoring—is strengthened by proximity to others. Course content sometimes overlaps, and consultations among instructors improve the quality of all courses. In addition, a central unit allows the staff to help train new staff members.

- Many learning centers have large drop-in populations. Students seldom know where to go for needed assistance if no designated center exists. Those who are not enrolled in developmental classes are more likely to visit if the learning center is visible and identified.

- A central unit lends name and place recognition to a program. The more students know about the center, the better able the center will be to reach students in need.

- Identification of the center as a cohesive entity with a special focus gives the staff a sense of direction. As a unit the center can give its teaching staff the kind of support that a lone person teaching study skills in a school of education might not have.

- The existence of a designated center emphasizes the institution's commitment to reading, study skills, writing, and tutoring. Delegating these services to the school of education or to a freshman English class may make these activities seem less important.

- Administrative time is better employed if three or four subunits are grouped together than if each is functioning separately in diverse locations. This structure makes central accountability and standardized evaluation much more feasible.

Another important factor in determining the best location for a learning center within the institution's organization is whether the center will be offering courses for credit. Roueche and Snow (1977) and Sullivan (1978) found that an increasing number of colleges were offering credit for learning center classes. Roueche (1983) notes that successful developmental programs offer classes for credit and make sure they appear as such on the students' transcripts.

If the center does not offer classes for credit, it may be viewed as having a student service function rather than an academic function. In this case, the learning center is administered through a student service office, such as the counseling unit, which acts on the belief that students' academic problems are seldom purely academic. If the center is associated with the counseling unit, referrals between program services are easier and the student service orientation of the center is maintained.

Most learning centers that offer developmental classes for credit are under the supervision of an administrator in academic affairs because other administrative units (such as student affairs or student services) do not grant credit for developmental activities (Walker, 1980). For these programs, reporting to an academic department or division chair might enhance the learning center's credibility with the faculty, but it would have several drawbacks as well. For instance, a center that was part of the school of education and reported directly to its dean would have the strength of the school behind it; teaching staff would be on the education faculty, and courses would be listed under education. However, the student service orientation of the center might be lost in a school or department whose primary interests are research and teacher training. Certainly, the center would lose some of its separate identity and assume the flavor and reputation of its administrative home. A similar set of advantages and disadvantages applies to centers that are part of the English department.

If the center is to serve the entire academic community, it is best for it not to be tied to any one department or school. That way, students in all major areas realize that the center is there to serve their needs, as do faculty and administrators. Another benefit to this system is that it enhances tutoring in various areas and working relationships with faculty members in diverse departments. In addition, it keeps any one department

Carpenter and Johnson

or school from having to shoulder the financial burden of a center designed to serve the entire institution. This structure also allows the center to develop programs with an institutionwide appeal, rather than catering to the interests of one academic view or focusing on a student services orientation. A direct administrative relationship to the vice president for academic affairs or the dean of undergraduate studies would eliminate many of the problems associated with a departmental or school association. If the center offers services for graduate students, a separate reporting relationship for those activities could be established with the dean of graduate studies. Ideally, the center should report to the highest ranking academic officer to ensure autonomous and diversified assistance for all registered students.

Program Emphasis: Remedial or Developmental?

Cross (1976) divided learning assistance programs into two types: remedial and developmental. She defined *remedial* programs as those whose purpose is to overcome students' academic deficiencies. Many institutions view the mission of their learning centers in this light. Open admission policies and federal funding that enables a wide diversity of students to participate in higher education have led many institutions to offer remedial services for their high-risk students. In some cases, the remedial courses are mandatory and must be successfully completed in order to continue enrollment at the institution (Cashen, 1983). In other cases, students attend regular college classes in addition to their remedial activities (Roueche & Snow, 1977). Often remedial courses do not carry academic credit; if credit is available, it is sometimes institutional or internal credit, in which case it counts toward the students' course load and grade point average but not toward graduation requirements (Helm & Chand, 1983).

Cross (1976) defined *developmental* programs as those whose activities are designed to develop students' diverse academic talents. Boylan (1983) agreed and further defined developmental education as a professional specialty concerned with promoting educational opportunity, academic skills development, and educational efficiency at the postsecondary level. Some learning centers offer both remedial and developmental services, clearly delineating the difference by offering credit for developmental classes but not for the remedial activities (Rosen, 1980). Often, high-risk students must successfully complete their remedial programs before they are allowed to participate in developmental activities.

A large number of learning centers label their programs developmental. At times the term developmental is used simply to avoid the stigma of calling a program remedial. Also, financial considerations often dictate use of the term developmental since state legislatures often discourage or even prohibit institutions from offering remedial courses at the postsecondary level. (Ironically, these same legislatures expect their institutions of higher learning to successfully educate all who enroll.)

The recent drop in postsecondary enrollment caused by declining numbers of high school graduates means that institutions must do all they can to retain the students who do enroll on their campuses. Developmental programs have been the mainstay of higher education's retention efforts. Since the 1960s, learning center administrators have expected increased retention, as well as improved grade point average, as a payoff from developmental education programs (Clymer, 1978).

All kinds of students, even good ones, have problems adjusting to the academic demands of college (Walker, 1980). Therefore, whenever possible, learning centers offer a variety of services: remedial support, developmental education, and enrichment opportunities. By offering learning opportunities at all levels, learning assistance educators provide intervention and support for all students in developing their learning skills and abilities to the fullest.

Student Placement and Enrollment

Colleges and universities use a variety of methods to determine which students should enroll in learning assistance centers or programs. Some schools make enrollment mandatory for certain students; others ask students to enroll on a voluntary basis.

Placement by testing.   About 60 percent of postsecondary institutions pretest all entering freshmen and use the results in assigning students to remedial or developmental classes (Roueche, Baker, & Roueche, 1984). As many as 90 percent of 2-year colleges assess students, although not all of these tests are mandatory (Woods, 1985). These test sequences assess reading, writing, and mathematics.

In four regional and national studies analyzed by Gabriel (1989), the Nelson-Denny Reading Test was the most commonly administered test for reading, while essays or locally developed tests were more common for writing and mathematics. Learning center personnel also may administer pretests, but generally they are more interested in using tests as diagnostic instruments to help them in directing students to the most appropriate developmental classes, introducing students to tutors who will be able to assist them, or designing an individualized instructional program.

Other placement procedures.   In the absence of a locally administered testing program, institutions often rely on American College Testing program (ACT) or Scholastic Aptitude Test (SAT) scores, along with high school records, in making class assignments. Academic advisors also may ask students for a self-assessment to use as an aid in making class selection decisions.

Whenever possible, a combination of information sources is used to place entering freshmen in classes in which they can function academically. Maxey and Sawyer's (1981) study indicated that ACT test scores and high school grades are useful predictors of freshman grade point average in college, although they are slightly less accurate for minorities. The authors also determined that the combination of test scores and self-reported high school grades predicts college freshman GPA with greater accuracy than does either measure alone.

Research by McDonald and Gawkoski (1979) supports the use of SAT tests for predicting the performance of incoming freshmen. Chissom and Lanier (1975) produced similar results earlier. Apparently, both ACT and SAT scores can be used in combination with high school grades to predict GPA with a moderate degree of success.

Many institutions have guidelines for mandated placement in a learning assistance program. A student who scores below a certain level on the ACT or SAT, has a high school GPA below a specified minimum, or scores below a designated score on a pre-enrollment placement test may be required to participate in specific learning center activities before matriculation. At some institutions, the student may be allowed to enroll in regular classes while still being required to take specific learning center classes (Committee on Learning Skills Centers, 1976; Maxwell, 1979). Roueche (1983) reported that mandatory completion of specific developmental courses assigned on the basis of basic skills achievement levels is one of the earmarks of a successful learning center.

Voluntary placement. At some institutions, entering students are not required to participate in learning center programs, no matter what their test results or previous grades are. Students are advised of the available opportunities, but use of the learning center is voluntary. Jones (1959) proposed that involvement in developmental activities be completely voluntary, maintaining that students will be successful only if they want to be and not because the are forced. But when skills assistance is offered solely on an elective basis, programs may not reach all students who need them. In a study conducted at an open-admission junior college, Reed (1989) found that 62 percent of students scoring below the ninth grade level on the Nelson-Denny Reading Test said they did not need help with their reading. Students' inaccuracy in assessing their need for help was made evident at the end of the year. Of the students reading below the ninth grade level, those who had said they needed help with their reading achieved higher GPAs than students who had said they might need help, who in turn achieved higher GPAs than students who had said they did not need help.

After experience with both required and voluntary programs, Shaw (1961) concluded that freshmen generally were incapable of determining if they should enroll in a skills course. He further noted that once enrolled, students were unable to determine whether they needed to continue. On the other hand, he said, if students resist taking the course, they should be allowed to drop it as they would any other course.

Whenever possible, learning centers offer credit for regularly scheduled classes. Those who support required programs generally recommend that credit be granted for developmental classes (Roueche & Snow, 1977). Faculty and administrative politics sometimes make granting credit for a course difficult; however, research indicates that awarding credit for developmental classes increases the overall effectiveness of the program. Boylan (1983), in his review of the effectiveness of programs based on analysis of program reports, research, and literature, found that the programs reporting the greatest student gains all offered credit for developmental courses.

In a national study, Roueche (1983) used survey questions to identify program and course elements common to institutions that reported the most positive outcomes. He found that among the skills development programs reporting the most complete and encouraging retention data, all awarded credit for developmental courses, and all counted the credit as transcript credit (counting toward graduation requirements).

Types of Learning Assistance Programs

Learning assistance programs may be categorized according to the facilities for instruction (e.g., regularly scheduled classes or a center/lab program), their connection with other services or courses on campus (e.g., outreach workshops or adjunct courses), or the delivery of instruction within a classroom or lab (e.g., individualized or small group instruction).

Organizational Patterns

Learning assistance programs may consist of classes that are similar to other college classes in appearance and that meet in regular classrooms. Alternatively, programs may be located in a designated lab or learning center that students visit individually or in small groups. As a third option, facilities may consist of several rooms housing a variety of learning assistance programs. The structure of the program often affects the services offered.

Laboratory instruction. Laboratory instruction may be offered to the entire college community or only to those enrolled in special programs for underprepared or at-risk students. It may be required of students taking regularly scheduled learning assistance classes or it may be offered on a drop-in basis. It may also be the only learning assistance provided on a campus.

Regularly scheduled classes. Learning assistance programs often consist of regularly scheduled classes because many underprepared students require more structure than is provided in drop-in programs (Roueche, Baker, & Roueche, 1984). In addition, these courses are, in the short run, less costly for the college to provide. Classes may be structured similarly to regular courses, running for a full quarter or semester, counting for 2 or 3 hours' credit, and involving comprehensive development of reading and study skills. Conversely, they may be a series of short, 1-hour credit classes that emphasize specific skills such as listening and notetaking, test taking, or spelling improvement. These classes often have a laboratory component, and additional assistance from tutors or faculty is readily available.

A program in New Mexico exemplifies a novel approach in which local public school reading specialists teach at the university program without outside laboratories or tutoring (Hamberg & Rubin, 1986). Using the Nelson-Denny Reading Test for placement and progress assessment, the public school teachers employ commercial materials, magazine articles, students' regular course materials, and sustained silent reading in their instruction. They teach reading and study skills directly to the whole class rather than using individualized work packets. The course is open to all university students.

At a Louisiana university, students receive 5 hours' credit for the recitation and lecture sections of either a lower or an upper level course in developmental reading (Dillard, 1989). In the lower level courses, students read and report on material on their major and on fiction. They also learn test taking skills, develop vocabulary, work on their reading rates, and receive lessons from the instructor. When students reach the upper level course, they learn to use a study plan, text structures, and writing patterns. The instructors provide individual guidance and small group work in the classroom and in the library. Students use both regular state-adopted textbooks and texts designed for reading classes.

Research supports the use of regularly scheduled classes in learning assistance programs. Beal (1980) has found that students who participate in such classes show improved study habits and attitudes toward learning. Students also improve their grade point averages and express positive feelings toward the institution and education.

Drop-in services. A well-advertised, centralized learning center encourages students to drop in for assistance any time during the semester. Most learning centers have staff members available to help students with specific learning difficulties, put them in contact with a tutor, or guide them into a focus group or class (Beal, 1980).

Adjunct classes. Special classes are sometimes initiated in conjunction with a specific academic department (Dempsey & Tomlinson, 1980; Elliottt & Fairbanks, 1986). For instance, a course designed to aid students in a nursing program would be specifically aimed at the reading, writing, vocabulary, and study techniques required in nursing classes. Sometimes a developmental educator team jointly teaches a class with a faculty member in a specific department. In a course called Introduction to Industrial Technology, for instance, a member of the industrial technology faculty might teach a portion of the class, introducing students to the discipline and giving them assignments designed to add to their information base. In the other part of the class, a developmental educator would instruct students in the reading and study techniques they needed to complete assignments, master the course content, and ultimately attain their academic goals.

At the University of Cincinnati, a psychology professor and two faculty members from the reading and study skills program collaborated on delivering two courses, one in psychology and one in reading and study skills. The two classes offered five credits and were listed under a single course number to facilitate scheduling (Bullock, Madden, & Harter, 1987).

At St. Cloud State University in Minnesota, students whose high school grades are below the 50th percentile in their class must take a "paired class" for two quarters of their freshman year (Rauch, 1989). With Modern Technology and Civilization, for example, they take a reading and study skills course. The program also includes a voluntary tutorial service.

The literature strongly supports the use of adjunct classes in learning assistance programs. Tomlinson and Green (1976) report beneficial outcomes from integrating reading and study skills classes with content area classes. Dempsey and Tomlinson (1980) describe different formats used to teach adjunct classes and maintain that the concurrent development of process skills and content understanding achieved through adjunct programming is a powerful tool for improving both instruction and student academic performance. In the Bullock, Madden, and Harter (1987) study, students taking the adjunct course had a better perception of their reading and study abilities and higher scores on standardized reading tests than their counterparts who took psychology without the adjunct course.

A program at the University of Missouri at Kansas City has been adopted in 34 states (Blanc, DeBuhr, & Martin, 1983; Wolfe, 1987). In this program, learning center instructors conduct review sessions in which they integrate learning skills instruction with course content. The instructors also attend the course lectures, take notes and complete the readings. They also schedule three or four supplementary instruction (SI) sessions per week for students who elect to attend. Students in need of further assistance receive tutoring. In one study, students who attended one or more SI sessions achieved significantly higher course test grades, course final grades, and overall GPAs for the semester than students who wished to take the sessions but could not because of schedule conflicts (Blanc et al.).

Carpenter and Johnson

After training at the University of Missouri program, Wolfe (1987) conducted a pilot study in a history class at Arundel Community College in Arnold, Maryland. She found that although participants in the SI program had received lower SAT scores than did nonparticipants, they achieved significantly higher GPAs and final course grades in history than did nonparticipants.

Outreach programs. A large learning assistance center may offer a variety of outreach programs. Instructors may offer workshops to various groups on campus, such as classes, fraternities, sororities, and residence hall gatherings. They may work with faculty members on dealing with reading and learning in their classes. For example, McKinley (1990) obtained release time from teaching to meet individually with the 65 full-time faculty members of Laramie County Community College in Cheyenne, Wyoming. She provided readability information about the textbooks they were using and informed them about the reading classes students could take. In some cases she shared some techniques they could use to help students comprehend their textbooks.

Methods of Instruction

According to Roueche, Baker, and Roueche (1984), 60 percent of respondents to their survey employed some form of individualized learning assistance instruction. Forty percent employed either whole class activities, such as lectures and class discussions, or small group activities. Whether instructors work within a classroom or a learning center lab, they may employ any of these instructional delivery systems.

Individualized instruction. Based on a pretest, diagnostic test, or professional evaluation, students may be given an individualized program designed either to correct specific skill deficiencies or to develop overall educational efficiency. The program may include readings, workbook pages, lab assignments, computer-assisted instruction, or a combination of these activities in conjunction with other instructional materials. These types of programs date back as early as the 1940s (Triggs, 1942) and still are in use today.

Although individualized instruction often is set in a lab that students attend regularly, it may occur in a scheduled class. In upstate New York, for example, 60 innercity students enrolled in a community college educational opportunity program in which they took a biology course and a developmental reading course. In the reading course students used a microcomputer to develop their knowledge of biology terms, increase their reading rate, and improve their comprehension of the biology text (Balajthy, Bacon, & Hasby, 1985).

In a more traditional individualized course with a strong computer-assisted instruction component, students participated in planning individualized programs of study with their instructors (Kincade et al., 1989). A total of 423 students enrolled in 24 sections of a one-semester college reading improvement course evaluated over a six-semester period. In addition to using computer programs that provided vocabulary practice and diagnostic information on 25 comprehension skills, students worked with comprehension kits, workbooks, and audiotapes. In this case, researchers found little gain in reading ability as measured by the Nelson-Denny Reading Test. Furthermore, 27.4 percent of the students failed to complete the course. The researchers were unable to explain the study's poor results.

One of the problems of computer-assisted instruction in the college reading and learning center is the dearth of materials designed for such use. To help meet the need, computer software on using college biology and psychology textbooks effectively was developed and evaluated at Indiana University (Adams & Mikulecky, 1989). Students at a community college and a 4-year college completed three lessons over a 3-week period. They learned to determine key concepts, compare and contrast these concepts, and graphically represent the relationships among them. Treatment groups significantly outperformed control subjects on chapter tests. The authors concluded that certain reading and learning strategies could be taught effectively with computer-assisted instruction.

With sequenced individualized assistance, students may be expected to complete designated parts of a program before they are assessed to determine whether they should continue in the same sequence. They may receive instructional supervision, tutorial help, and aid from lab assistants, or they may be expected to complete the assignments with little supervision and meet the faculty only for evaluation purposes. Rupley, Clark, and Blair (1979) discuss an individualized program that differentiates and coordinates personnel, time, and available resources to maximize the reading development of all learners.

Small group instruction. At times a number of students need to gain expertise in the same skills (Spaulding, 1975). Small groups may be used to teach time management, effective listening skills, efficient notetaking, or a variety of other developmentally oriented skills. Students receive feedback not only from the teacher but also from other group members. These groups may be advertised campuswide or formulated specifically for students already enrolled in learning center activities. Focus groups are usually short term associations, but students often participate in more than one focus group in order to strengthen different academic abilities. Heerman (1984) employed small groups in an individualized lab setting.

Dempsey and Tomlinson (1980) suggest that small groups can provide a place for experimentation, creativity, and innovation. Small groups also enable the learning center staff to provide very specific help to a wide variety of students without expending the time required for an ongoing class or for individual counseling.

Tutoring. Learning centers often provide content area tutoring to assist students with specific academic classes (Beal, 1980; Clymer, 1978). Often the institution pays the tutors, while the learning center is responsible for selecting, training, and monitoring them. At some colleges, students must pay for tutor assistance, and learning center personnel act as both program administrators and brokers, bringing the student together with a tutor who is proficient in the required subject area. Tutors also are usually available to help students engaged in learning center activities. Reading and study skills tutors may help students with specific developmental assignments or assist in the reading and study skills lab.

Tutoring is a familiar component of larger comprehensive programs for high-risk students. McHugh, Jerigan, and Moses (1986) employed tutoring in a multifaceted program that included study skills and writing courses in addition to regular freshman courses. Anderson and Smith (1987) used peer tutors in a developmental college reading laboratory.

Tutoring for a particular course most often is done on an individual basis. Many students need to contact a tutor only once for help with a specific problem. However, students often return to a tutor weekly for continuing assistance with a difficult subject. In these circumstances, a learning center staff member or the tutor may form tutoring groups, encouraging all individuals who need help with a specific class to meet weekly at a regular time and place.

Tutors may be graduate or upper division students with expertise in a specific subject, full- or part-time teachers, members of the community, or retired faculty members. Continuous training in the skills areas, empathy, assertiveness, and record keeping ability enable tutors to be of maximum assistance (Carpenter, 1984).

Researchers at Los Angeles City College found that students who worked with tutors showed a higher rate of achievement than students who did not (Gold, 1980). The same study reported strong support from faculty for the tutoring program. Similar results were reported at Los Angeles Pierce College (Schulman, 1981), where half the students indicated that they would have failed or dropped courses without tutoring help. Peer tutors in the study by Anderson and Smith (1987) helped students achieve higher grades, increase attendance in the reading laboratory, and improve reading posttest scores.

Ingredients of Successful Programs

Investigating successful programs. Many published program descriptions now report some form of evaluation, and the sophistication of program evaluation appears to be improving. Components of successful learning assistance programs, as determined by several research reviews, are listed in Table 1.

One of the first major efforts to investigate the components of successful developmental programs resulted from the federally-funded National Project II: Alternatives to the Revolving Door, which involved a consortium of institutions with successful developmental programs. In his report of project activities, Donovan (1975) found that the more successful programs included (1) a wide variety of personal and academic developmental services; (2) a dual emphasis on personal counseling and academic skills development; and (3) frequent staff contact with students.

Roueche and Snow (1977) attempted to identify model developmental programs using the survey technique. In programs identified as being particularly effective, they found the following components: (1) diagnostic services, (2) an emphasis on learning skills development, (3) personal counseling to support learning skills development, and (4) individualized learning opportunities provided through small classes or laboratories.

Grant and Hoeber (1978) investigated the effectiveness of developmental programs through an extensive review of the literature and research. Their findings were reported in two categories: instructional and programmatic. Under instructional components, the authors listed five important features: (1) clearly written, well-articulated objectives made available to the students; (2) continuous and systematic planning based on feedback and program monitoring; (3) attention to individual needs, personal styles of learning, and rates of growth; (4) close attention to appropriate matches of learners, teachers, methods, and materials; and (5) intensive efforts to identify how and under what learning conditions students transfer knowledge.

Under the heading of programmatic considerations, the authors found the following to be important: (1) faculty development in specific awareness skills and teaching-learning strategies, (2) development and refinement of diagnostic instru-

Table 1

Components of Successful Learning Assistance Programs

Component	Donovan (1975)	Roueche & Snow (1977)	Grant & Hoeber (1978)	Maxwell (1979)	Boylan (1983)	Roueche (1983)
Strong administrative support						X
Assessment/diagnosis/placement		X	X	X	X	X
Structured courses						X
Award of credit					X	X
Flexible completion strategies						X
Multiple learning systems		X				X
Written, disseminated objectives			X			
Continuous faculty training			X			X

Carpenter and Johnson

Table 1 (continued)

Components of Successful Learning Assistance Programs

Use of peer tutors	X		X			
Student contact/monitoring	X	X		X		X
Preparation for subsequent courses	X					
Program evaluation/research	X		X	X		
Variety of academic developmental services		X	X	X	X	X
Personal counseling	X		X	X	X	X

ments, (3) sophisticated and sensitive research designs, and (4) comprehensive curricular revision.

Based on her own experience in working with developmental students as well as a review of the literature, Maxwell (1979) recommends that effective learning assistance programs include (1) diagnosis of students' strengths and weaknesses as learners, (2) tutorial services, (3) personal counseling, (4) basic reading and study skills instruction, and (5) built-in evaluation activities.

In his review of the effectiveness of developmental programs, based on an analysis of program reports, research, and literature, Boylan (1983) found that programs reporting the greatest student gains (1) provided a comprehensive array of services, (2) had a high degree of student participation, (3) made participation mandatory at the outset of the college careers of high-risk students, (4) offered credit for developmental courses, and (5) emphasized the development of students' reasoning skills in addition to basic content skills.

Roueche (1983) conducted a national study to determine how colleges and universities responded to underprepared students. Among other objectives, Roueche sought to identify which program and course characteristics were shared by the institutions that reported the most positive outcomes. Roueche identified 11 common elements: (1) strong administrative support; (2) mandatory assessment and placement; (3) structured courses having scheduled days and times with attendance requirements; (4) award of credit without exception; (5) flexible completion strategies, including the use of incompletes; (6) multiple learning systems; (7) volunteer instructors who receive special training in developmental studies and consider counseling an integral part of the instructional effort; (8) use of peer tutors; (9) monitoring of student behaviors; (10) preparation for subsequent courses, including awareness of their demands; and (11) program evaluation.

Investigating the investigations. Inspection of Table 1 and the literature reviews brings to mind several observations. First, without some objective means of identifying which reports of program evaluations to include, the analyses might be

Carpenter and Johnson

subject to bias, either intentional or inadvertent. Second, some important factors may have failed to make the list or may have been identified in only one or two analyses. Third, the content of instruction seems to be irrelevant to the success of a program, although this appearance may be due simply to difficulty in defining reliably what the content was. Fourth, some components of successful programs may be components of nearly all programs, successful or unsuccessful. Even components that are associated only with success may not be the reason for success. For instance, routine success with applying a diagnostic-prescriptive approach may indicate only that the instructors who choose this approach tend to be well educated in the field and thus knowledgeable about recommended techniques.

A metaanalysis of studies selected according to strict criteria is the logical alternative to the above informal procedures. In their metaanalysis, Kulik, Kulik, and Shwalb (1983) found only 60 studies that met their criteria out of more than 500 available in the research literature. They found that college programs for high-risk and disadvantaged students produced a small but positive effect on GPA and retention rates. Effects were stronger for new programs than for older ones, which led them to postulate that much of the effect was due to the novelty of the program rather than its instructional effectiveness. In community colleges, learning assistance programs were relatively ineffective. Because the effects reported in published journal articles were larger than those reported in ERIC documents, the researchers concluded that even the small overall improvements found in GPA and retention might have been overly optimistic, noting that many studies without significant effects might not have been published at all.

These review studies suggest that for learning assistance programs to be effective, much care must be taken in their design, implementation, and evaluation. Apparently it is all too easy for programs to have little lasting effect on the students they serve.

Assessing program effectiveness. The consensus in the increasing body of research in developmental education is that improving student learning skills is a unified process rather than a set of individual activities. Programs with isolated and unrelated services are far less likely to be successful than those with a comprehensive, systematic approach. Furthermore, programs that emphasize personalization of the learning process and attend to the affective as well as the cognitive dimensions of learning are more likely to succeed (Maxwell, 1979).

Research reports also suggest that the greater the variety of services provided, the more likely students are to show gains in test scores, grade point averages, and retention. Skill development groups or classes are effective if they are coupled with counseling or tutoring (Burgess, Cranney, & Larsen, 1976; Martin & Blanc, 1981; Randlett, 1983; Starks, 1982).

Learning centers in higher education need to assess the value of their programs and services. Formative and summative evaluations of each aspect of existing programs should lead to valuable information for growth and change (see Boylan & George, this volume). Longitudinal research tracking student GPA, perseverance, and graduation might indicate which types of programs are the most successful, which approaches yield the best results, and which instructional practices produce the most efficient learners (Morante, 1986).

Even though aiding students in becoming efficient learners is the main objective of developmental educators, school administrators might be more impressed if researchers followed Tucker's (1982) lead and initiated projects that would justify the cost of developmental programs. For instance, studies comparing matched groups of students suggest that the attrition rate is lower among students who participate in developmental programs than among those who do not (Kulik, Kulik, & Shwalb, 1983; Obler, 1980; Starks, 1982).

Programs that cater specifically to high-risk students particularly need to conduct careful research projects to determine the effectiveness of the services provided. Since some educators believe that money would be better spent in other endeavors that show visible benefits, those involved in high-risk student retention must carefully justify the worth of their programs.

Conclusions and Implications

Learning assistance has been a part of American higher education since the nineteenth century. Then, as now, institutions provided specific educational programs to assist their academically underprepared students. Learning assistance programs were not spawned because of open admission policies; bridging the academic preparation gap has long been part of the traditional, if not the formal, mission of higher education.

Differences in philosophical orientation, program organization, and external and internal structure are as numerous as learning centers themselves. No two programs are identical because each is tailored to fit the requirements of the institution, the needs of the students, and the expertise of the professional staff. Educators in learning assistance programs continue to search for more efficient teaching strategies, a more effective structuring model, and an ideal pattern of program organization that fits their unique circumstances.

Since research has not yet indicated the desirability of one theoretical model over all others or even the best combination of several models, individuals who are just beginning to work in learning assistance or who wish to expand their services in a learning center must make the best of what research and information is available. Adopting successful activities into new or expanding centers could strengthen programs while eliminating the trial-and-error approach necessarily employed by professionals who began their learning centers in earlier years.

When initiating or expanding a learning center, administrators need to assess the needs of their students, their faculty, and their institution (Castelli & Johnson, 1984). One of the theoretical models previously discussed might serve as a guide for development; on the other hand, a combination of models might more nearly address the needs of these groups. Only those actively involved in the project can adequately determine what the most pressing needs are and initiate activities to meet them. Attempting to duplicate the programs of another learning center may not be the most effective approach.

Whatever approach administrators use, they should take care not to promise more than their program can deliver. They should initiate activities based on the resources available, with additional services added as they become feasible. It is important to perform advertised activities well in order to build confidence in the center's ability to increase student learning and achievement. If a program offers too many services in relation to the resources available, the center's staff may not be able to perform any of the promised activities adequately. Students, as well as the reputation of the center, will suffer.

Whenever possible, input from students, faculty, and midlevel administrators should be encouraged. Regular meetings of an advisory board comprising several students, faculty from each area of the institution, and interested administrators will strengthen the center, add new ideas, and make programs more visible. In addition, keeping supervisory administrators informed and involved should increase their commitment and support to the center and its activities.

Formative and summative evaluations (Peterson, 1983) can further increase support from the administrative and academic communities. These evaluations should be conducted on a regular basis, involve all aspects of the center's activities, and be made available to the public. Evaluations are a valuable tool in assessing the quality of the services being offered as well as in indicating areas of concern. The type of evaluation tools should be varied, as should the evaluators, in order to acquire reliable, new, and useful information (Clowes, 1984; Somers, 1987).

In addition to conducting regular and periodic evaluations, we encourage professionals to become involved in research activities. Research in the field of postsecondary learning assistance is relatively new, and little information was published prior to 1960. Since that time, much of what has been written has been descriptive. Some excellent survey research has described what is being done in learning centers; however, more empirical research is needed.

Empirical research examining the different types of programs would aid professionals in determining the most effective

Carpenter and Johnson

delivery systems and instructional methods. Both qualitative and quantitative research which could be replicated would provide useful information to educators in learning assistance. Past research has provided some basic information, but it is now time to test hypotheses about models of organization and methods of instruction. What is determined through research could assist educators in all academic areas in providing quality educational opportunities to all students.

Professionals in learning centers have a responsibility to assist students in achieving their academic goals. They also can become campus leaders in initiating new learning experiences, sharing teaching techniques, and providing developmental activities for teachers as well as students. By offering insights and expertise to other faculty members in a nonthreatening atmosphere, they can make a narrowly focused learning assistance program a true learning center where learning is enhanced for everyone.

References and Suggested Readings

Adams, S.M., & Mikulecky, L. (1989). Teaching effective college reading and learning strategies using computer assisted instruction. *Journal of College Reading and Learning, 22,* 64-70.

Anderson, O.S., & Smith, L.J. (1987). Peer tutors in a college reading laboratory: A model that works. *Reading Improvement, 24,* 238-247.

Balajthy, E., Bacon, L., & Hasby, P. (1985, November). *Introduction to computers and introduction to word processing: Integrating content area coursework into college reading/study skills curricula using microcomputers.* Paper presented at the Conference on Microcomputers and Basic Skills in College, New York. (ED 273 941)

Beal, P.E. (1980). Learning centers and retention. In O.T. Lenning & R.L. Hayman (Eds.), *New roles for learning assistance* (pp. 59-73). San Francisco, CA: Jossey-Bass.

Bengis, L. (1986, April). *College discovery prefreshman summer program, 1985: An evaluation.* New York: City University of New York, Office of Student Affairs and Special Programs. (ED 278 287)

Blanc, R.A., DeBuhr, L.E., & Martin, D.C. (1983). Breaking the attrition cycle: The effects of supplemental instruction on undergraduate performance and attrition. *Journal of Higher Education, 54,* 80-90.

Boylan, H.R. (1982). The growth of the learning assistance movement. In H.R. Boylan (Ed.), *Forging new partnerships in learning assistance* (pp. 5-16). San Francisco, CA: Jossey-Bass.

Boylan, H.R. (1983). *Is developmental education working? An analysis of research.* Report prepared for the National Association for Remedial and Developmental Studies in Postsecondary Education. Boone, NC: Appalachian State University.

Boylan, H.R. (1986). Facts, figures, and guesses about developmental education programs, personnel, and participation. *Research in Developmental Education, 3,* 1-6.

Boylan, H.R., & White, W.G. (1987). Educating all the nation's people: The historical roots of developmental education (Part 1). *Research in Developmental Education, 4,* 1-4.

Brier, E. (1984). Bridging the academic preparation gap: A historical view. *Journal of Developmental Education, 8,* 2-5.

Bullock, T., Madden, D., & Harter, J. (1987). Paired developmental reading and psychology courses. *Research and Teaching in Developmental Education, 3,* 22-31.

Burgess, B.A., Cranney, A.G., & Larsen, J.J. (1976). Effect on academic achievement of a voluntary university reading program. *Journal of Reading, 19,* 644-646.

Cahalan, M., & Farris, E. (1986). *College level remediation.* (Report No. cs-86-218; frss-r-19). Washington, DC: Department of Education, Office of Educational Research and Improvement. (ed 274-290)

Carpenter, K. (1984). *Tutor selection, training, and supervision.* Unpublished manuscript, Kearney State College, Kearney, NE.

Carter, H.L.J. (1959) Effective use of textbooks in the reading program. In O.S. Causey & W. Eller (Eds.), *Starting and improving college reading programs* (pp. 155-163). Fort Worth, TX: Texas Christian University Press.

Cashen, C.J. (1983). The University of Wisconsin-Parkside college skills program. In J.E. Roueche (Ed.), *A new look at successful programs* (pp. 49-58). San Francisco, CA: Jossey-Bass.

Castelli, C., & Johnson, D. (1984). Learning center assessment: Managing for change in the '80s. *Journal of College Reading and Learning, 17,* 30-42.

Chissom, B.S., & Lanier, D. (1975). Prediction of first quarter freshman gpa using sat scores and high school grades. *Educational and Psychological Measurement, 35,* 461-463.

Christ, F.L. (1971). Systems for learning assistance: Learners, learning facilitators, and learning centers. In F.L. Christ (Ed.), *Proceedings of the Fourth Annual Conference of the Western College Reading Association* (pp. 32-41). Whittier, CA: College Reading and Learning Association.

Clowes, D.A. (1984). The evaluation of remedial/developmental programs: A stage model of program evaluation. *Journal of Developmental Education, 8,* 14-15, 27-30.

Clymer, C. (1978). A national survey of learning assistance evaluation: Rationale, techniques, problems. In G. Enright (Ed.), *Proceedings of the Eleventh Annual Conference of the Western College Reading Association* (pp. 21-30).Whittier, CA: College Reading and Learning Association.

Committee on Learning Skills Centers. (1976). *Learning skills centers: A cccc report.* Urbana, IL: National Council of Teachers of English.

Cranney, A.G. (1987). The improving professionalization of postsecondary developmental reading. *Journal of Reading, 30,* 690-700.

*Cross, K.P. (1976). *Accent on learning.* San Francisco, CA: Jossey-Bass.

Dempsey, J., & Tomlinson, B. (1980). Learning centers and instructional/curricular reform. In O.T. Lenning & R.L. Nayman (Eds.), *New roles for learning assistance* (pp. 41-58). San Francisco, CA: Jossey-Bass.

Dillard, M.L. (1989). Changing a college developmental reading program from three to five semester hours' credit: What's involved? *Forum for Reading, 20,* 26-31.

Donovan, R.A. (1975). *National Project II: Alternatives to the revolving door.* Unpublished manuscript, Bronx Community College, New York.

Elliott, M.K., & Fairbanks, M. (1986). General vs. adjunct reading/study skills instruction for a college history course. *Journal of College Reading and Learning, 19,* 22-29.

Enright, G., & Kerstiens, G. (1980). The learning center: Toward an expanded role. In O.T. Lenning & R.L. Nayman (Eds.), *New roles for learning assistance* (pp. 1-24). San Francisco, CA: Jossey-Bass.

Fairbanks, M.M. (1974). The effect of college reading improvement programs on academic achievement. In P.L. Nacke (Ed.), *Interaction: Research and practice for college-adult reading* (pp. 105-114). Clemson, SC: National Reading Conference.

Gabriel, D. (1989). Assessing assessment. *Review of Research in Developmental Education, 6*(5), 1-5.

Gold, B.K. (1980). *The LACC tutoring program: An evaluation* (Research Study No. 80-4). Los Angeles, CA: Los Angeles City College. (ED 182 465)

Gordon, B., & Flippo, R.F. (1983). An update on college reading improvement programs in the southeastern United States. *Journal of Reading, 27,* 155-163.

Grant, M.K., & Hoeber, D.R. (1978). *Basic skills programs: Are they working?* Washington, DC: American Association for Higher Education.

Hamberg, S., & Rubin, R. (1986). Profiles of a successful college reading program. *New Mexico Journal of Reading, 7,* 25-27.

Heerman, C.E. (1984). Reading gains of students in a college reading laboratory. *Reading Horizons, 24,* 186-192.

Helm, P.K., & Chand, S. (1983). Student success at Triton College. In J.E. Roueche (Ed.), *A new look at successful programs* (pp. 43-48). San Francisco, CA: Jossey-Bass.

Jones, E. (1959). Selection and motivation of students. In O.S. Causey & W. Eller (Eds.), *Starting and improving college reading programs* (pp. 25-34). Fort Worth, TX: Texas Christian University Press.

Kincade, K.M., Kleine, P.F., Johnson, I.T., & Jacob, C.T., Jr. (1989). Individualizing a college reading course with the aid of computers. *Journal of College Reading and Learning, 23,* 71-80.

*Kulik, C.C., Kulik, J.A., & Shwalb, B.J. (1983). College programs for high-risk and disadvantaged students: A metaanalysis of findings. *Review of Educational Research, 53,* 397-414.

Landward, S., & Hepworth, D. (1984). Support systems for high-risk college students: Findings and issues. *College and University, 59,* 119-128.

Martin, D.C., & Blanc, R. (1981). The learning center's role in retention: Integrating student support services with departmental instruction. *Journal of Developmental & Remedial Education, 4,* 2-4.

Maxey, J., & Sawyer, R. (1981). *Predictive validity of the ACT assessment for Afro-American/black, Mexican-American/Chicano, and Caucasian-American/white students* (Research Bulletin No. 81-1). Iowa City, IA: American College Testing Program.

*Maxwell, M. (1979). *Improving student learning skills.* San Franciso, CA: Jossey-Bass.

McDonald, R.T., & Gawkoski, R.S. (1979). Predictive value of SAT scores and high school achievement for success in a college honors program. *Educational and Psychological Measurement, 39,* 411-414.

McHugh, F., Jernigan, L., & Moses, K. (1986). Literacy first: A successful opportunity program. *College Teaching, 34,* 83-87.

McKinley, N. (1990). Reach out to community college faculty. *Journal of Reading, 33,* 304-305.

McMurtrie, R.S. (1982). Effects of training in study skills for specific content courses as reflected in actual course enrollment, grades, and withdrawals of high-risk college freshmen. *Yearbook of the American Reading Forum, 2,* 64-65.

Morante, E.A. (1986). The effectiveness of developmental programs: A two-year follow-up study. *Journal of Developmental Education, 9,* 14-15.

Obler, S.S. (1980). Programs for the underprepared student. In. J.E. Roueche (Ed.), *A new look at successful programs* (pp. 21-30). San Francisco, CA: Jossey-Bass.

*Perry, W.G. (1959). Students use and misuse of reading skills: A report to the faculty. *Harvard Educational Review, 29,* 193-200.

Peterson, P. (1983). Success: A model for the planning and evaluation of college learning. *Journal of College Reading and Learning, 16,* 39-54.

Pollock, J.E., & Wilkinson, B.L. (1988). Enrollment differences in academic achievement for university study skills students. *College Student Journal, 22,* 76-82.

Pugh, S. (1985). Comprehension and comprehension monitoring by experienced readers. *Journal of Reading, 28,* 292-300.

Randlett, A.L. (1983). Peer tutor training in reading and study skills: A research review. *Yearbook of the American Reading Forum, 3,* 53-57.

Rauch, M. (1989). Encouraging students to use tutorial services. *Journal of Reading, 32,* 55.

Raygor, A.L. (1977). Keynote address: Meeting the individual needs of students. In G. Enright (Ed.), *Proceedings of the Tenth Annual Conference of the Western College Reading Association* (pp. 6-10). Whittier, CA: College Reading and Learning Association.

Reed, K.X. (1989) Expectation vs. ability: Junior college reading skills. *Journal of Reading, 32,* 537-541.

Reedy, V. (1973). Maximized individualized learning laboratory. *Community and Junior College Journal, 43,* 34.

Robyak, J.E., & Patton, M.J. (1977). The effectiveness of a study skills course for students of different personality types. *Journal of Counseling Psychology, 24,* 200-207.

Rosen, S.S. (1980). College level developmental reading and study skills programs: Survey report and overview. *Forum for Reading, 12,* 3-12.

Roueche, J.E., Baker, G.A. III, & Roueche, S.D. (1984). College responses to low-achieving students: A national study. *American Education, 20,* 31-34.

*Roueche, J.E., & Snow, J.J. (1977). *Overcoming learning problems.* San Francisco, CA: Jossey-Bass.

Roueche, S.D. (1983). Elements of program success: Report of a national study. In J.E. Roueche (Ed.), *A new look at successful programs* (pp. 3-10). San Francisco, CA: Jossey-Bass.

Rupley, W.H., Clark, F.E., & Blair, T.R. (1979). A model for individualizing instruction. In G. Enright (Ed.), *Proceedings of the Twelfth Annual Conference of the Western College Reading Association* (pp. 117-121). Whittier, CA: College Reading and Learning Association.

Schmelzer, R., & Brozo, W.G. (1982). A skills therapy approach for developmental learning in college. *Journal of Reading, 25,* 646-655.

Schulman, S. (1981) *A description of a developmental program for high risk students in a community college.* Woodland Hills, CA: Los Angeles Pierce College.

Shaw, P. (1961). Reading in college. In N.B. Henry (Ed.), *Development in and through reading* (pp. 336-337). Chicago, IL: University of Chicago Press.

Simpson, M.L. (1983). Recent research on independent learning strategies: Implications for developmental education. *Forum for Reading, 15,* 22-29.

Smith, G.D., Enright, G.D., & Devirian, M. (1975). A national survey of learning and study skills programs. In G.H. McNinch & W.D. Miller (Eds.), *Reading: Convention and inquiry* (pp. 67-73). Clemson, SC: National Reading Conference.

Smith, L., & Smith, G. (1988). A multivariate analysis of remediation efforts with developmental students. *Teaching English in the Two-Year College, 15,* 45-52.

Somers, R.L. (1987). Evaluation of developmental education programs: Issues, problems, and techniques. *Research in Developmental Education, 4,* 1-4.

Spaulding, N.V. (1975). Five minicourses in study skills. In R. Sugimoto (Ed.), *Proceedings of the Eighth Annual Conference of the Western College Reading Association* (pp. 179-181). Whittier, CA: College Reading and Learning Association.

Starks, G. (1982). *Community college retention in the '70s and '80s: Reasons for the withdrawl and effects of remedial and developmental programs.* Unpublished manuscript, University of Minnesota, Crookston, MN.

Sullivan, L.L. (1978). *A guide to higher education learning centers in the United States and Canada.* Portsmouth, NH: Entelek.

Sullivan, L.L. (1980). Growth and influence of the learning center movement. In K.V. Lauridsen (Ed.), *New directions for college learning assistance: Examining the scope of learning centers* (pp. 1-8). San Francisco, CA: Jossey-Bass.

Tomlinson, B.M., & Green, T. (1976). Integrating adjunct reading and study classes with the content areas. In R. Sugimoto (Ed.), *Proceedings of the Ninth Annual Conference of the Western College Reading Association* (pp. 199-203). Whittier, CA: College Reading and Learning Association.

Townsend, B.S. (1983). Assessment of a college reading course for academically deficient students. *Yearbook of the American Reading Forum, 3,* 41-42.

Triggs, F.O. (1942). Remedial reading programs: Evidence of their development. *Journal of Educational Psychology, 33,* 678-685.

Tucker, J. (1982). The cost-effectiveness of programs that teach people how to learn: An economic perspective. *Journal of Learning Skills, 4,* 28-34.

Walker, C. (1980). The learning assistance center in a selective institution. In K.V. Lauridsen (Ed.), *Examining the scope of learning centers.* San Francisco, CA: Jossey-Bass.

White, W.F. (1984). The college program to ameliorate developmental lag. *The College Board Review, 133,* 7-29.

Wolfe, R.F. (1987). The supplemental instruction program: Developing learning and thinking skills. *Journal of Reading, 31,* 228-232.

Woods, J.C. (1985). *Status of testing practices at two-year postsecondary institutions.* Iowa City, IA: ACT Publications. (ED 264 907)

Wright, D.A. (1985). *Many college freshmen take remedial courses* (Report No. NCES-85-211b). Washington, DC: National Center for Educational Statistics. (ED 262 742)

3

Program Evaluation

Hunter R. Boylan
Anita P. George
Barbara S. Bonham

I n its most basic sense, the term *evaluate* means to establish the value of something. In the sense of educational evaluation, the term generally refers to establishing the value of a particular program, technique, or set of materials on the basis of some known criteria.

The process of establishing value can have several purposes. Rossi and Freeman (1985) consider the major purpose of evaluation to be "to judge and to improve the planning, monitoring, and efficiency of educational activities" (p. 19). Cronbach (1983), however, suggests that the intent of evaluation is to influence thought or action in both the short and the long term. Anderson and Ball (1978), in discussing educational program evaluation, list six purposes: (1) to make decisions about program installation, (2) to make decisions about program continuation, (3) to rally support for a program, (4) to rally opposition to a program, (5) to revise or refine a program, or (6) to understand basic processes.

While each of these descriptions differs somewhat, several elements are common to each. First, evaluation should describe what is being done. Second, it should describe how well it is being done as measured against some relevant criteria. Third, it should provide information that may be used in decision making. This chapter focuses on evaluation methods that provide all three elements. The information provided here is designed to assist practitioners who are considering evaluation activities as well as those who are already engaging in such activities.

The first section of the chapter provides an overview of the changing role of educational evaluation over the past 50 years. It also is intended to explain some of the reasons evaluation has become such an important issue for college reading programs. In the second section, we discuss different types of evaluation and when they should be used. This discussion is followed by a review of several theoretical models of evaluation. The third section is designed to explore the strengths and weaknesses of various models commonly applied to the evaluation of postsecondary education programs. The fourth section discusses attempts by reading and study skills professionals to apply some of these models to the evaluation of their activities. Examples of the research and literature in the field are described and critiqued. In the fifth section we review the implications for practitioners of both the theoretical and the praxeological literature. Based on this review, we offer recommendations for those who are engaged in program evaluation activities. The chapter's final section explores future trends in the evaluation of postsecondary reading programs. We expect these trends to affect both the ways in which evaluation is carried out in college reading and study strategies programs and the issues that such evaluation will explore in the future.

The Changing Role of Evaluation

Efforts to evaluate college reading programs are a relatively recent phenomenon. In fact, the emergence of the entire field of educational evaluation is rather recent (Anderson & Ball, 1978).

Fifty years ago, few people in postsecondary education bothered to evaluate what they were doing in any formal or systematic fashion. It was taken for granted that those teaching in or managing educational programs were able to determine how well things were working on the basis of observation and experience. Furthermore, institutions and their faculty were much more autonomous than they are now. Not only were few external forces advocating evaluation, few were holding institutions and their faculties accountable for their actions.

Even when some sort of evaluation was desired, few commonly accepted tools and models were available. Those that were available were borrowed from the biological sciences and were heavily oriented toward testing and statistics (Clowes, 1981). Such models often required data that were hard to obtain and calculations that were difficult to perform. Evaluation in postsecondary institutions of the time was an extremely labor-intensive activity.

Obviously, times have changed. Program evaluation has become almost a cottage industry in most postsecondary schools. The evaluation of reading and study strategy programs is only one component of a vast array of evaluation activities taking place on college and university campuses.

At least three forces have had a major impact on the increasing volume and sophistication of evaluation activity. The first is the rise of state education systems. The second is the federal government's expanding role in funding postsecondary education. The third is the financing crisis experienced by many states in the 1970s and 1980s. Each of these factors has contributed to the importance of describing what we do, measuring its impact, and using evaluation data in the process of program development, refinement, and improvement.

The Rise of State Systems

As the number of state-supported colleges and universities grew in the 1950s and 1960s, most state legislatures established coordinating agencies for postsecondary education. While the roles of these agencies varied widely from state to state, all of them exercised some responsibility for assessing educational activities. As these agencies grew, so did their desire for data and evaluative assessment.

The information these agencies required included such basics as the number of minority students enrolled, the types of courses and services offered, and the number of faculty members with doctorate degrees. The purpose for collecting this data was consistent with Anderson and Ball's (1978) notion of understanding basic processes. Without this information on what was being accomplished with state tax revenues, it was practically impossible for the coordinating agencies to discharge their legislatively mandated responsibility to monitor state education activities.

Since these agencies did not have the staff to collect their own data, they relegated this responsibility to the institutions under their control. Pressure for evaluation at the state level was thus "top-down." Initially, the agencies wanted only data that described what was taking place in each institution so they could understand basic processes and develop a statewide picture of postsecondary education activity. Later, this information was used in a more sophisticated fashion consistent with Rossi and Freeman's (1985) notion of incorporating evaluation data into program planning and development. The information also was used to make decisions about program expansion, continuation, or elimination. Individual institutions, therefore, had to provide information in order to ensure that their needs were considered in statewide planning efforts.

The establishment of state coordinating agencies had two effects. First, it made individual institutions accountable for providing information to a higher authority. Within the institution, central administrators held department chairs and program directors accountable for providing this information. Thus, gathering data was added to the job description of middle managers in postsecondary education.

A second effect was that college administrators began to use evaluation data for more than just descriptive purposes. They began to gather information for decision making. They also began to see evaluation as being linked to decisions made by state coordinating agencies about their particular institutions.

The Growth of the Federal Education Bureaucracy

A second force in the expansion of evaluation was the increased federal role in funding postsecondary education during the latter half of the twentieth century. While the federal government has always had some role in funding postsecondary education (e.g., the Morrill Acts of 1862 and 1890, the National Defense Education Act of 1958), the Higher Education Act of 1965 probably was the most comprehensive modern piece of legislation involving federal funding for colleges and universities. Its various titles authorized hundreds of millions of dollars for program development; student financial aid, assistance to the disadvantaged; capital improvements on college campuses; library facilities; and special programs for women, ethnic minorities, and adults. The federal education bureaucracy expanded rapidly to coordinate and support these programs.

With this expansion came an increased need for information to help in coordinating, refining, and improving this vast body of educational endeavors. Again, initial evaluation activity was designed to describe what existed or to understand basic processes—in this case, to quantify what the public was receiving for its tax dollars. Programs were expected to provide data on the type and number of students served, the nature of services provided, the gains made by students in various programs, and student retention rates. Like the state bureaucracies, the federal bureaucracies needed maintenance data to show returns for the money spent.

Later, as new programs were proposed and new budget authorizations were debated, evaluative data were needed for political and decision-making purposes. Officials who supported the expansion of special programs and services wanted evaluation data to rally support for their positions. Those who opposed special programs looked to evaluation as a means of establishing that such programs were ineffective and should not be supported.

At the same time, legislative mandates for improved planning and coordination of the federal education bureaucracy caused those responsible for monitoring federal education programs to seek even more evaluative data. Their needs were to understand exactly what was being provided in various federal programs so that efforts could be coordinated and refinements planned.

In both cases, the burden for providing data was placed on the institutions receiving funds. Again, the pressure for providing evaluation data came from the top (the federal government) down (the individual institutions). By the early 1970s, most colleges and universities were providing data for two levels of bureaucracy—state and federal. Both reinforced the notion that evaluation activity was important. Now, however, the importance of evaluation was not only to understand basic processes or to monitor and refine programs but also to justify continued funding of these programs.

The Impact of Financial Crises

By the mid-1970s, a variety of financial pressures began to affect postsecondary education. After the baby boom generation passed through postsecondary institutions, there was no large pool of applicants to replace them. Enrollment shortfalls became commonplace for colleges and universities.

These shortfalls led to a number of financial problems. Since most public institutions were funded according to a formula based on full-time students enrolled, the loss of enrollment resulted in a commensurate loss in revenue from state subsidies. The financial problems caused by lost revenues from enrollment shortfalls were soon exacerbated by the pressures of inflation during the late 1970s. The recession of the early 1980s brought about a decline in state tax revenues, making matters still worse.

As a result of these factors, institutions had to face some difficult decisions they had been able to avoid during the time of financial plenty. Retrenchment became a buzzword among postsecondary administrators during the 1970s. Retrenchment meant that colleges and universities would have to eliminate some programs and consolidate others—and, in the process, cut back some faculty positions. It also meant that the limited financial resources available had to be watched more carefully and allocated more objectively. When dollars were scarce, it was necessary to gather as much information as possible to decide where to spend them in order to obtain maximum benefits for the institution.

These financial crises led to a new set of purposes for institutional evaluation: institutional planning, assessment of cost/benefit ratios and cost-effectiveness, and evaluation of program outputs. Given that these demands for evaluative data came from institutional administrators, they were top-down in origin, at least as far as the faculty and program directors who had to respond to these demands were concerned. To a certain extent, however, much of this evaluation pressure was also bottom-up.

Faculty, department chairs, and program directors at the bottom began to understand that their funding was related to the information they provided to institutional administrators at the top. The more thoughtful individuals implemented their own data collection and evaluation activities in order to prove that the money given to their programs was well spent. They wisely concluded that if they did not initiate such activities, someone else might do it for them. To many program administrators, it seemed better to set their own criteria for evaluation than to leave the decision to outsiders or institutional administrators.

Boylan, George, and Bonham

Furthermore, as concerned professionals, many of these individuals sincerely wanted to find out how well their programs' objectives were being met and how their programs might be refined or improved. Thus, evaluation pressure originating from the bottom and directed toward the top of the institutional hierarchy became more common. By providing evaluative data, these program administrators not only were assessing program performance, they also were attempting to influence the thoughts and actions of institutional decision makers (Cronback, 1983).

This situation had several implications. For one, it meant that evaluation was not always forced on faculty and program administrators by those at higher levels. Program administrators began to see evaluation activities as a means of controlling their own destinies. Another implication of this changed view was that program development and refinement were added to the list of reasons for conducting evaluations. Previously, most evaluations had been done to satisfy the mandates of external agencies or local administrators. Many program administrators now recognized that this same data could be used to describe what the program was doing, who it served, and what impact the services had. This information then could be used to monitor and refine program activities. Evaluation became not only a function of external mandates but also a force for program research and development.

The combination of financial crises and the growth of federal and state education bureaucracies during the past 30 years has changed both the scope and the focus of evaluation activities. What was once an activity undertaken primarily for the purpose of scholarly research or in response to federal, state, or administrative mandates is now a regular feature of many college reading and study strategies programs. In her survey of postsecondary reading and study skills programs for nontraditional students, Cross (1976) found that fewer than 20 percent included an evaluation component. By the mid-1980s, Spann and Thompson (1985) found that more than 80 percent of these programs included some kind of evaluation component.

What was once being mandated from the top down for the purposes of description and monitoring is now being initiated from the bottom up to influence opinion and action, to understand basic processes, and to refine and improve program operations. Evaluation is now seen as an activity that can help individual reading instructors and program managers measure the impact of their work, explore the effectiveness of their treatments, and monitor and revise their activities while planning for future changes.

Fortunately, as the role of evaluation has expanded and changed in postsecondary education, the amount of theory and research on the topic also has expanded. The following section reviews the more salient aspects of this theory and research as a guide to those who are contemplating either initiation or revision of evaluation efforts.

Types of Evaluation

Two areas that bear review regarding different types of evaluation are the issues of formative versus summative evaluation and quantitative versus qualitative evaluation. Although formative and summative evaluation are generally presented as being on opposites ends of a continuum, the line between the two often is difficult to draw. Similarly, in current practice quantitative and qualitative evaluation no longer are regarded as polar opposites but as complementary activities.

Formative and Summative Evaluation

The notions of formative and summative evaluation are useful in deciding which evaluation activities are appropriate at a given time in a program's development. According to Stake (1967), summative evaluation is "aimed at giving answers... about the merits and shortcomings of a particular curriculum or a specific set of instructional materials" (p. 24). Such an evaluation provides a summary of the program's real, rather than potential, accomplishments and benefits. Summative evaluation, therefore, is most appropriate when a technique or program has been fully implemented. The strengths and weaknesses of a particular program or approach can be accurately determined only after it has been revised, refined, and adjusted to meet local needs and realities.

Frequently, a novel approach to instructional delivery or the use of new instructional materials either will be unsuccessful at first or will not yield its potential benefits until after revisions have been made. Methods and materials borrowed from other programs often need major adjustment to work properly in a new setting. Similarly, methods or materials that should work in theory often need considerable refining before they work in practice.

Too often, new programs are subjected to summative evaluation before these adjustments have been made. As a general rule, new programs, methods, or materials should not be subjected to summative evaluation until they have been fully implemented. Full implementation does not occur until enough time has passed for the innovation to be reviewed, refined, and adjusted. Until this point has been reached, the most appropriate forms of evaluation are formative.

Stake (1967) refers to formative evaluation as that which "seeks information for the development of a curriculum or instructional device," further noting that "the developer wants to find out what arrangements or what amount of something to use" (p. 23). Formative evaluation should be conducted to understand how programs, techniques, and materials are working and to use this understanding to modify and improve them. Formative evaluation, therefore, generally should precede summative evaluation. In fact, results from formative evaluation activities will tell program directors and staff when it is appropriate to conduct summative evaluation.

This does not mean that formative evaluation should cease once an innovation has been fully implemented. In fact, as Fitz-Gibbon and Morris (1978) point out, a major function of formative evaluation is "to persuade staff to constantly scrutinize and rethink assumptions and activities that underlie the program'' (p. 14). Generally speaking, formative evaluation should be an ongoing process. Summative evaluation, on the other hand, should take place at specific intervals.

Formative evaluation addresses one of the major purposes of evaluation for college reading programs; it provides information to be used in modifying and improving the program. It also can provide information about exactly what the program is doing. While formative evaluation can determine how well a program is working, it provides this information only for a given point in time. It does not provide information about the program's full potential.

Summative evaluation addresses another major purpose of evaluation for college reading programs: it determines how well the program, its techniques, and its materials are working once they have been implemented. Summative evaluation is therefore more generalizable than formative evaluation. It provides publishable information that can be used to make institutionwide or systemwide decisions about the efficacy of various approaches. Summative evaluation studies should include the best and most credible information available to enable decision makers to accurately assess the value of a particular approach or set of materials.

Qualitative and Quantitative Evaluation

Until recently, most evaluation efforts were quantitative in nature. They relied on the presentation of numbers, percentages, and statistical analysis. As Maxwell (1979) and Walvekar (1981) point out, reports of gains on reading assessments from pretest to posttest have been the standard means of evaluating reading programs for the past 50 years. Grade point averages, course completion rates, and retention rates also have become standard in the evaluation of reading programs over the past two decades (Boylan, 1981).

Such measures do have limitations, however. The actual meaning of gains from pretest to posttest is often difficult to ascertain given the limitations of assessment instruments. So many factors contribute to course completion and retention that it is difficult to isolate the effects of reading programs on student performance in these areas. Nevertheless, the reporting of such data does provide information that can be useful for program evaluation purposes. Furthermore, the inclusion of such data in evaluation reports has become almost universal in the industry. It would be difficult to have an evaluation report taken seriously if such information were missing.

It is becoming increasingly apparent to evaluation experts, however, that quantitative data alone are insufficient to provide a complete picture of the strengths, weaknesses, successes, and failures of a given program. To add depth and meaning to an evaluation, qualitative data are needed. Patton (1980) defines qualitative evaluation as follows:

> Qualitative data consist of detailed descriptions of situations, events, people, interactions, and observed behaviors; direct quotations from people about their experiences, attitudes, beliefs, and thoughts; and excerpts or entire passages from documents, records, and case histories....Qualitative measures permit the evaluation researcher to record and understand people in their own terms. Qualitative data provide depth and detail'' (p. 22).

In the 1960s, many new programs for nontraditional students—concerned as they were with self-concept development and attitudinal change—tended to use only qualitative data to report the outcomes of their efforts While this strategy could demonstrate that students liked their experiences and felt good about themselves, it could not document whether the programs actually helped students improve their academic performance. This failure to include quantitative data in program reports caused many educators, legislators, and administrators to question the worth of all special programs for nontraditional students. The exclusive use of qualitative data at the expense of quantitative data is a case of too much of a good thing—a case that unfortunately is still true of many programs today.

While both quantitative and qualitative evaluation methodologies have their shortcomings, they can be extremely powerful and informative when combined. In fact, Walvekar

(1981) considers this eclectric approach the most beneficial method of evaluating college learning skills programs. The combination of quantitative and qualitative data can be used appropriately for both formative and summative evaluation. Student feedback obtained from formative evaluation activities can be most helpful in revising or improving program performance. When a program attempts to establish its worth or validate its accomplishments at the summative stage of evaluation, testimonials from students regarding the program's impact on their beliefs, attitudes, and values are important sources of documentation.

The issues of formative versus summative and quantitative versus qualitative evaluation have considerable impact on when and how program evaluations should be conducted. Some of the more common theoretical perspectives that affect evaluations are discussed in the following section.

Theoretical Models of Evaluation

Several authors have attempted to describe typologies of evaluation theories or models. Stufflebeam et al. (1971) identified four types of evaluation based on the purpose each was designed to serve: context, input, process, and product. Context evaluation helps to determine objectives for planning, input evaluation helps to determine project designs, process evaluation helps to determine project operations and policies, and product evaluation helps to refine and improve project operations. These categories do not represent evaluation models so much as purposes for evalution. In many respects, they can be likened to Anderson and Ball's (1978) purposes of evaluation, cited earlier in this chapter.

Cronbach (1983) suggests that two types of evaluation methodologies exist, one supporting the scientific ideal and the other supporting the humanistic ideal. The former uses the scientific method and is concerned with objectivity, while the latter uses qualitative methods and allows for subjective impressions. Cronbach further suggests that most evaluation designs can be plotted on a continuum between these two conflicting schools of thought.

Campbell and Stanley (1966) are the most frequently cited proponents of the scientific school of evaluation. They argue that "true" scientific designs fall into one of two categories: experimental or quasiexperimental. Experimental designs provide for full control of the factors that affect results, such as internal and external validity and reliability. Quasiexperimental designs are used in situations in which full control is not possible. It must be noted that Campbell and Stanley's models were designed to govern research activities, not evaluation activities. While much of what they say is relevant to evaluation, particularly evaluation designed to understand basic processes, their work was never intended as a guideline for program evaluation.

Moore (1981) developed a typology of 10 evaluation frameworks based on the ways evaluators assess programs. His typology, which combines several of the models presented by other authors, includes the following categories: (1) experimental research design, (2) quasiexperimental research design, (3) professional judgment, (4) measurement methods, (5) congruency comparison, (6) cost-effectiveness approaches, (7) behavioral taxonomies, (8) systems analysis, (9) informal evaluation, and (10) goal-free, or responsive, evaluation.

Moore's typology appears to be one of the more comprehensive in the literature; it includes the works of most major authors in the field of evaluation. While all these models probably have been applied to some degree in college reading and study strategies programs, we believe that six of them are particularly applicable for the purposes of this chapter. Table 1 summarizes the advantages, disadvantages, and uses of each of these six models. Fuller descriptions appear in the following pages.

Professional Judgment Designs

Professional judgment designs rely on the subjective ratings of individuals or panels of experts and peers. Before the

Table 1
Comparison of Evaluation Models

Model	Advantages	Disadvantages	Purposes/Uses
Professional Judgment Subjective ratings by peers, panels, or individual experts	Direct and easy; usually results in clear recommendations for action	Lacks reliability and generalizability; is not an objective model	Answers specific questions when other models are inappropriate and provides good formative information
Experimental Scientific approach providing control of specific factors that may affect results	Controls for internal and external validity	Requires quantifiable and measurable data, specific sample size, and selection procedures; focuses only on reliable, objective data	Is appropriate for answering specific questions regarding individual program components; is most appropriate when program is in a mature state of development
Quasiexperimental Similar to experimental model but lacks full experimental control	Controls some factors affecting validity; uses scientific strategies similar to those used in experimental designs	Includes potential sources of internal and external invalidity	Useful in determining causal relationships in situations requiring more formal research in natural social settings

Boylan, George, and Bonham

Table 1 (Continued)
Comparison of Evaluation Models

Model	Advantages	Disadvantages	Purposes/Uses
Congruency Comparison Based on comparison of program objectives with observed outcomes	Is easy and direct as well as reliable and generalizable; can be integrated with instructional processes	Has a rather narrow focus that may overlook certain desirable effects	Useful in refining programs and determining program effectiveness; is particularly appropriate for competency-based programs
Cost-Effectiveness Used to determine the financial benefits of a total program and/or its components	Provides cost factors for program components and the total program; provides useful data for program budgeting and accountability	Excludes program activities that are not observable and measurable in terms of cost; requires some specific training in cost accounting procedures	Useful in assessing program benefits versus costs
Goal-Free/Responsive Reviews programs from a broad perspective including all areas and activities; emphasizes actual outcomes independent of program goals or objectives	Useful for programs with varied purposes and activities; is flexible and adaptable to unstructured situations.	Does not provide information that may be required for reporting purposes, such as program intent, goals, or objectives	Useful for investigating strategies that work best for particular individuals or groups of students

advent of more scientific evaluation designs in the 1960s, professional judgment was the primary method of evaluation in postsecondary education (Walvekar, 1981). Even today, it is widely used, particularly among federally funded programs.

Accreditation teams, doctoral review committees, grant proposal reviewers, and professional journal referees all illustrate the professional judgment evaluation design (Moore, 1981). Another example is the panel method, described by Campbell and Stanley (1966) as "observations made at a single point in time" and strengthened by "waves of interviews," thus providing individual observations over a span of time (pp. 66-67).

Professional judgment designs also include "structured visitations by peers," as described by Stake (1967). In this model, visiting experts assess a program on the basis of their knowledge of the program's particular field of endeavor. This method, by itself, has often been considered a complete model of program evaluation (Provus, 1971; Stufflebeam et al., 1971). Provus, however, points out that even evaluation based on a reconciliation of the judgments of several individuals are subject to questions about the standards used for such judgments—both those of the judges and those of the program being evaluated.

Two other forms of evaluation that fall within the category of professional judgment are the opinions of program staff and the opinions of those affected by a program. Maxwell (1979) suggests that evaluations based on the opinions of a program's participants put those persons in the role of participant-observer. She describes the evaluation process as follows: each participant systematically records his or her reactions to a program, after which all of these reactions combined are used to assess the program's strengths and weaknesses.

Used alone, this design would not meet the total evaluation needs of a college reading and study strategy program—particularly one subject to the scrutiny of colleagues oriented toward scientific evaluation. Its lack of sophistication, reliability, objectivity, and generalizability are obvious disadvantages

(Stufflebeam et al., 1971). Nevertheless, there appears to be some merit to the inclusion of expert, subjective judgments in program evaluation, particularly when this is the best way to collect data on specific questions that are unanswerable by other methods (Maxwell, 1979). In this context, professional judgment is perhaps better included as a component of systematic evaluation rather than as a design in itself.

Experimental Research Designs

Program evaluation strategies that employ the research model derive from experimental or scientific research designs. Campbell and Stanley (1966) maintain that only three "true" experimental research designs exist: the Pretest-Posttest Control Group Design, the Solomon Four-Group Design, and the Posttest-Only Group Design. These designs are "true" in that they provide controls for internal and external validity and random assignment of subjects to groups.

Campbell and Stanley (1966) also explore what they refer to as "pre-experimental" designs. Such designs lack some of the major controls necessary for statistical validity. Although these designs are used frequently, Campbell and Stanley consider them to be of little scientific value.

The issue of experimental designs versus qualitative designs, or "hard" versus "soft" evaluation data, has been a source of considerable debate among evaluation specialists. This debate has been explored by a variety of experts in the field. Clowes (1981), for instance, distinguishes between hard and soft data used for evaluation purposes. Hard data in this context are defined as objective data, while soft data are defined as those based on perceptions. Clowes considers the application of an experimental research design an example of hard evaluation.

Maxwell (1979) asserts that experimental research designs are generally used for determining causal relationships; for collecting objective, reliable, and valid data; and for analyzing data through statistical techniques. She cautions against the inclination to stereotype hard and soft evaluation and suggests that evaluation techniques be chosen according to their appropriateness to specific evaluation questions. For instance, soft data, such as student reports or colleague impressions, may be entirely appropriate in assessing students' perceived quality of experience during their participation in a program. Hard data, such as analysis of score gains on standardized measures, may be more appropriate for assessing program impact on student performance.

Stufflebeam et al. (1971) point out several disadvantages of equating the empirical research methodology with evaluation techniques. They suggest that this practice could leave unaddressed some of the needs met by a good evaluation or by good empirical research. They note the difference between actual situations that the evaluator wants information about and contrived situations or laboratory settings from which "universally true principles" are established (p. 23). Research design methodologies, according to these writers, are intended to occur in context-free laboratories that exclude all influences except those under study. They assert, on the other hand, that the purpose of evaluation is to identify all the influences on the learning process and that evaluation should therefore occur in a context-rich environment.

There are several other arguments against using experimental research designs to evaluate college reading programs. One argument is that these designs are usually used as a form of final evaluation. Rossi and Freeman (1985) maintain that important information about a program during its formative stages is missed if the evaluation employs an experimental design. As an example of this problem, Provus (1971) notes that an astounding number of evaluations comparing control groups with experimental groups yield "no significant difference" (p. 98). These results suggest that many programs were evaluated before there were fully implemented.

Sample size and selection in college reading and study strategy programs also contribute to problems with implementing experimental research designs. Frequently the numbers of students involved in a program are insufficient to provide for an appropriate sample or selection (Kamil, 1984). According to Kamil, sample size is one of the factors contributing to numerous findings of "no significant difference." Stufflebeam et al. (1971) emphatically address this same notion, stating, "When a technique continually produces findings that are at variance with experience and common observation, it is time to call that technique into question" (p. 8). This appears to be the case in many instances in which evaluators have relied on the experimental model to assess college reading and study strategy programs.

Experimental research designs are not always appropriate for evaluating such programs. When explanatory information is required, when conditions exist that allow the use of true experimental evaluation models, when sample size is sufficient, and when a program is in a mature state of development, experimental designs may be appropriate. Otherwise, they are unlikely to produce significant results.

Moore (1981) states that there is often no practical or economical way to "conduct true experiments in learning assistance programs" (p. 35). This also appears to be the case in college reading and study skills programs. In many situations, quasiexperimental or other models may be more useful for evaluation of these programs.

Quasiexperimental Research Designs

The application of quasiexperimental research techniques to answer specific questions or to evaluate specific components of a program has been proposed by several authors. Campbell and Stanley (1966) recommend quasiexperimental research designs for use in natural social settings where full experimental control is impossible. They propose 10 such models, emphasizing the importance of understanding the variables for which these models fail to control.

Myers and Majer (1981) provide a rationale for the use of a quasiexperimental research methodology to answer practical questions in evaluating learning assistance centers. They propose that the overall purpose of evaluation is to answer important questions concerning program improvement, accountability, funding, cooperation, and knowledge. The authors provide several examples of such questions and suggest experimental and quasiexperimental techniques as ways to obtain answers to these questions.

Akst and Hecht (1980) stress that preprogram and postprogram measures must be a part of an objective evaluation of college remedial programs. According to these researchers, the measurement and evaluation of learning are critical to program evaluation. Measurement of learning involves determining how well the content has been mastered, while the evaluation of learning entails judging the quality of learning against some standard.

Akst and Hecht recommend four comparative evaluation designs for measuring learning in which groups are compared to those qualifying for but not participating in programs. These are: single-group pretest-posttest, remediated-unremediated, marginally remedial, and marginally exempted designs. For evaluating learning, the authors suggest remediated-exempted, cross-program, historical, norm-group, and regression-discontinuity comparison. Akst and Hecht also provide a summary table with ratings of each design, appropriate preprogram and postprogram measures, feasibility problems, possible biases, and a judgment of design suitability.

Quasiexperimental designs may be appropriate for the assessment of selected components of a particular program. Maxwell (1979) suggests that the various purposes of program evaluations may determine the areas where quasiexperimental designs are appropriate. She provides a chart outlining which research designs may yield the best results with certain applications (pp. 450-455). She recommends the use of quasiexperimental designs for the following activities:

- making decisions about program continuation, expansion, or accreditation;
- determining the effectiveness or sequencing of curriculum components;

- determining the effectiveness of presentation methods, pacing, and length;
- selecting and placing students;
- training and evaluating instructors and administrators;
- obtaining evidence to rally support for or opposition to a program; and
- contributing to the understanding of basic processes in educational, social, psychological, or economic areas.

It is important to note that many of the objectives of college reading and study strategy programs relate to affective and personal growth factors, many of which are not typically assessed through quasiexperimental approaches. Caution must be exercised to ensure that these factors are not overlooked in the overall evaluation process. A research-based judgment, while preferred by many, may be inappropriate for assessing many worthwhile program components (Dressel, 1976). Other designs, such as congruency comparison, cost-effectiveness models, or goal-free, responsive designs may be more effective in such cases.

Congruency Comparison Designs

Congruency comparison designs are included in the large class of "general" evaluation models that are applicable to many contexts and users (Borich, 1974). They involve comparing a program's objectives or standards with data derived from observation of the program to determine congruence or lack of congruence. A measure of congruence reveals whether intended transactions or outcomes did occur (Stake, 1967).

The discrepancy evaluation model (Provus, 1971) is one of the best known examples of a congruency comparison design. Since its original development, it has been revised substantially to accommodate explorations and critiques from several sources. The revised model is described in terms of five stages:

(1) design, (2) installation, (3) process, (4) product, and (5) program comparison.

Stages 1 through 4 are used to evaluate programs that are already under way. Stage 5 is an optional step that allows for comparisons of two or more programs. The process of this design involves working through the stages while simultaneously examining the program's input, process, and output. In other words, program design and installation are assessed to determine who is entering the program, what is happening in the program, and what outcomes the program produces.

A significant feature of congruency observations, comparisons, and judgments is that they are replicable, generalizable, and appropriate for competency-based programs (Moore, 1981). Moore provides the example of comparing student outcomes against stated behavioral objectives as a straightforward application of the congruency approach.

Stufflebeam et al. (1971) consider this model to have both advantages and disadvantages. The disadvantages include placement of the evaluator in a technical role, the focus on evaluation as a terminal process, and a narrow focus on objectives, as well as the elevation of "behavior as the ultimate criterion of *every* instructional action." The model's advantages include a "high degree of integration with the instructional process, data available on both student and curriculum, possibility of feedback, objective referent and built-in criteria, and the possibility of process as well as product data" (p. 15).

This type of evaluation appears to be relatively easy and direct, which are distinct advantages, although this directness means that such evaluation may not address incidental (but desirable) effects not specified in a program's objectives. This technique may be appropriate for evaluations designed to refine programs as well as those designed to determine program effectiveness. In addition, the opportunity for feedback makes this model appropriate for administrators of college reading and study skills programs who want to revise program content and processes. Those who want to determine the financial benefits of their activities, on the other hand, may be better served by cost-effectiveness design.

Cost-Effectiveness Designs

Cost-effectiveness designs are considered by some to be among the most effective approaches to program evaluation. The notion of evaluating program effectiveness in terms of costs has its origins in business and industrial evaluation, where costs and products are easier to measure. Nevertheless, when used properly, this model can be applied to teaching, learning, and human behavior.

Land (1976) delineates a problem classification schema in applying the cost-effectiveness approach to the evaluation of education programs. His classification includes discussions relating to the problems of estimation, investment decisions, measurement of achievement, cost allocation, and program control.

Haller (1974) outlines an expanded notion of program costs that goes beyond the usual definition of dollars and cents. In this model, costs are considered to be "benefits lost" (p. 408). In other words, what might have happened had a particular program or intervention not been in existence? Three implications arise from this point of view:

- the costs of a given action (or inaction) are directly related to the decision about whether to take that action;
- the consequences of doing or not doing something must be adequately defined in order for cost-effectiveness to be measured; and
- since absolute accuracy in measuring costs is impossible, approximate measures must be accepted in determining cost-effectiveness (p. 409).

This design would certainly be attractive to college administrators who are responsible for fiscal accountability and planning because it provides cost factors for discrete program components as well as for the total program. Cost-effectiveness evaluations do present certain problems, however.

The disadvantages of this approach, noted by Moore (1981) and Land (1976), relate to the fact that it is frequently used ineffectively. Ineffectiveness results from time constraints and the exclusion of program components from the evaluation process because they may not be directly observable.

We agree with this criticism and would not recommend this design for college reading and study skills programs because many worthwhile components are not observable or measurable. In addition, few program directors have the expertise or fiscal training to apply this type of design successfully to an overall program evaluation.

The cost-effectiveness design is discussed here because administrators and legislators often pressure reading and study strategy programs to apply this design. But while this model may satisfy the needs of administrators to document what is gained from dollars spent, it does not satisfy the needs of program personnel to determine the impact of program activities and ways in which this impact may be enhanced. A more effective method to accommodate this need might be to apply goal-free or responsive evaluation designs.

Goal-Free/Responsive Designs

A sixth evaluation design model represents a "laissez-faire perspective" of evaluation unencumbered by the language of intent, goals, and objectives (Borich, 1974). Moore (1981) combined goal-free and responsive designs because of the similarity of these two models. They are combined in this review for the same reason.

Goal-free and responsive designs are distinguished by their emphasis on the importance of an external, objective evaluator. This evaluator looks for the actual results or outcomes of a program, not its intent. Borich (1974) describes the goal-free evaluator as viewing program development and evaluation from a broad, general perspective that includes all of a program's areas and activities. This view differs only slightly from the professional judgment model of evaluation discussed earlier. The major difference is that with a goal-free approach, evaluators base their judgments not on their own expertise but on the extent to which all program activities are integrated into some meaningful whole.

Scriven (1967)—a proponent of goal-free evaluation—distinguishes between evaluation that incorporates values into a model, thus giving weight to both description and judgment, and the casting of the evaluator in a decision-making role. Stake (1967), on the other hand, believes that the evaluator should not be a part of the decision-making team. While this may be true in theory, the fact is that the evaluator is often called on to make decisions. It seems more sensible to acknowledge this role by formally including the evaluator in the decision-making process than to pretend that such a role does not exist.

A possible problem encountered by administrators who receive goal-free reports is that such reports may be difficult to relate to their goals for a program. In spite of this difficulty, the varied purposes and intents of college reading and study strategy programs make goal-free and responsive evaluation more suitable than other evaluation approaches. These designs are flexible and adaptable to relatively unstructured situations. Moore (1981) comments that all "processes, outcomes, resources, and objectives are potentially relevant" in goal-free/responsive evaluation, and that these models are people-centered rather than system-centered (p. 41).

Ethnographic approaches that evaluate program effectiveness for individuals and groups also should be included in this category. Guthrie (1984) explains ethnographic methods in terms of participant observation, interviews, quantification schemes, diary studies, case studies, and the use of technology. He particularly recommends ethnographic designs for the evaluation of reading programs when the objective is to determine what is really happening between the teacher and individual students or a particular group of students.

It is certainly important for the staffs of college reading and study strategy programs to understand what works best for each group of students enrolled in their programs. Ethnographic and other goal-free/responsive evaluation research may be a valuable tool for investigating such programs. Unfortunately, the literature does not, at present, provide any examples of its use in college reading programs.

Typical Evaluation Studies of College-Level Programs

The literature reflects relatively few examples of the various evaluation methodologies that can be applied to college reading and study skills programs. A review of the last five volumes of the four major reading journals and three related journals, as well as a detailed Educational Resources Information Center (ERIC) search, yielded only a handful of articles on the evaluation of college reading and study strategy programs.

Of those reported in the literature, the vast majority are either experimental or quasiexperimental in design. This preponderance is probably the result of two factors. First, many journals show a preference for research articles using experimental or quasiexperimental methods. Second, many articles discussing program evaluation activities using alternative methodologies do not yield statistically quantifiable results. Both of these factors militate against the publication of articles dealing with alternative evaluation models.

We found no studies that compared the effectiveness of various evaluation designs for college reading and study skills programs. The studies that follow represent a sampling of the published accounts of systematic efforts to apply either experimental or quasiexperimental designs to the evaluation of these programs.

Experimental Research Studies

One of the earliest articles featuring the experimental approach is provided by Behrens (1935). He investigated the effects of a course on how to study, comparing students who had taken the course with those who had not. He found that students in the experimental group that took the course obtained better grades than students in the control group.

In a later and more extensive study, Mouly (1952) also attempted to assess the effects of a university remedial reading program on student grades. The experimental group consisted of 155 students who took remedial reading for one semester. This group was further divided into two subgroups: students who successfully completed the course and students who either failed or did not complete the course. The control group was made up of students who did not take the remedial course. This group was subdivided into those who were advised to take the course and decided not to and those who were randomly selected to be excused from the course.

Only slight differences were reported in the combined grade point averages of the total experimental and the total control group; in addition, these groups' dropout rates and average number of credits accumulated during the period under study were almost identical. When the results were broken down by subgroup, however, a different picture emerged. The experimental subgroup that successfully completed the remedial course earned a significantly higher combined GPA than the total control group. Mouly (1952) concluded that "a remedial reading program can result in improvement in academic grades for those persons who take the course seriously" (p. 466). Mouly noted further that in institutions where enrollment in remedial reading courses is voluntary, the benefits of such courses are lost to many students. In considering the results of this study, however, it should be noted that it did not control for possible pretreatment differences between experimental and control groups.

Haburton (1977) provides another example of a common experimental design in reading research. This design involves providing one treatment to the experimental group and another treatment to the control group. Haburton found that students who participated in an experimental reading development course obtained a higher combined GPA than those who received individual tutoring. His results suggest that reading development courses can help high-risk community college students improve their academic performance.

A more recent study using this design was conducted by Maring, Shea, and Warner (1987). The authors compared three experimental groups taking reading and study strategy courses with two control groups not taking these courses. Their purpose was to assess the impact of the courses on such factors as student GPA, retention, and satisfaction. Although a major part of the study used an experimental design featuring objective statistical data, the authors also collected subjective data from students. They found no significant difference between the grade point averages of the experimental and the control groups. However, students in the experimental groups had higher retention rates and expressed greater satisfaction with their college experiences then did students in the control groups.

The Maring, Shea, and Warner (1987) study provides an excellent example of an experimental design used in conjunction with subjective data and analysis. The authors offer a number of recommendations for those who wish to implement this design in evaluating reading, study strategy, and learning assistance programs. This design appears to be one of the most powerful evaluation models reported in the recent reading literature.

Quasiexperimental Design Studies

Several reading and study skills programs at the college level have been evaluated using quasiexperimental designs. Studies are classified as quasiexperimental when the subjects are not randomly assigned to groups or when full control of variables is not possible (Cook & Campbell, 1979).

In one quasiexperimental study, Borich (1974) analyzed the relationships of selected intellective and nonintellective variables to the academic success of educationally and economically disadvantaged freshmen. The subjects participated in a special summer transitional program before enrolling as freshmen the following fall semester. The special program involved instruction in regular freshman English and history courses, remedial courses in mathematics and reading/study skills, peer counseling, and professional counseling. Academic achievement was measured by changes in pretest and posttest scores during the special summer program. Measures of achievement, study habits and attitudes, self-concept, and intelligence were administered. Other variables studied were IQ, high school GPA, gender, preliminary American College Testing (ACT) score, and selected demographic variables.

Significant predictors of postprogram achievement were reported to be pretest scores and IQ. The best predictors of fall GPA were found to be high school GPA, gender, IQ, and self-concept. The study also concluded that successful and unsuccessful students showed significant differences on cognitive variables but not on self-concept or demographic variables.

Chand (1982) attempted to assess the impact of a comprehensive developmental program on student retention and GPA. Students were selected for participation in the program on the basis of ACT scores, standardized reading tests, and a writing sample. Students who fell below a certain cutoff score on these instruments were assigned to a regimen of developmental courses, counseling, and tutoring. Chand found that students who received regular tutoring and who successfully completed one or more developmental courses had higher retention rates and higher grade point averages than those who did not.

Freeley, Wepner, and Wehrle (1987) conducted a quasiexperimental study designed to test the impact of direct exposure to test items on the performance of students taking the reading section of the New Jersey College Basic Skills Placement Test. The experimental group took a reading course that used direct quotations from the test as reading passages. The control group was given reading passages that covered topics similar to those on the test but that were not direct quotes. The authors found that although the scores of both groups on the New Jersey College Basic Skills Placement Test improved significantly over pretest scores, there was no significant difference between the two groups' posttest scores. These results suggest that a reading and study strategy program focusing on preparing students for standardized tests need not involve direct "teaching to the test" to be successful.

Wolfe (1987) used a quasiexperimental design in comparing the impact on student performance of a course using the supplemental instruction technique. The experimental group received tutoring and special study sessions after a course, while the control group took the same course without this treatment. Of those students participating in the experimental group, only 16 percent withdrew from the course or received grades of D or F. Of those students not receiving supplemental instruction, 55 percent either withdrew from the course or received D or F.

While the studies cited here provide data that can be used for program evaluation purposes, they also represent examples of research designed to understand basic processes. The Borich (1974) study, for instance, was clearly designed to explore the effect of intellective and nonintellective variables on student performance—not necessarily to assess the quality of the program in which the students were enrolled. Similarly, the Wolfe (1987) and Freeley, Wepner, and Wehrle (1987) studies were designed to assess a particular strategy for improving student performance. Nevertheless, each study provides a good example of how quasiexperimental design can be used to assess program components.

Nonexperimental Studies

Although the literature clearly favors studies that take an experimental or quasiexperimental approach to program evaluation, we did find several examples of other approaches. Spivey (1981) provides an example of a congruency comparison model for program evaluation. Using a system known as Goal Attainment Scaling, students in a learning center were asked to establish goals for their participation in the center. The goals were discussed with a counselor, quantified in terms of measurable outcomes, and then reviewed at the end of each semester. Stu-

Boylan, George, and Bonham

dents and counselors then jointly agreed on the extent to which these goals had been accomplished or the degree to which student performance matched expectations. In addition to serving as a program evaluation tool, this system had a positive impact on student performance.

Smith & Brown (1981) used a version of congruency comparison to evaluate staff performance in a reading and study strategies program. Using a modified version of Management by Objectives (McConkey, 1975), staff members negotiated their performance objectives with supervisors. These objectives were then quantified and weighted. At the end of each year, staff members met individually with supervisors to determine the extent to which these objectives had been accomplished. The authors concluded that this system not only improved the quality of program management but also boosted staff motivation.

Boylan (1978) provides an example of cost-effectiveness evaluation in learning centers. He developed a formula to determine the costs of producing gains in scores on various standardized instruments. The performance of the program could then be judged on a year-to-year basis in terms of costs compared with gains. His results suggest that mature programs generally reach a "point of maximum return." At this point, the program has reached maximum efficiency and can no longer increase gains without increasing the resources allocated to program operations.

Another example of cost-effectiveness evaluation is found in the work of Levin, Glass, and Meister (1987). These authors attempted to determine the cost-effectiveness of computer-assisted reading instruction—as measured against peer tutoring, increased instructional time, and reduced class size—as a means of improving scores on reading tests. Results were reported as the score gains achieved for each $100 spent per student. Peer tutoring was found to be the most cost-effective approach, with computer-assisted instruction just slightly behind. Increasing instructional time and reducing class sizes were found to be the least cost-effective methods.

Silverman (1983) used a goal-free/responsive evaluation approach in attempting to determine which variables affected students' self-esteem and academic performance. Using student interviews combined with performance data, she determined that positive academic self-concepts were directly related to academic performance. Additional factors such as motivation, peer influence, and faculty influence also affect self-concept. The information collected with this evaluation approach has useful implications for the design and refinement of basic skills programs as well as for counseling interventions designed to support them.

Another example of a goal-free/responsive approach is Suen's (1979) evaluation of a Special Services Program at the University of Wisconsin-Oshkosh. Suen first applied an experimental research methodology to determine the effects of the program on the cumulative grade point averages of participants. After these were determined, he conducted a stepwise regression analysis to determine which features of the program had the greatest impact on student grades. His analysis revealed that basic English, reading, and mathematics courses appeared to have the greatest impact; career counseling also seemed to have a significant effect. The statistical analysis segment of the study was goal-free in that it attempted to explore the weight of individual factors contributing to success in addition to measuring the overall impact of the program.

Implications for Practice

The studies reviewed in this chapter include evaluations of a variety of program components, reading courses, techniques, and approaches. Few of these studies are comprehensive since they tend to focus on one or more aspects of a given program. Most of these studies used either hard (objective) or soft (subjective) data. We believe that comprehensive program evaluation should include both objective and subjective data.

This notion is consistent with the views of Cronbach (1983), who suggests that evaluators need not choose between humanistic and scientific schools of thought. Certain settings require objective, reproducible, concentrated evaluation, while others demand broad, phenomenological, flexible evaluation. The choice of approach should reflect the purpose of the evaluation. There appears to be no agreement among experts in the field as to the best design for evaluation. This lack of consensus is particularly true for college reading and study strategy programs, whose goals, objectives, and methods are so diverse.

While it is impossible to recommend a single evaluation model for college reading and study skills programs, those who must select and implement evaluation activities for their programs may find the following general guidelines useful:

- A clear statement of realistic, attainable objectives is essential to program development and, consequently, to program evaluation.
- Both formative and summative evaluations are necessary for successful overall program evaluations.
- Evaluations conducted by external experts who know and understand various reading and study strategies and their functions should be a substantial part of formative evaluations.
- A summative evaluation at the end of some phase of a program is probably the best place for objective, quantitative, data-based information regarding program effectiveness.
- Traditional experimental designs are less appropriate than other designs for evaluating reading programs because these programs are typically unable to assign students randomly.
- Evaluations should consist of multiple criteria; evidence of success should be sought on several dimensions.

Aside from choosing a model, those involved in reading and study strategy programs must consider several other issues before beginning an evaluation. Important considerations include choosing an evaluation strategy that will encourage use by decision makers, deciding how much information to include, and determining the evaluation criteria.

Encouraging Utilization of Evaluation Reports

If the personnel of a reading and study strategy program have gone to the trouble of completing an evaluation and reporting their findings, naturally they want administrators to use those findings in making decisions that affect the program. In an extensive study on the use of evaluation reports, Cousins and Leithwood (1986) found that decision makers are more apt to utilize evaluation information under the following circumstances:

- Evaluation activities are considered appropriate in approach and methodology to the issues being investigated.
- The decisions to be made directly affect the users of evaluation information and are of the sort normally made on the basis of evaluation data.
- Evaluation findings are consistent with the beliefs and expectations of the decision makers.
- Decision makers have been involved in the evaluation process and have shown commitment to the benefits of evaluation.
- Decision makers consider data reported in the evaluation to be relevant to the problem being explored.
- Information from other sources conflicts minimally with the results of evaluation.

These findings are consistent with the notions of Clowes (1983) and Keimig (1984) regarding the importance of administrator involvement in the planning of program evaluation. Both authors note that it is essential for institutional decision makers to be involved in the evaluation process from the outset. Such decision makers should be thoroughly familiar with the purposes of evaluation, the issues to be evaluated, the methodologies to be used, and the objectives to be accomplished through evaluation. They should be consulted at each step in the evaluation process, and the results of the evaluation should be presented in a manner consistent with their need for information.

Keeping It Simple

In determining how much information to present in an evaluation report and how this information should be presented, there is a fine line between too little and too much. The information should be sufficient to provide administrators with appropriate data to make decisions or to understand the program being evaluated. It should not, however, be so extensive that it becomes difficult to extract necessary information.

A 100-page report filled with graphs, charts, and statistical analysis may be appropriate if administrators want to know the exact status of every program activity. On the other hand, if the only decision to be made on the basis of the report is whether to change diagnostic instruments, such a thorough review is too cumbersome to be useful.

Care should be taken to ensure that those reading the evaluation reports are able to understand them. Not all administrators are statisticians. It may take a fairly sophisticated statistical analysis to determine which of two techniques is more effective in raising student scores on a standardized instrument, but the key part of this information is simply that different groups of students scored differently. While a T-test or an analysis of variance procedure might be conducted to determine statistical significance, decision makers do not need to read the calculations or see the charts and tables used to arrive at the final figures. They really only need to know that one technique worked better than another and that a valid technique was used to determine these results.

The point here is that it is possible to obscure important findings by spending too much time presenting statistical analysis and not enough time dealing with the implications of the analysis. As a general rule, raw data should be explained in the simplest terms possible, regardless of how sophisticated the methods of analyzing them were. The purpose of evaluation is, after all, to generate useful information—not to impress superiors with one's ability to perform statistical calculations.

Evaluation Criteria

One of the major tasks in designing a program evaluation is the selection of evaluation criteria. Maxwell (1979) lists eight common criteria for evaluating college reading and study strategies:

1. extent to which students use the program,
2. extent to which users are satisfied with the program,
3. grades and grade point averages of those who use the program,
4. year-to-year retention rates of students in the program,
5. test scores and gain scores of those who use the program,
6. faculty attitudes toward the program,
7. staff attitudes toward the program, and
8. impact of the program on the campus as a whole.

In addition to these criteria, we would add three others: grades in follow-up courses, course completion rates, and "serendipitous benefits." If a reading and study strategy program is designed to improve student performance, its effectiveness can best be measured by assessing the grades students receive in subsequent reading-oriented courses. If students who complete the program tend to do well in later courses requiring advanced reading skills, the program has accomplished its objective.

The extent to which students who enter reading and study strategy courses complete these courses is another valid indicator of program success. Low course completion rates often indicate that something is wrong with the delivery of the course. High completion rates usually indicate that students see the course as valuable and perceive that they are obtaining benefits as a result of their participation. It also should be noted that those who participate in a reading and study strategy program but do not complete it should not be counted in measuring the program's subsequent impact. The impact of a given treatment can be measured accurately only for those students who experienced the full treatment.

Serendipitous benefits are unanticipated positive results from a program. By their very nature, evaluation of these benefits cannot be planned. A good evaluator should be constantly aware of potential benefits that may not be part of an evaluation plan. An unanticipated benefit of a college reading and study strategy program, for instance, might be increased faculty awareness of the reading levels of texts used in their courses. Instructors in community college General Equivalency Diploma (GED) programs have found that participants often use their newly acquired reading skills to teach other family members how to read. Benefits of this type are unlikely to be listed as program evaluation objectives. Nevertheless, they are valid measures of program impact.

The State of the Art in Program Evaluation

For a variety of reasons, reading programs are more frequently called on to evaluate their efforts than are most other academic units on a college or university campus. In spite of the current emphasis on accountability, the sociology department is seldom asked to prove that students know more about sociology after completing introductory courses than they did beforehand. This type of request accompanies practically all efforts to improve the basic skills of underprepared college students. In terms of evaluation quantity, reading and study strategy programs probably rank near the top among postsecondary programs.

The quality of these evaluation efforts, however, often leaves much to be desired. Control groups seldom are used in assessing the relative merits of program activities. Too much emphasis is placed on either quantitative data or qualitative data, without an appropriate mix of each. Programs either report gain scores and retention rates without asking students their opinion of the program or they rely on student testimonials without reporting sufficient data on student performance. Where statistical treatment of data takes place, it is often inappropriate—either too sophisticated for the issues being considered or not sophisticated enough to generate valid conclusions. Frequently, evaluation reports are prepared without the benefit of adequate data collection systems. Consequently, the results are either fragmentary or meaningless. In their metaanalysis of remedial programs for high-risk college students, Kulik, Kulik, and Shwalb (1983) had to discard the results of 444 out of 504 program evaluation reports because they suffered from "serious methodological flaws."

In addition, many college reading programs attempt summative evaluation at inappropriate points, without enough formative data to inform the evaluation. Often these programs are called on to provide annual reports for institutional, state, or federal administrators. Their reports summarize what the program is doing and assess the program's activities as if all of them were fully developed. Program staff and institutional administrators alike treat these reports as summative evaluations.

This misguided approach can produce seriously flawed results. A newly acquired computer-assisted reading package is evaluated in the same way and against the same criteria as a set of reading textbooks that have been used successfully for a decade. A newly implemented learning laboratory is assessed in the same manner and using the same standards as reading classes that have been in operation for 20 years. As a result, many promising innovations are judged as failures because they have been subjected to summative evaluation standards before they have been fully implemented.

In essence, then, the state of the art in college reading and study strategy program evaluation is generally poor. Although a great deal of evaluation activity takes place in these programs, much of it is done poorly, much of it is unsystematic,

Boylan, George, and Bonham

and much of it yields inaccurate or misleading results. Further-more, evaluations often take place at the wrong time for the wrong reasons and ask the wrong questions. As a result, judg-ments regarding the effectiveness of college reading and study strategy programs are often inaccurate.

There is much room for improvement in the quality of evaluation in these programs. Nevertheless, the personnel in-volved in college reading and study skills programs are to be commended for being among the first in academia to take eval-uation seriously. The early experiences and pioneering efforts of college reading programs in this area will serve them well in the future as evaluation becomes an increasingly critical com-ponent of all postsecondary education ventures.

Future Issues in the Evaluation of College Reading Programs

During the remainder of this century, college reading and study strategy programs must come to grips with a number of issues relating to program evaluation. Some of the more im-portant of these issues are discussed in the following pages.

Focus on Purpose

College reading and study skills programs have a variety of origins. Some stemmed from attempts by counseling centers to help students who were doing poorly in school. Some grew out of efforts to facilitate the adjustment of military veterans re-turning to campus. Some began as a component of college learning assistance centers. Some originated as content area courses—either independent courses or segments of basic skills or remedial/developmental courses. Regardless of their origins, however, many of these programs initially stated their goals in "broad and rather vague terms...making it unlikely that an eval-uation plan [could] be implemented consistent with these goals" (Rossi & Freeman, 1985, p. 65).

In many cases, programs were established in response to some local condition such as an increase of nontraditional stu-dents in the campus population or a shortfall in enrollment leading to a desire for greater student retention. Frequently, these local conditions have changed but the content and processes of the reading and study strategy program have remained the same. In many cases, little thought has been given to program purpose since the program was originally established.

As higher education changes, it is reasonable to expect that college reading and study strategy programs also will change. In the coming years, it will become increasingly important for these programs to focus on their purposes. Program coordinators and staff will have to rethink what their programs are supposed to accomplish, how they plan to do it, and how they will assess whether they are successful.

This rethinking will undoubtedly result in new roles, new goals, and new objectives for these programs. Evaluation designs must reflect these changes. An evaluation designed to assess gain scores from pretest to posttest, for instance, is perfectly appropriate if the goal of the program is to improve students' reading rates. If the goal of the program changes to enhancing retention, however, such a design is no longer appropriate. A major issue for personnel in college reading and study strategy programs will be to reconsider their focus and perhaps to redesign their activities. This refocus and redesign will have a substantial impact on the nature of evaluation activities, the type of data collected, and the analysis techniques used in these programs.

Focus on Integration

College reading and study strategy programs often function independently rather than as part of a larger effort to assist underprepared students. For instance, a great many college reading and study strategy programs were designed excusively to teach reading skills independently of other activities and courses. As Thomas and Moorman (1983) note, "The most striking characteristic of most programs is the isolation of reading from the rest of the...curriculum" (p. 15). As a result, the activities of these programs often were not well integrated into the total structure of campus academic support activities.

As pressures for college and university accountability mount, college reading and study strategy programs will be asked to document not only what they do but also how their activities contribute to overall campus efforts to assist students. If the efforts of these programs take place in a vacuum, their contribution will be extremely hard to document. It will become increasingly important, therefore, for such programs to be integrated with other campus activities designed to assist underprepared students. These programs must be conceived of and operated as one component of a larger effort rather than as an independent unit.

The personnel of reading and study strategy programs must interact with their colleagues more often, participate in joint planning efforts on a more regular basis, and conceive of their efforts from a more global perspective. When this is done, the nature of evaluation activity may change. The direction of this change—from assessment of a single activity to assessment of the activity as part of a series —will have a significant impact on evaluation designs. Such designs will, of necessity, explore more variables, investigate more interactions, and pool larger amounts of data to determine a total picture of the forces that affect student performance.

Focus on Long Term Outcomes

As Robinson (1950) pointed out more than 40 years ago, "Academic performance is clearly the sine qua non for the validation of remedial courses...in the final analysis remedial instruction must necessarily stand or fall on the basis of this single criterion" (p. 83). In recent years, the definition of student performance has expanded from performance measured at a given time to performance measured over a period of time (Levitz, 1986).

In spite of this change, most college reading and study strategy programs are evaluated according to short term performance criteria such as gain scores or grade point averages for a given semester. If student performance is the major evaluation criterion for these programs, performance must be measured over time rather than at a single point in time. Thus, long term and longitudinal evaluation must be undertaken to assess the impact of programs.

Such longitudinal evaluation should involve tracing student performance over several semesters—preferably, through graduation. Particular attention should be paid to student performance in the semester immediately following participation in a reading and study strategy program. Attempts should be made to determine not only whether participation in such programs has some immediate impact but also whether the skills learned in these programs are transferred to other courses.

Focus on the Affective Dimension

Previous researchers (Bliss & Mueller, 1987; Haburton, 1977; Mouly, 1952) have noted the lack of correlation between what students know about study skills and how they actually study. As Maxwell (1979) notes, if students are instructed to respond to study skills inventories as if they were excellent students, their responses will indicate a fairly sophisticated knowledge of good study habits. This suggests that the affective dimension of reading and study habits is at least as important as the cognitive dimension. The key is not only to teach students how to study but also to get them to put what they learn to use.

An effective program, therefore, must be concerned not only with teaching reading and study strategies but also with developing the attitudes, beliefs, and values that shape how students use those skills. While some efforts to accomplish this goal already have been made (Brozo & Curtis, 1987; Butkowski & Willow, 1980), more research in this area is needed. As the results of this research become available, the current focus on measuring and evaluating cognitive skills may be replaced by a focus on measuring a combination of cognitive skills and affective development.

Focus on Component Analysis and Ethnographic Evaluation

For much of the past three decades, evaluation reports have dealt with the issues of whether a program works to improve reading or study skills, to what degree it works, and the extent to which its outcomes benefit students. In the next several decades, attention will be given to the question, "What works for whom?" As Cross (1976) points out, we will move from a concept of education for all to one of "education for each" (p. 129).

In order to discover what works for whom, we will have to explore a number of issues more fully and use our existing knowledge more effectively. Areas that need this type of work include the specific characteristics of students and the extent to which these characteristics influence learning, the degree to which demographic factors may influence the effectiveness of certain kinds of instructional programs, and the components of such factors as motivation and aptitude.

The acquisition and use of this information will require the analysis of individual program components and treatments as well as expanded use of ethnographic evaluation techniques. Also, more advanced statistical treatments such as factor and regression analysis will be required in program evaluation. This change may result in a shift of program evaluation priorities from determining how well a program works to improving our understanding of the basic processes that make it work. We know that reading and study skills programs tend to work. In the future, we may place more emphasis on discovering why they work, and who they work for, as part of the overall evaluation process.

Focus on Eclectic Evaluation Methodologies

As this analysis makes clear, there is no single best method of evaluating college reading and study strategy programs. Evaluators employ a wide range of methods in assessing such programs, and there is little agreement among experts as to which designs have the most promise. Furthermore, college reading and study strategy programs (like all programs concerned with human learning) involve extremely complex sets of personal, contextual, content, and process variables. No single evaluation design can explore all these variables and find definitive answers.

It appears that the most promising designs will incorporate a combination of several research methods. At present, selection of evaluation methods for reading and study strategy programs is generally random. Often the choice is based on which method a particular program administrator happens to know about or which one a particular consultant recommends. Evaluation activities of the future will likely be far more systematic as well as far more eclectic than those in use today.

As our understanding of evaluation grows, designs will become tools of the evaluation process as opposed to structures for that process. No standard design will exist for the evaluation of college reading and study strategy programs of the future. Instead, there will be a series of choices to be made about the purposes, intents, goals, and objectives of a program or course in the planning of evaluation activities.

Evaluation practitioners will have to become more familiar with the many design tools available to them to be able to select the most appropriate ones for their purposes. This eclectic approach to evaluation will enable individual programs to explore issues specific to their particular needs, contexts, and circumstances.

Conclusion

It is apparent throughout this chapter that the evaluation of college reading and study strategy programs is an extremely complex enterprise. It is a field with few standard models and little agreement on what variables, techniques, or questions should take precedence. In addition, evaluation is not an area in which many reading specialists are well trained. Program evaluation is becoming a profession in and of itself. It is no longer something that anyone with graduate training can be expected to be able to do; the available evaluation methods have become too diverse, the application of these methods too specific, the statistical methods for analyzing data too complicated, and the planning and implementation decisions involved too numerous.

As pressure for program evaluation continues to expand, as the need for understanding basic processes becomes more apparent, and as the population of American colleges and universities becomes more diverse, reading professionals will face several new challenges. They will need to improve their own knowledge of the research and evaluation literature. They will need to place more emphasis on investigating what they do, analyzing and reporting what they find, and sharing their results with others. They will need to establish links with colleagues in other related areas—particularly those in graduate schools of education and university research centers—to ensure that basic research on the evaluation of college reading programs continues and the results are disseminated.

As Christ (1985) points out, "any activity worth doing should be evaluated." According to the dictionary, to evaluate something is to determine its value. If we value what we do, we should want to know how well we do it. We ought to be interested in the impact of what we do. We ought to be able to describe and measure what we do. We ought to be able to explore what works and why. These are the challenges presented by program evaluation. They are challenges that can only enhance the professionalization of those who work in college reading and study strategy programs.

References and Suggested Readings

Akst, J., & Hecht, M. (1980). Program evaluation. In A.S. Trillin & Assoc., *Teaching basic skills in college.* San Francisco, CA: Jossey-Bass.

Anderson, S., & Ball, D. (1978). *The profession and practice of program evaluation.* San Francisco, CA: Jossey-Bass.

Behrens, H. (1935). Effects of a "how to study" course. *Journal of Higher Education, 6,* 195-202.

Bliss, L., & Mueller, R. (1987). Assessing study behaviors of college students: Findings from a new instrument. *Journal of Developmental Education, 11*(2), 14-19.

Borich, G. (Ed.). (1974). *An investigation of selected intellective and nonintellective factors as predictors of academic success for educationally-economically disadvantaged college freshmen.* Unpublished manuscript, Mississippi State University, Starkville.

Boylan, H. (1978, April). *Evaluating cost-effectiveness for learning center operations.* Paper presented at the annual conference of the American College Personnel Association, Detroit, MI.

Boylan, H. (1981). Program evaluation: Issues, needs, and realities. In C. Walvekar (Ed.), *New directions for college learning assistance, vol. 5: Assessment of learning assistance services* (pp. 3-16). San Francisco, CA: Jossey-Bass.

Brozo, W., & Curtis, C. (1987). Coping strategies of four successful learning disabled college students: A case study approach. In J. Readance & R. Baldwin (Eds.), *Thirty-Sixth Yearbook of the National Reading Conference* (pp. 237-246). Rochester, NY: National Reading Conference.

Butkowski, I., & Willow, D. (1980). Cognitive-motivational characteristics of children varying in reading ability: Evidence of learned helplessness in poor readers. *Journal of Educational Psychology, 72,* 408-422.

*Campbell, D., & Stanley, J. (1966). *Experimental and quasiexperimental designs for research.* Chicago, IL: Rand McNally.

Chand, S. (1982). The impact of developmental education at Triton College. *Journal of Developmental Education, 9*(1), 2-6.

Christ, F. (1985, August). *Managing learning assistance programs.* Symposium conducted at the Kellogg Institute for the Training and Certification of Developmental Educators, Boone, NC.

Clowes, D. (1981). Evaluation methodologies for learning assistance programs. In C. Walvekar (Ed.), *New directions for college learning assistance; vol. 5: Assessment of learning assistance services* (pp. 17-32). San Francisco, CA: Jossey-Bass.

Clowes, D. (1983). The evaluation of remedial/developmental programs: A stage model for evaluation. *Journal of Developmental Education, 8*(1), 14-30.

Cook, T., & Campbell, D. (1979). *Quasiexperimentation: Design analysis for field settings.* Chicago, IL: Rand McNally.

*Cousins, B., & Leithwood, K. (1986). Current empirical research on evaluation utilization. *Review of Educational Research, 56,* 331-364.

*Cronbach, L. (1983). *Designing evaluations of educational and social programs.* San Francisco, CA: Jossey-Bass.

Cross, K.P. (1976). *Accent on learning.* San Francisco, CA: Jossey-Bass.

Dressel, P. (1976). *Handbook of academic evaluation.* San Francisco, CA: Jossey-Bass.

Fitz-Gibbon, C., & Morris, L. (1978). *How to design a program evaluation.* Beverly Hills, CA: Sage.

Freeley, J., Wepner, S., & Wehrle, P. (1987). The effects of background information on college students' performance on a state developed reading competency test. *Journal of Developmental Education, 11*(2), 2-5.

Guthrie, J. (1984). A program evaluation typology. *The Reading Teacher, 37*(8), 790-792.

Haburton, E. (1977). Impact of an experimental reading-study skills course on high risk student success in a community college. In P.D. Pearson (Ed.), *Twenty-Sixth Yearbook of the National Reading Conference* (pp. 110-117). Clemson, SC: National Reading Conference.

Haller, E. (1974). Cost analysis for program evaluation. In W.J. Popham (Ed.), *Evaluation in education* (pp. 17-23). Berkeley, CA: McCutchan.

Kamil, M. (1984). Current traditions of reading research. In P.D. Pearson (Ed.), *Handbook of reading research* (pp. 3-19). New York: Longman.

Keimig, R. (1984). *Raising academic standards: A guide to learning improvement* (Report No. 3). Washington, DC: American Association for Higher Education.

Kulik, J., Kulik, C., & Schwalb, B. (1983). College programs for high-risk and disadvantaged students: A meta-analysis of findings. *Review of Educational Research, 53,* 397-414.

Land, F. (1976). Economic analysis of information systems. In F. Land (Ed.), *We can implement cost-effective systems now* (pp. 2-17). Princeton, NJ: Education Communications.

Levin, M., Glass, G., & Meister, G. (1987). Cost-effectiveness of computer-assisted instruction. *Evaluation Review, 2,* 50-72.

Levitz, R. (1986, March). *What works in student retention.* Keynote address presented at the annual conference of the National Association for Developmental Education, New Orleans, LA.

Maring, G.H., Shea, M.A., & Warner, D.A. (1987). Assessing the effects of college reading and study skills programs: A basic evaluation model. *Journal of Reading, 30,* 402-408.

*Maxwell, M. (1979). *Improving student learning skills.* San Francisco, CA: Jossey-Bass.

McConkey, D. (1975). *MBO for nonprofit organizations.* New York: American Management Associates.

Moore, R. (1981). The role and scope of evaluation. In C. Walvekar (Ed.), *New directions for college learning assistance, vol. 5: Assessment of learning assistance services* (pp. 33-50). San Francisco, CA: Jossey-Bass.

Mouly, C. (1952). A study of the effects of remedial reading on academic grades at the college level. *Journal of Educational Psychology, 43,* 459-466.

Myers, C., & Majer, K. (1981). Using research designs to evaluate learning assistance programs. In C. Walvekar (Ed.), *New directions for college learning assistance, vol. 5: Assessment of learning assistance services* (pp. 65-74). San Francisco, CA: Jossey-Bass.

*Patton, M. (1980). *Qualitative evaluation methods.* Beverly Hills, CA: Sage.

*Provus, M. (1971). *Discrepancy evaluation for educational program improvement and assessment.* Berkeley, CA: McCutchan.

Robinson, F. (1950). A note on the evaluation of college remedial reading courses. *Journal of Educational Psychology, 41,* 83-96.

*Rossi, H., & Freeman, E. (1985). *Evaluation: A systematic approach.* Beverly Hills, CA: Sage.

Scriven, M. (1967). The methodology of evaluation. In R.E. Stake (Ed.), *Perspectives of curriculum evaluation* (pp. 2-14). Chicago, IL: Rand McNally.

Silverman, S. (1983). Qualitative research in the evaluation of developmental education. *Journal of Developmental and Remedial Education, 6*(3), 16-19.

Smith, K., & Brown, S. (1981). Staff performance evaluation in learning assistance centers. In C. Walvekar (Ed.), *New directions in college learning assistance, vol. 5: Assessment of learning assistance services* (pp. 95-110). San Francisco, CA: Jossey-Bass.

Spann, M., & Thompson, C. (1985). *A national directory of exemplary developmental education programs.* Clearwater, FL: H & H Publishing.

Spivey, N. (1981). Goal attainment scaling in the college learning center. *Journal of Developmental and Remedial Education, 4*(2), 11-13.

Stake, R. (1967). The countenance of educational evaluation. *Teachers College Record, 68,* 523-540.

Stufflebeam, D., Foley, W., Gephard, W., Guba, E., Hammond, R., Merriam, H., & Provus, M. (1971). *Education evaluation and decision making.* Itasca, IL: F.E. Peacock.

Suen, H. (1979). Special services evaluation. *Journal of Developmental and Remedial Education, 3*(1), 7-8.

Thomas, K., & Moorman, G. (1983). *Designing reading programs.* Dubuque, IA: Kendall/Hunt.

Walvekar, C. (1981). Educating learning: The buck stops here. In C. Walvekar (Ed.), *New directions in college learning assistance, vol. 5: Assessment of learning assistance services* (pp. 75-94). San Francisco, CA: Jossey-Bass.

Wolfe, R.F. (1987). The supplemental instruction program: Developing learning and thinking skills. *Journal of Reading, 31*(3), 228-232.

4

Reading Tests

Rona F. Flippo
Madlyn L. Hanes
Carol J. Cashen

W ith the rapid growth of college reading assistance
programs throughout the United States, assessing
the reading abilities and reading needs of entering college students has become a fairly standard practice. An estimated one-
third to one-half of incoming freshmen and reentering students
in postsecondary institutions are in need of reading assistance. In
response to the need, a vast majority of colleges—as many as 75
percent of the nation's 4-year public institutions—offer developmental and/or remedial programs in reading. As great as it is now,
the need for such programs is likely to increase over the next
decade as colleges step up recruitment of disadvantaged students
(Kerstiens, 1990; Ross & Roe, 1986; Sullivan, 1980).

Reading tests are the most common type of assessment
instrument used to determine who needs such programs. Many

postsecondary institutions, even those with open admissions policies, require incoming students to take tests as part of the admissions process. Reading tests are often among the exams administered. The extent to which reading tests are used varies from institution to institution and from state to state; some states require all students entering postsecondary schools within the state system of higher education to take reading tests (Abraham, 1987; Ross & Roe, 1986; Wood, 1988).

Although we believe that reading tests are and should be only a part of reading assessment, their widespread use (and often misuse) warrants exclusive attention. In this chapter, we focus on the use, selection, and limitations of reading tests for various assessment purposes.

The prevalence of reading tests in postsecondary institutions is not solely attributable to their use as assessment instruments. Reading tests are popular largely because they often provide data for the institution's academic profile of its students and thus provide a standard against which stability or change in the student body can be measured. In this way, reading tests can influence high-level administrative decisions. They are given serious consideration in determining the staffing and programmatic needs for academic assistance and other retention initiatives, which, in turn, influence decisions about institutional budgeting and enrollment management.

In addition, reading tests have been found to have a predictive value similar to that of such robust measures as the Scholastic Aptitude Test (SAT) and the American College Test (ACT). Consequently, they hold significant standing alongside these more traditional admissions criteria (Carney & Geis, 1981; Malak & Habeman, 1985; Noble, 1986). Having found their way into the decision-making process—both as part of the institution's academic profile and as a possible predictor of academic success— reading tests, for good or bad, are here to stay.

Reading tests are certainly not free of problems, however. Practitioners are cautioned throughout this chapter about the pitfalls of misusing these tests, particularly when the tests are to serve as a basis for evaluating student progress or program effectiveness. Research studies on college populations, particularly programmatic and instructional research studies, traditionally use reading tests as dependent variables, and their findings should be evaluated with caution.

Ideally, college reading tests should assess readers' ability to deal with the academic demands of college-level coursework—in other words, the ability to derive, synthesize, and sustain meaning from lengthy texts that vary in content, vocabulary, style, complexity, and cognitive requirements (Smith & Jackson, 1985). The long-standing concern associated with most reading tests is that they may not adequately reflect the actual reading demands of academic coursework. Consequently, their use as the definitive tool for assessing reading performance among college populations and for designing and evaluating programs to address performance deficiencies has been questioned (Wood, 1988).

This chapter delineates several critical issues related to the shortcomings of conventional reading tests. Our purpose in raising these issues is to engage college reading practitioners and administrators in the kind of deliberation that is needed to make informed decisions about test selection. We examine test specifications, technical and structural considerations, and the types and purposes of many available tests to help practitioners make optimum use of these resources. An appendix of selected commercial tests with test specifications appears at the end of this chapter to guide practitioners in selecting appropriate tests.

Origins of College Reading Tests

The need to evaluate students' reading abilities is not a new phenomenon. In the early 1900s, there was a sweeping movement in the United States to develop measures for sorting students into ability tracks for college admission and for promotion purposes.

Readence and Moore (1983) traced the history of standardized reading comprehension tests, noting that reading tests grew out of a movement to assess skill levels. The original reading tests followed one of three formats: asking students to solve written puzzles, reproduce a passage, or answer questions. Burgess (1921), Kelly (1916), and Monroe (1918) developed tests comprised of written puzzles. These puzzles demanded reasoning skills and painstaking adherence to specific directions. Starch (1915) developed a reading test that required students to read a 30-second passage and then write everything they could remember. Students were allowed all the time they needed for this exercise. Any words they wrote that were not related to the text (either incorrect or new information) were not counted by the scorer. A test developed by Gray (1919) required students to read a passage and then write or retell its content. He eventually added questions to the test.

Thorndike (1914), a major proponent of having students answer questions, saw the need for more objective and convenient measures of students' abilities. To that end, he developed the Scale Alpha for students in grades 3 through 8. The test consisted of a series of short paragraphs with questions of increasing difficulty. The question/answer format appeared reasonable on several counts:

- Answers could be scored quickly and objectively.
- Questions could tap information at various levels.
- Questioning was a common school activity.
- Questioning was adaptable to the multiple choice format that became popular during the 1930s.

Questioning continued to gain popularity because it seemed to offer educators the most convenient, economical, and objective format for assessing comprehension. By the 1930s, it was the predominant means for making such assessment.

Researchers in the 1930s had already investigated the shortcomings of tests and the testing process in general (Bloom, Douglas, & Rudd, 1931; Eurich, 1930; Robinson & McCollom, 1934; Seashore, Stockford, & Swartz, 1937; Shank, 1930; Tinker, 1932). By the 1940s researchers were questioning reading tests—specifically the validity of these tests (Bloomers & Lindquist, 1944; Langsam, 1941; Robinson & Hall, 1941; Tinker, 1945).

These concerns have not abated. Kingston (1955) cites the weaknesses of standardized reading assessments noted in early studies. Triggs (1952) states that assessment of reading ability is limited by the "scarcity of reliable and valid instruments on which to base judgments" (p. 15). Farr and Carey (1986) charge that neither reading tests nor the ways in which we use them have changed significantly in the past 50 years, even though advances have been made in the areas of validity and reliability measurement.

Selecting the Appropriate Test

To choose the best test for a given circumstance, college reading and study skills instructors must be aware of the different types of tests that are available. Several pairs of choices exist, including survey versus diagnostic tests, formal versus informal tests, instructor-made versus commercial tests, and group versus individual tests. Once they know what their options are, instructors can assess their purposes for testing and the skills they want to test in order to select the most appropriate mix of exams.

Types of College Reading Tests

Survey and diagnostic tests. College reading tests are generally broken down into two broad categories: the survey test (or screening instrument), which is meant to provide information about students' general level of reading ability, and the diagnostic test, which is meant to provide more in-depth information about students' specific reading strengths and weaknesses (Kingston, 1955). Both types of test have a place in the college reading program.

Since the advent of open-door admissions in the 1960s, colleges have been accepting a greater number of students with a wider range of reading abilities than ever before. A screening instrument allows colleges to provide reading assistance services early on to those who need it. Despite the fact that, without further probing, screening instruments provide little more than a general idea of reading ability or achievement, they do provide a fast way of broadly screening students to see if they need the assistance of the college reading specialist.

Once students have been identified as needing reading or learning skills assistance, in-depth diagnosis is needed to determine the proper course of instruction. (Flippo, 1980a, 1980c). Thus, valid diagnostic measures of reading abilities are important. Of course, even with the best available tests, the results will not yield all the answers. The information gleaned from these tests must be analyzed and interpreted by a knowledgeable reading specialist and combined with other student evaluation data.

Formal and informal tests. Within the two broad categories of reading tests, survey and diagnostic, many different types of test exist. One way of classifying tests is as formal or informal. Formal tests are usually standardized instruments with norms that provide the tester with a means of comparing the students tested with a norm group representative of those students' particular level of education and other related factors. This comparison, of course, is valid only to the extent to which the characteristics of the students being tested resemble those of the norm group.

Informal tests, which are usually teacher-made, do not provide an outside norm group with which to compare students. These informal tests are usually criterion referenced—that is, the test maker has defined a certain passing score or level of acceptability against which individual students' responses are measured. Students' scores are compared to the criterion (rather than to the scores of an outside norm group of students). Again, the results are valid only to the extent to which the criteria reflect the reading skills and strategies students actually need to accomplish their own or their instructors' goals.

Instructor-made and commercial tests. Another way of classifying tests, already alluded to, is as teacher-made or commercially prepared tests. This distinction refers to whether a test has been developed locally by a teacher, department, or college, or whether it has been prepared by a publishing or test development company.

When appropriate commercially prepared tests are available, colleges usually use one of those rather than going to the expense and trouble of developing their own. After evaluating the available commercial tests, however, colleges (or reading specialists) may decide that none of these materials adequately test the reading skills and strategies they want to measure. In these cases, a teacher-made or department/college-made test is developed.

Group and individual tests. The final way of classifying reading tests is as group or individual tests. These terms refer to whether the test is designed to be administered to a group of students during a testing session or to one student at a time. Most college reading programs rely primarily on group tests because they are perceived to be more time efficient given the large number of students to be tested.

Most survey tests are designed and administered as group tests. Diagnostic tests can be designed either for group administration or for individual testing, and most diagnostic tests can be used both ways. Similarly, formal, informal, teacher-made, and commercially prepared tests can all be designed specifically for either group or individual administration, but sometimes can be used both ways.

Matching the Test to the Purpose

As the breakdown of test categories shows, the purpose for testing should determine the type or types of tests selected or developed. Therefore, a key question to ask when the issue of testing arises is "What purpose are we trying to accomplish with this testing?" Although this question may sound trivial at first, the answer is not as simple as it seems. Guthrie and Lissitz (1985) emphasize that educators must be clear about what decisions are to be made from their assessments, and then form an appropriate match with the types of assessments they select.

Three major purposes cited for testing college students' reading ability are to conduct an initial screening, to make a diagnostic assessment, and to evaluate the effectiveness of the instruction resulting from the assessment. The purpose of screening is often twofold: (1) to determine if the student has a reading problem or a need for reading assistance, and (2) to determine placement in the appropriate reading course or in special content courses or sections.

Diagnostic testing examines the various skill areas in greater depth and determines the relative strengths and weaknesses of the reader in performing these skills. This type of assessment provides an individual performance profile or a descriptive account of the reader's abilities that should facilitate instructional planning based on individual needs.

Evaluation of the instruction's effectiveness has two functions: (1) to assess individual students' progress and determine appropriate changes in teaching/remediation, and (2) to assess or document the overall success of the college reading program and identify needed changes.

If the required function of testing is gross screening to determine whether students need reading assistance, testers should probably select an appropriate instrument from the available commercially prepared standardized group survey tests. If the screening is to be used for placement, the college should probably develop instruments to measure students' ability to read actual materials required by the relevant courses. If the purpose of testing is diagnostic assessment, an appropriate instrument should be selected from the commercially prepared group or individual tests, or one should be developed by the instructor or the college. Finally, if the purpose for testing is to evaluate the effectiveness of the instruction or the program, an appropriate instrument may be selected either from among the commercially available tests or tests developed by the instructor or college.

Guthrie and Lissitz (1985) indicate that while formal, standardized reading tests are helpful for placement or classification of students as well as for program accountability purposes, they do not provide the diagnostic information vital to making informed decisions about instruction. Consequently, using such tests "as a basis for instructional decisions raises the hazard of ignoring the causes of successful learning, which is the only basis for enhancing it" (p. 29). On the other hand, they note that while informal assessments such as teacher judgments and observations are helpful to the instructional process, they are not necessarily satisfactory for accountability or classification purposes.

One note of caution: if a college elects to develop its own test, it should do so with the expertise of a testing and measurement specialist. Such tests must undergo rigorous review and field testing by the content and reading faculty involved. Colleges must be prepared to commit the necessary resources to this effort. It is not in the realm of this chapter to describe the process of developing a test; however, given the faults of so many existing commercial tests, colleges wishing to develop their own tests should enlist as much expertise and use as much care as possible.

What Should Be Tested?

In addition to determining the purpose of testing, college reading and study strategy instructors must address a second question before selecting a reading test: "What reading skills and strategies should be tested for this population?" Again, the answer to this question is not as obvious as it may seem. In fact, after years of research and discussion, reading authorities still do not agree on this point (Flippo, 1980b).

The popular trend at present is to view reading from a whole language or holistic perspective rather than as a set of isolated subskills. However, those who administer and teach in college reading programs must make a decision on the basis of their particular situation. They must define the reading skills, strategies, and theory relevant for student success in their college courses and determine the reading needs of the population they serve before selecting the most appropriate tests for their program (Flippo, 1982b). If an appropriate test is not available, the college should develop its own test rather than use an evaluation instrument that is poorly suited to the program's purposes, theory of reading, and students.

Review of the Literature

The literature related to reading tests for college students raises a number of important issues. It is important for college reading instructors to understand these issues and what the literature says about them in order to clarify their assessment needs and the criteria for selecting the most appropriate tests for their programs. Some of the literature reviewed refers to groups other than college reading students. These studies were included because they appear germane to problems and issues involved in the testing and diagnosis of college students' reading.

One very basic but sometimes overlooked question the literature addresses is "What is reading?" Early reading tests were largely atheoretical, with no grounding in a consensus of what was to be measured. This fact, however, did not deter researchers from going about the business of measuring reading, despite the lack of a theoretical basis for defining it.

The major problem identified by researchers reviewing early reading tests was the lack of agreement regarding the nature of the reading process. As Cronbach (1949) stated, "no area illustrates more clearly than reading that tests having the same name measure quite different behaviors" (p. 287).

The assumptions behind standardized tests are threefold: that these tests provide a standardized sample of an individual's behavior; that by observing this sample we will be able to make valid inferences about the students; and that appraising certain aspects of reading abilities will give us insight into overall reading achievement. However, if we cannot agree on the essential skills involved, we cannot agree on the measurement of reading (Kingston, 1955).

Issues in the Literature

Among the many issues cited in the literature, three specifically affect reading programs for college students. The first is the debate about whether reading is a product or a process. Which definition practitioners accept for reading will influence the instruments they select to evaluate students. The second issue relates to the special reading needs college students have. Finally, researchers raise the issue of how college reading tests should be norm-referenced.

Product versus process. Since the 1940s, researchers have debated the question of what can be measured in reading. One group suggests that reading is a product. This group includes Gates (1935) and Gray (1919), who investigated reading testing through the skills approach; Clymer (1968) and Wolf, King, and Huck (1968), who explored the taxonomy approach; Cleland (1965), Kingston (1961), Robinson (1966), and Spache (1962), who studied the models approach; and Farr (1969), who researched the measurement approach.

By far the most product-oriented research has been conducted on the factor-analytic approach. Using this model, researchers attempted to isolate the factors that make up reading to determine whether reading is composed of a number of discrete skills that can be measured separately or if it is a more generalized, pervasive skill that cannot be subdivided into bits and pieces.

Factor-analytic researchers identified a variety of subskills they thought could be measured separately (Burkart, 1945; Davis, 1944, 1947, 1968; Hall & Robinson, 1945; Holmes, 1962; Holmes & Singer, 1966; Lennon, 1962; Schreiner, Hieronymous, & Forsyth, 1969; Spearritt, 1972). Although the research has identified from 1 to 80 separate factors that can be measured, agreement is centered somewhere between 2 and 5 factors. Yet researchers cannot agree what these factors are (Berg, 1973).

Another group of researchers investigating the factor-analytic model concluded that reading cannot be divided into separate subskills that can be neatly measured. Instead, they

Flippo, Hanes, and Cashen

suggest reading is a global skill (Thurstone, 1946; Traxler, 1941). One of these researchers, Goodman (1969), suggests that reading is a form of information processing that occurs when a reader selects and chooses from available information in an attempt to decode graphic messages.

Early attempts to study reading as a process begin with Huey (1908), followed by the works of Anderson (1937), Buswell (1920), and Swanson (1937). More recent research into reading as a process includes work by Freedle and Carroll (1972), Gibson and Levin (1975), Goodman (1968, 1976), Kintsch (1974), Rumelhardt, Lindsay, and Norman (1972), Schank (1972), Smith (1973, 1978), and Winograd (1972).

While disagreement continues as to whether reading is global or can be segmented into discrete skills, most reading professionals now agree that to measure reading achievement, comprehension must be measured. Factor-analytic studies assume that reading comprehension occurs if the reader has some particular skills (such as word knowledge or the ability to grasp the author's expressed ideas) that can be measured discretely. These studies look upon reading as a product that can be fragmented to determine in which areas students have achieved a particular level of development. The implication here is that each of the subskills is independent from each of the others; in other words, theory suggests that the ability to grasp the author's meaning is unrelated to word knowledge which, in turn, is unrelated to reasoning in reading. Factor-analytic studies negate the relationship one skill has to another in the total reading process, and thus negates reading as an interactive process (Cashen, 1980).

Currently, most reading assessments are group-administered, multiple choice, paper and pencil tests that deal solely with the products of reading. This is due largely to teachers' and administrators' demands for tests that are easy to administer, score, and interpret. Curtis and Glaser (1983) agree that these product-oriented tests pose problems because "the discrepancy between what is needed to diagnose difficulties in reading and what is provided by the achievement tests makes

those tests impractical for many instructional purposes"
(p. 143).

Although research from the 1980s suggests that reading
is now viewed as a process involving a network of interrelated
skills, little progress has been made in developing tests to measure reading as a process (Glaser, 1981; Guthrie & Lissitz, 1985;
Squire, 1987; Valencia & Pearson, 1987). According to Squire,
we are still trying to measure process-oriented learning with
product-oriented measures—measures that remain "mired at
the skills level" (p. 724).

A few practitioners, however, are developing new methods of measuring students' reading process. Smith and Jackson
(1985) describe such a procedure in which students read an
800-word passage from a college sociology textbook, taking
notes and rehearsing the information in the text much as they
would for work in a college course. Then they write a reconstruction of the passage without looking back at the original
text or their notes. The reconstructions are scored for important generalizations, details, and the quality of the text.

While some movement toward measuring reading as a
process is evident, Johnston (1984b)—an advocate of this
movement—notes that process-oriented methods of assessment
will require substantial revision of current assumptions in both
assessment and teacher training. Johnston recognizes that current testing instruments and methods support a discrete skill or
product orientation rather than the cognitive process orientation he favors. Other researchers (Squire, 1987; Valencia &
Pearson, 1987) indicate similar concerns.

Special needs of college students. A second issue raised
by the literature relates to the special reading needs of college
students. Two primary needs are the ability to read sustained
passages of text and the ability to relate prior knowledge to text
being processed.

Regarding the first of these needs, Perry (1959) warned:
"The possession of excellent reading skills as evidenced on conventional reading tests is no guarantee that a student knows
how to read long assignments meaningfully" (p. 199). For this
reason, Perry developed an instrument that used a college read-

ing assignment to assess the reading and study strategies of students at Harvard University. This instrument is still in use today.

Most current reading tests measure only minimal skills such as vocabulary, reading rate, and comprehension without attempting to evaluate long term memory of material or the comprehension of longer text. Smith and Jackson (1985), echoing Perry, maintain that testing students' ability to handle college-level texts requires the use of longer passages taken directly from college textbooks.

Research on the effect of prior knowledge demonstrates that comprehension is heavily influenced by what students already know (Anderson et al., 1977; Carey, Harste, & Smith, 1981; Drabin-Partenio & Maloney, 1982). Simpson (1982) concludes that diagnostic processes for older readers need to consider both their prior knowledge and their background information; few instruments are available to serve those objectives.

Johnston (1984a) cautions against assuming that it is possible to construct a reading comprehension test with scores immune to the influence of prior knowledge. Prior knowledge is an integral part of the reading process; therefore, any test on which prior knowledge did not affect performance would not measure reading comprehension. The alternative is to concede that prior knowledge can be responsible for biasing the information the evaluator gains from reading comprehension tests and to factor that bias into the interpretation of the test results.

Norm-referenced and criterion-referenced tests. A third issue raised by the literature is the question of test norms. Until recently, instructors had no real choice about whether to use a norm-referenced instrument or a criterion-referenced one, as none of the latter was commercially available for the college population. Anderson (1972) reminds instructors that norm-referenced tests are intended to rank students and discriminate maximally among them, while criterion-referenced tests are intended to determine students' level of skill and knowledge.

Popham (1975) recommends norm-referenced tests as the best measures available for looking at one student in relation to others of similar age and educational level. Maxwell

(1981), however, encourages institutions to develop their own norms based on the performance of students on their own campuses. (Once again, the expertise of a testing and measurement specialist would help in developing local norms.)

Problems Cited in the Literature

In addition to raising the three major issues surrounding reading assessment, the literature cites numerous problems in assessment. One such problem is the lack of expertise of many college reading instructors in the area of testing, which results in the misuse of reading tests and in attempts to match readers' assignments to grade equivalencies. Another problem is the technical deficiencies found in many reading tests used for the college population. A third problem is the lack of available, appropriate tests.

Misuse of reading tests. Perhaps the most critical problem cited in the literature is college reading instructors' lack of expertise in the testing of reading (Flippo, 1980a; 1980b). In a survey of 300 college reading instructors, Goodwin (1971) found that 60 percent used the standardized reading test administered to their junior college students at the beginning of the term as a diagnostic instrument. However, the four tests they most often reported using were, in fact, survey tests. Only 27 percent of the instructors correctly reported that their tests measured reading achievement rather than diagnosing specific skills needs.

Ironside (1969) notes that while survey tests can be appropriately used for prediction, screening, and comparison, they are inappropriate for assessing achievement or performance. Support of Ironside's theory is found in studies by Anderson (1973), Brensing (1974), Feuers (1969), Florio (1975), Freer (1965), Rice (1971), Schoenberg (1969), Taschow (1968), and Wright (1973).

On the other hand, some studies and program descriptions have reported success in using survey tests for diagnostic and achievement purposes (Anderson, 1971; Bloesser, 1968; Cartwright, 1972; Stewart, 1970). Experimenting with a cut-time administration of the Nelson-Denny Reading Test (NDRT), Creaser et al. (1970) suggested that the test may be useful for screening, prediction, diagnosis, and assessment. Most researchers, however, caution against using survey tests for diagnosis.

The NDRT is the test most widely used by college reading instructors in the United States (Carsello, 1982; Sweiger, 1972). A nationwide survey by Sweiger found that the Diagnostic Reading Test was the next most popular test. These tests, as well as others, are often used incorrectly. Goodwin (1971) and Sweiger both conducted national surveys showing that college instructors used survey instruments to test the broad skills of comprehension and vocabulary. (As noted previously, however, many of these instructors thought these tests were meant to be diagnostic.) Surveys in Georgia (Lowe & Stefurak, 1970) and Florida (Landsman & Cranney, 1978), plus a survey of 588 institutions in the southeastern United States (Gordon & Flippo, 1983), support the studies by Goodwin and Sweiger. In addition, a newer study (Van Meter, 1988) found that of the 90 percent of community/junior colleges in Maryland that used the Nelson-Denny, 40 percent reported using it (inappropriately) for diagnostic purposes.

Matching assignments to grade equivalencies. A problem that has plagued reading researchers for years is the attempt to match readers to text through the use of grade equivalencies determined from students' test results. As one cause of this problem, Daneman (1982) points to the two foci of standardized reading tests: one focus is on differentiating readers with the goal of predicting their success, and the other is on measuring the difficulty of the text with the goal of determining whether the material will be comprehended by its intended audience. In 1981, the International Reading Association issued a statement warning against the misuse of grade equivalencies. Nevertheless, the majority of the college reading tests used today allow the instructor to convert students' reading scores to grade equivalencies.

Readability formulas allow educators to convert test passages into grade equivalencies. The problem occurs when instructors assume that students' scores on a standardized reading test can be matched to the grade equivalencies of text as measured by a readability formula. Bormuth (1985) concludes that it is currently impossible to match readers to materials economically and efficiently.

The real problem with attempting this match occurs at two levels of reading. In the early grades, attempts to match students to materials on the basis of their standardized reading test scores do not succeed because readability formulas underestimate the ability of young readers to comprehend elementary materials. The opposite problem occurs when an instructor attempts to match high school seniors and college freshmen to texts; students' reading ability is generally overestimated at this level. Carver (1985a, 1985b) recently cited this problem with the relatively new Degrees of Reading Power Test, which came out in 1983. Dale and Chall (1948) observed this phenomenon in their readability formula early on; Chall (1958) warned that all readability formulas suffer from the same problem.

Researchers have concluded that none of the 50-plus readability formulas now available is a perfect predictor of readability. These formulas neglect two essential components of reading comprehension: the information processing demands of the text and the readers' processing characteristics (Daneman, Carpenter, & Just, 1982; Kintsch & Vipond, 1979).

Technical problems. Another problem noted in the literature is the incidence of technical deficiencies in reading tests. Test validity has been the concern of numerous researchers. Farr (1968) concluded from his study of convergent and discriminant validity that total test scores are more valid and more reliable than subtest scores. Since then, however, Farr and Carey (1986) have noted that they have observed some advances in the technology of testing. They indicate that in recent years test developers have done a better job of fine-tuning their tests.

Benson (1981) reminds instructors that validity extends beyond test content to the structure of the test, including item wording, test format, test directions, and item readability. Recent researchers encourage test users to evaluate not only validity but also reliability, usability, and normative data (Gordon, 1983; Schreiner, 1979; Webb, 1983).

Lack of appropriate tests. A third problem cited in the literature is the need for better and more appropriate tests for college students (Flippo, 1980a, 1980b). A number of studies have found that most available tests do not assess all necessary dimensions of reading behavior. These include studies by Alexander (1977), Coates (1968), Cranney and Larsen (1972), Janzen and Johnson (1970), Ketcham (1960), Kingston (1965), Pardy (1977), Phillips (1969), and Tittle and Kay (1971). In addition, as noted earlier, many reading authorities argue that current tests completely fail to assess the more important process dimensions of reading.

Many specific suggestions and criticisms concerning the appropriateness of postsecondary reading tests appear in the literature, from both the product and the process perspective. For instance, Ironside (1969) called for diagnostic tests that would measure subskills and provide interpretation of the resulting information for the instructor. Farr (1969) suggested tests that would give information on higher reading skills such as interpretation, critical reading, and comprehension of the author's intent. Tittle and Kay (1971) implied a need for special reading tests that could adequately measure the lower half of the achievement distribution, where judgments about remediation and reading needs are most often made.

Raygor and Flippo (1981) noted the need for tests that allow for relative item success on at least half the test items. They suggested that one way of judging the appropriateness of a reading test for a given population was students' ability to finish at least half the test correctly, which would indicate an appropriate level of difficulty.

The flaws of existing tests have been widely documented. Evans and Dubois (1972) and Flippo (1980c, 1982a) expressed concern that the tests being used for underprepared students are not diagnostic. Kerstiens (1986b) was troubled about the number of time-critical standardized tests. He indicated that these timed tests are not appropriate for finding out the true reading abilities of students—particularly the lower achieving developmental college students with whom they are frequently used. Ahrendt (1975) also called for more diagnostic standardized reading tests and for tests that would measure reading achievement in specific subjects.

After studying the Nelson-Denny Reading Test, Chester, Dulin, and Carvell (1975) suggested changes in comprehension questions. Raygor and Flippo (1981) also examined the NDRT and found that the test was much too difficult for college students with significant reading problems. Van Meter and Herrman (1986-1987) reviewed the literature more recently and concurred with the Raygor and Flippo findings. In addition, a study by Noble (1986) indicated that reading skill as measured by the NDRT (Forms C and E) can be predicted with moderate accuracy from the American College Test Social Studies Reading and English Usage subtests, suggesting that if the ACT were used initially for college admissions purposes, additional NDRT data would not be necessary.

Summary of the Literature

In reviewing the literature on reading tests generally, and college reading tests specifically, three themes continue to surface. First and foremost, researchers are still unable to agree on what reading is or how to measure it. Second, college reading instructors need to be better informed about reading tests and their uses. Finally, there is a scarcity of appropriate tests to measure the special reading needs of college students.

Some years ago, Farr (1968) concluded that reading evaluation is far behind other aspects of the field. He called for new reading tests, refinement of reading tests currently on the market, and the application of theory and empirical assumptions about reading to the evaluation of reading. In a more recent book, Farr and Carey (1986) conclude that after almost 20 years little has changed.

The needs Farr cited in 1968 are particularly relevant to the testing of college-level reading. Few reading tests have been written specifically for college students. Even in revised versions, standardized test makers have applied little, if any, of current reading theory or empirical assumptions to tests for college students. Farr and Carey (1986) believe that we must strive to improve existing tests. They predict that new forms of assessment will evolve from present tests rather than from the development of totally different alternatives.

Evaluating Commercial Group Tests

Given the issues and problems surrounding reading tests reported in the literature, it is safe to say that there is a need not only for new and revised reading tests for college students but also for more appropriate selection of the tests that are available. While in this chapter we can do little to meet the first need, we can make recommendations to help college reading instructors make informed choices from among the more recent commercially available tests. To accomplish this task, we have included with this chapter an appendix that contains a selective review of commercially available group tests that were published or revised in 1970 or later. These tests include both those that are commonly used for college reading programs (as reported in the literature) and other tests that seem to be applicable to college populations.

The purpose of this test review is to help practitioners select the most appropriate tests for their specific program purposes and populations. Although we acknowledge that many reading researchers consider the currently available commercial tests to be weak, inappropriate, or limited, we also acknowledge that college reading instructors still need to assess large numbers of students. Until better commercial tests are available, these instructors must either choose from the currently available instruments or revise or design their own assessments with the support and assistance of appropriate college personnel or test developers. The recommendations of such researchers as Guthrie and Lissitz (1985) and Farr and Carey (1986) are our prime motivators. These researchers maintain that until new instruments are developed, research will have to concentrate on how to use current tests effectively and avoid the most flagrant misuses.

The reviews that are included in the appendix were done by directly examining each test and the information presented in the test manuals. We did not rely on reviews done by others. However, other recommended reviews are cited in the appendix and should be consulted for additional important comments on the tests.

A number of reading tests that traditionally have been used with college students over the past decade are not included in this review. These include the Nelson-Denny Reading Test, Forms A and B (1960); the McGraw-Hill Basic Skills Reading Test (1970); the Davis Reading Test (1961); the Diagnostic Reading Tests (1947); the Cooperative English Tests – Reading (1960); and the Sequential Tests of Educational Progress: Reading (1969). The first four tests were excluded from the review because they are out of print. The last two tests were excluded because they are no longer available as separate tests; both are now part of multiple test booklets. An earlier IRA publication (Blanton, Farr, & Tuinman, 1972) reviews all of these tests, except the McGraw-Hill, up to the most current revisions available at that time.

Practitioners still using one of those dated instruments should consider the more up-to-date tests reviewed here. Although we acknowledge deficiencies and problems with all of these commercial instruments, we suggest that the newer instruments are probably more appropriate than their dated counterparts. Recent work by Farr and Carey (1986) supports this recommendation.

Each of the tests listed in the appendix has been reviewed to provide the following information:

- name and author(s) of the test
- type
- use(s) of the test
- skills or strategies tested

- recommended population
- overall theory of reading
- readability and source of passages
- format of test/test parts
- testing time/number of items
- forms
- levels available
- types of scores available
- norm group(s)/tryout group(s)
- date of test publication or last major revision
- reliability
- validity
- scoring options
- cost
- ordering information
- recommended other reviews of the test
- weaknesses of the test
- strengths of the test

Careful analysis of this information should help practitioners select the most appropriate tests for their given situations and populations. We wish to note that we do not endorse any of these tests in particular. In fact, we find them all deficient in assessing most college reading needs and lacking in the components we believe are most important relating to reading. Our purpose is simply to present practitioners with detailed information regarding the commercially available choices to enable them to make the most informed decisions possible.

Normative Considerations

Most of the tests reviewed in the appendix are referenced. This means that norms, or patterns typical of a particular group, are employed to make comparisons between students. Comparisons are often made using percentiles, stanines, or grade equivalents. Test publishers usually report the procedures used to norm their instrument in the test manual. This information includes a description of the norming group in terms of age, sex, educational level, socioeconomic status, race, geographical setting, and size.

Peters (1977) reminds us that without this information, it is impossible to determine whether the test results are applicable to the population to be tested. For example, if all students to be tested are college freshmen from a low socioeconomic rural population, the use of a test that was normed with high school students from an upper middle class metropolitan area would have to be questioned. Even if the norm group and the group tested are comparable, the normative data must be current. For example, a group of college freshmen tested in the 1950s might differ from the same population tested in the 1980s. Therefore, unless both the test and the normative data are continually updated, validity becomes questionable.

Reliability Considerations

Test reliability, usually reported in "reliability coefficients," is a measure of how consistently a test measures whatever it is measuring. A test is considered reliable to the extent that students' test scores would be the same each time they took the test (assuming, of course, that no learning would take place between test administrations and that the students would remember nothing about the test at the next administration). If a test is highly reliable, we can assume that test scores will probably be an accurate measure of students' performance rather than a fluke. The coefficient of stability, or a report of test-retest reliability, is an indication of this stability in performance over time.

Most reading tests also report other types of reliability. One of these is internal consistency reliability, which measures the relationship between items on a test and looks at the consistency of performance on the various test items. Internal consistency is usually calculated with the Kuder-Richardson KR-20 or KR-21 formulas or by using "split-half reliability." With the split-half method, reliability is computed by dividing the test into two parts and comparing or correlating scores on the parts.

Another type of reliability reported for many reading tests is the coefficient of equivalence (also called parallel forms reliability, or alternate forms reliability). This method is used when a test has two forms. To compute reliability, both forms are given to the same sample group, and then the scores are correlated.

Of course, no test can be 100 percent reliable. Variability is inevitable when dealing with human beings. The higher the reliability coefficient for a test, however, the more confident we can be that the test will accurately measure students' performance. Testing and measurement authorities advise that one way to determine whether a particular test's reliability score is acceptable is to measure it against the highest score attained by a similar test. As Brown (1983) put it, "the reliability of any test should be as high as that of the better tests in the same area" (p. 89). However, Brown also indicates that performance measures with reliability values of .85 - .90 are common. Peters (1977) notes that .80 or higher is a high correlation for equivalent, parallel, or alternate form reliability.

On a final note, users must remember to analyze what a given test actually measures. Even if a test is highly reliable, if it does not measure the appropriate skills, strategies, abilities, and content knowledge of the students to be tested, it is of no value.

Validity Considerations

A test is considered valid to the extent that it measures what the test user is trying to measure. If a test measures the skills, strategies, abilities, and content knowledge that the college or program deems important for a given population's academic success, it is a valid instrument. If the test also measures extraneous variables, its validity is weakened proportionately. A test cannot be considered valid unless it measures something explicitly relevant both to the population being tested and to the purpose of the testing. Of course, a test that is not reliable cannot be considered valid.

As pointed out earlier, validity considerations must extend beyond content validity to include appropriateness of the test's structure and materials. Item wording, test format, test directions, length and readability of passages, and content materials must all be analyzed to determine their appropriateness for the given population and the purposes of the testing.

Test developers and publishers use different terminology to describe the validity of their tests. This terminology actually describes different types of validity. Type of validity is usually a function of the way the test publisher determined that the test was valid for a given purpose. It is important for test users to know something about the different types of validity in order to understand the terminology reported in test manuals.

Often test publishers report only one or two types of validity for their tests. One type of validity cannot be generalized to another. However, if you know why you are testing, what you are testing for, and the needs of the population being tested, you can usually determine the validity of a test for yourself even when given limited information. Of course, as Peters (1977) points out, reading instructors should demand appropriate validity documentation in test manuals. If an instrument does not provide validity information, it really should not be used; purchasing such a test only perpetuates the assumption made by some test publishers that this information is of little importance.

Types of validity. According to Brown (1983), the numerous types of validity generally fall into three main classes: criterion-related validity, content validity, and construct validity.

The basic research question for the criterion-related validity measure is "How well do scores on the test predict performance on the criterion?" (Brown, 1983, p. 69). An index of this predictive accuracy, called the "validity coefficient," measures the validity of the particular test. What is of ultimate interest is the individual's performance on the criterion variable. The test score is important only as a predictor of that variable, not as a sample or representation of behavior or ability. An example of criterion-related validity is use of the SAT to predict college grade point average. Concurrent validity and predictive validity are two types of criterion-related validity often noted in test manuals.

Concurrent validity refers to the correlation between test scores and a criterion measure obtained at the same (or nearly the same) time; therefore, it measures how well test scores predict immediate performance on a criterion variable. Predictive validity examines the correlation of test scores with a criterion measure obtained at a later point in time.

The most frequently used method of establishing criterion-related validity is to correlate test scores with criterion scores. A validity coefficient is a correlation coefficient; the higher the correlation, the more accurately the test scores will predict scores on the criterion task. Thus, if the choice is between two tests that are equally acceptable for a given population and purpose, and one test has a validity coefficient of .70 while the other has a validity coefficient of .80, the test user should choose the latter. According to Peters (1977), a test should have a validity coefficient of .80 or above to be considered valid. Any coefficient below this level, he says, should be considered questionable.

The basic question researched for content validity is "How would the individual perform in the universe of situations of which the test is but a sample?" (Brown, 1983, p. 69). The content validity of a test is evaluated on the basis of the adequacy of the item sampling. Since no quantitative index of sampling adequacy is available, evaluation is a subjective process. In evaluating this type of validity, the test score operates as a sample of ability. An example of content validity is use of an exam that samples the content of a course to measure performance and ability in that course.

Face validity is often confused with content validity. A test has face validity when the items seem to measure what the test is supposed to measure. Face validity is determined by a somewhat superficial examination that considers only obvious relevance, while establishing content validity entails thorough examination by a qualified judge who considers subtle as well as obvious aspects of relevance.

The basic question researched for construct validity is "What trait does the test measure?" (Brown, 1983, p. 69). Construct validity is determined by accumulating evidence regarding the relationship between the test and the trait it is designed to measure. Such evidence may be accumulated in various ways, including studies of content and criterion-related validity. As with content validity, no quantitative index of the construct validity of a test exists. An example of construct validity is the development of a test to define a trait such as intelligence. Congruent validity, convergent validity, and discriminant validity are all types of construct validity that are cited in test manuals.

Congruent validity is the most straightforward method of determining that a certain construct is being measured. Congruence is established when test scores on a newly constructed instrument correlate with test scores on other instruments measuring a similar trait or construct. Convergent and discriminant validity are established by determining the correlation between test scores and behavioral indicators that are aligned theoretically with the trait (convergent validity) or that distinguish it from opposing traits (discriminant validity). For example, we would expect that scores on verbal ability tests would correlate highly with observed performance on tasks that require verbal skills. On the other hand, we would expect a low correlation between scores on manual ability tests and verbal behaviors, since these traits, in theory, are distinct. Ideally, if convergent validity is reported, discriminant validity is also reported.

Brown (1983) emphasizes that validity evidence will always be situation-specific. Therefore, any test will have many different validities. It must be remembered that validity is always established for a particular use of a test in a particular situation. As you review tests for possible use in your college reading program, always consider the particular situation and how the test is to be used.

Passage dependency. Although not usually mentioned in testing and measurement texts as an aspect of validity, the passage dependency of a test should be considered by reading test users. According to the more traditional testing and measurement perspective, if students can answer test items by recalling prior knowledge or applying logic without having to read and understand the passage, the test items are "passage independent," and the validity of the results should be questioned.

Reading instructors who adhere to this perspective would not want students to be able to answer test questions by drawing on past experience or information. That would defeat the instructors' purpose in conducting a reading assessment. They would argue that if test items are well constructed, students should have to read and understand the test passages in order to correctly answer questions based on those passages.

Of the commercial tests reviewed for this chapter, those that utilize a cloze procedure appear to be the most passage dependent. Reading tests using the traditional model—a brief paragraph followed by multiple choice questions—appear to be less passage dependent, as answers to questions are sometimes available from the examinees' background knowledge or reasoning ability.

Practitioners can best determine the passage dependency of a reading test by conducting their own studies of the reading materials. In these studies, the same test questions are administered to two groups of examinees; one group takes the test in the conventional manner with the reading passages present, while the other group attempts to answer the items without the reading passages. See the Examiner's Manual of the Nelson-Denny Reading Test (Brown, Bennett & Hanna, 1980) for one detailed plan to calculate passage dependency.

In contrast to the more traditional test perspective, some reading researchers consider it desirable to allow prior knowledge to affect reading assessment (Johnston, 1984a; Simpson, 1982). In addition, Wark and Flippo (1991) note the importance of logic as a skill necessary for the test taking success of college students.

Test users must decide for themselves the importance of prior knowledge, logic, and passage dependency as each relates to the measurement of reading comprehension. We recommend that practitioners learn as much as possible about any test they plan to use so they can more accurately analyze their results and better understand all the concomitant variables. As we know from psycholinguists' work with miscue analysis (analysis of word recognition deviations from text), some traits that are traditionally considered undesirable may not be undesirable at all. Miscues, for instance, may actually show reading strengths. Similarly, college students' use of logic or prior knowledge while taking a test may provide practitioners with insights into students' ability to handle textual readings.

Readability Considerations

In our appendix we used traditional readability formulas (Fry, 1977; Raygor, 1979) to compute the approximate readability of test passages whenever test publishers did not furnish this information. Nevertheless, we want to point out the limitations of these formulas. Traditional readability formulas consider only sentence and word length, with the assumption that the longer the sentence and the longer the words in the sentence (or the more syllables per word), the more difficult the passage will be for the reader. However, we believe that other factors also contribute to readability. These factors are less tangible and therefore more difficult to quantify and measure.

Those reviewing tests and materials for use in formal or informal assessment should consider several readability factors in addition to sentence and word length: (1) the complexity of the concepts covered by the material, (2) students' interest in the content, (3) students' past life experience with the content, (4) students' cognitive experience with the content, and (5) students' linguistic experience with the syntax of the material.

Optimizing the Use of Commercial Tests

If standardized, norm-referenced reading tests are to be used, they should be selected and used wisely. College reading professionals can use a number of strategies to maximize the usefulness of these commercially prepared group tests and achieve a better fit with local needs. In the following pages, we offer several suggestions that we judge to be both practical and timely. These ideas show promise in providing practitioners with additional ways of comparing tests, administering tests, and interpreting results.

Moreover, these suggestions address several of the issues and concerns raised in the literature, offering some resolution for the local setting. We recommend four strategies: (1) conducting item analyses to determine the appropriateness of test content and level of difficulty, (2) adjusting administrative time constraints, (3) developing local norms, and (4) using scaled scores.

Item Analysis

Reading tests that do not measure the content taught in reading courses may be inappropriate for evaluating program success. One way to determine the match between reading tests and reading courses is to analyze test items against course objectives. This technique is time consuming, but it may be helpful. Alexander (1977) recommends that learning assistance personnel take the reading test, examine each item to determine the skill or concept being tested, and compile a checklist of skills and concepts by item. Then they should compare the checklist with the objectives taught in the reading course. If the instructors think it is important to select an instrument on the basis of its match to reading course objectives, they can analyze several reading tests in this way to find the test with the closest match.

While this strategy may provide a viable way of evaluating program effectiveness, we caution practitioners that the content of many college reading courses themselves may not match the actual reading needs of college students. Unless the content and objectives of the reading course closely match the reading needs of the students in their regular college classes, this type of item analysis will not be worth the time it takes.

Wood (1989) suggests that test items be reviewed to examine the extent to which they represent "real" college reading. We strongly support this type of item analysis. Items should cover a variety of sources and subjects, be of adequate length, and reflect a level of difficulty typical of college reading assignments. Esoteric topics, according to Wood, prohibit students' use of prior knowledge and make tests unnecessarily difficult. Although practitioners are unlikely to find a perfect representation of actual college reading, this kind of review provides a good way of making relative comparisons among tests.

Raygor and Flippo (1981) suggest that practitioners analyze students' success rate on each item to determine the appropriateness of standardized reading tests for local populations. We concur. Some tests may be too difficult and some too easy to discriminate adequately among the full range of student performance. Analyzing the relative success rates (i.e., percentage of items answered correctly) of several widely used instruments, Raygor and Flippo found that the best discrimination occurs when approximately half of the students respond to at least 50 percent of the test items correctly. When tests meet this criterion, scores tend to be more normally distributed. Deficient readers as well as highly skilled readers are more likely to be identified under these circumstances.

Tests on which most students have a success rate of 50 percent or higher may be too easy and will tend to discriminate only among the lower performance ranges. On the other hand, tests on which most students have lower than a 50 percent success rate may be too difficult and will discriminate only among the more highly skilled readers (Raygor & Flippo, 1981). Practitioners should analyze possible test choices and select those that discriminate best for their populations.

Time Constraints

Several studies report that the time constraints imposed by many reading tests result in dubious performance scores for certain populations of college students. Developmental students have been found to have a slower response rate on timed tests, which may amplify relative performance discrepancies on time-critical reading tests (Kerstiens, 1986a, 1986b, 1990). Adult students and minority populations also appear to be penalized by time-critical factors inherent in standard test administration.

Davis, Kaiser, and Boone (1987) examined test completion rates among 8,290 entering students in Tennessee's community, 4-year, and technical colleges. The test used for the study was the Reading Comprehension Test of the Tennessee State Board of Regents. Performance differences in age and race were found in all three types of institutions. Adult students (those 22 years of age and older) demonstrated lower completion rates than their younger counterparts, and minority students had lower completion rates than whites. Davis recommended extending the test time allotted for completion to remove the performance bias that tends to work against these populations.

Stetson (1982) reported that pretest and posttest comparisons can be misleading. She used pretesting and posttesting to determine the effectiveness of programs designed to increase reading rates, and found that gains in posttest performance reflected an increase in the number of items attempted rather than an improvement in ability. By adjusting posttest scores to reflect accuracy levels based on pretest completion rates, she found that her students actually did worse on vocabulary and comprehension posttests than they had on the pretests. Test efficiency appeared to decrease with increased attention to rate or speed of response.

It may be of value to practitioners in the developmental setting to compare completion rates on posttests with those on pretests. If considerable discrepancies exist, it may well be worth investigating test efficiency to guard against artificial score inflation. Adjusting raw posttest scores on the basis of pretest completion rates (the farthest point to which the student progressed on the initial testing) will allow for a more direct comparison of pre- and posttreatment performance.

Local Norming

The match between the norm reference group on a standardized test and the college group being tested is critical to test interpretation. When the norm group and the college population are dissimilar, test results have no basis for comparison. Some test publishers will provide norms that are aligned with the characteristics of certain local populations, particularly in metropolitan areas; practitioners should inquire about the availability of these norms when national norms are not appropriate. Otherwise, developing local norms is strongly recommended.

Developing local norms requires the redistribution of local scores to simulate a normal curve. Raw scores can then be reassigned to standard units of measurement such as stanines or percentile rankings. Most test manuals and basic statistics texts provide the necessary information about normal distributions to guide the redistribution of local raw scores. For example, raw scores that account for the lowest and highest 4 percent of the range of scores can be reassigned to the first and ninth stanines, respectively. It is essential to use as large a data set as possible when establishing the local norm group. Repeated administration over time—for instance, scores for all incoming freshmen over 3 to 5 consecutive years—are preferable to ensure adequate representation.

Two other important points should also be considered. First, while the calculations involved in developing local norms may be straightforward, it is advisable to seek the assistance of professionals trained in psychometrics or educational measurement. Second, practitioners must keep in mind that local norms, once established, are meaningful only in making relative judgments about students at their own institutions.

Use of Scaled Scores

More local research is encouraged to assess the long term changes in students' reading abilities, particularly those changes resulting from intervention by developmental programs. The selection of reading tests may change in response to new local conditions or because of periodic revisions (new editions) of commercially available tests.

Because reevaluation is necessary to keep up with these changes, preserving old records is important. However, valuable data can be lost by preserving the wrong source of performance measures or scores. Keeping raw scores alone on record is not useful. It is far better to retain raw scores along with scaled scores, which will sustain their usefulness despite changes of instrumentation or revised editions of formerly adopted instruments. (We have already warned against the use of grade equivalent scores; these scores are misleading and have virtually no comparative value.)

Raw scores have value for measuring individual changes in performance on the same or equivalent forms of tests (e.g., pre- and posttesting). Because they are more sensitive to variations in performance than scaled scores, they can capture smaller (but still meaningful) gains. Raw scores, however, are meaningless when comparing performance on different tests. Normalized scaled scores, such as percentile rankings and stanines, are less sensitive to variations in performance because of the wider bands of scores forced into the comparison scales. Unequal differences between the rankings or stanines at either end of the scales and those in the middle range are also likely. However, the advantage of scaled scores is that they can be used effectively to make comparisons across groups and across tests.

Standard scores are the best alternatives for record keeping. They represent the conversion of raw scores to a form that ensures equal differences among converted values by comparing an individual student's score to the rest of the distribution of scores. They are also the most useful scores for longitudinal studies of performance. Like normalized scaled scores, they can be used for making comparisons with other standardized, norm-referenced tests as well as with revised versions of the same test. Most test publishers report test scores in terms of standard scores, percentile rankings, and stanines.

Evaluating Informal Reading Assessments

Because of the large number of students who participate in college reading programs, most programs limit their testing to standardized group instruments. However, we should point out that carefully designed informal reading assessments appropriate for college students can provide more diagnostic information, and probably more useful information, than any of the formal group tests currently available.

Informal assessments can be administered to groups or to individuals. Two of the tests in the appendix are examples of informal group assessments: the Degrees of Reading Power (1983) and the Reading Progress Scale (Carver, 1975). Both are group cloze instruments.

The use of informal group assessment has broad support in the literature. Rankin and Helm (1986), Sadden and Reid (1984), and Stephens et al. (1986) point out the advantages of using teacher-developed or program-developed group cloze instruments rather than the standardized commercial group tests. Rankin and Helm add that they have been able to show high validity on various measures with their cloze assessments. McWilliams and Rakes (1979) provide samples of informal group assessments relevant to the content areas, including cloze assessments as well as group informal reading inventories (IRIs). Glazer, Searfoss, and Gentile (1988) describe techniques for assessing comprehension through informal procedures such as retelling, think-aloud protocols, and ethnographic recording, and suggest these techniques as alternatives to standardized tests. Finally, Smith and Jackson's (1985) method of assessing college students' comprehension of passages with written retellings shows potential as a quality informal assessment. Most textbooks on reading in the content area or secondary reading education provide directions for developing group IRIs and cloze assessments.

Using individual IRIs with college students presents two problems: (1) they are time consuming to administer and analyze, and (2) few commercially available individual IRIs are even close to being appropriate for college populations. Although time consuming, an individual IRI may be appropriate for students exhibiting unusual or conflicting results on other assessments, or for students indicating a preference for more diagnosis. The practitioner or program director will have to decide when it makes sense to administer an individual IRI. This decision may have quite a lot to do with the philosophy of the program. Certainly, few reading authorities would deny the power of the IRI as a diagnostic tool. It may well be that the level of qualitative analysis one can get from an IRI will be worth the time it takes.

In our review of tests for this section, we searched for commercially prepared IRIs that might be appropriate for the college population. We found two commercially available IRIs that contain passages and scoring information through the twelfth grade level and may therefore be adapted for use with college students: the Burns/Roe Informal Reading Inventory (1985) for preprimer through twelfth grade, and the DeSanti Cloze Reading Inventory (1986) for grades 3 through 12. DeSanti's inventory is especially promising, combining elements of a cloze assessment developed for group or individual administration with an IRI.

A third IRI, the Advanced Reading Inventory (Johns, 1981), is available for seventh grade through college. Since this instrument was designed for use through the freshman college level, it should be examined by any college program interested in an IRI. Those interested in using a commercially available IRI should consult Jongsma and Jongsma (1981) for a listing of recommendations, and Pikulski and Shanahan (1982) for a critical analysis of the IRI and other informal assessment measures.

Given the dearth of commercial instruments designed for the college population, a program that seriously desires to use an IRI should consider designing its own. Although most program-developed assessments will have some flaws, the positive aspects should far outweigh the negative. A college could develop an assessment using actual reading materials from the students' introductory courses. Cloze procedures and written retellings can be used for more qualitative analyses. An institution-developed IRI or cloze procedure would be most desirable in that it would provide both an assessment of students' ability to read materials for their required courses and a powerful tool for qualitative diagnosis.

Most good reading methods texts include directions for constructing an IRI, analyzing the results, and using retellings. In addition, Pikulski and Shanahan (1982) are recommended for information on the IRI and cloze as diagnostic tools, Smith and Jackson (1985) are recommended for information on use of written retellings with college students, and Glazer, Searfoss, and Gentile (1988) are recommended for a discussion of other informal techniques.

Summary of Findings and Analysis

There is still no real agreement among reading educators as to whether reading is a global process or a series of discrete skills. It is evident that the majority of the standardized group tests reviewed here define reading as a product—a series of discrete skills whose composite score is considered the measure of the reader's achievement. Only two group tests reviewed, the Degrees of Reading Power (1983) and the Reading Progress Scale (Carver, 1975), view and measure reading as a process that cannot be fragmented into discrete skills—in other words, as a form of processing that occurs when a reader selects and chooses from available information in an attempt to decode graphic messages. Other informal assessments (cloze exams, IRIs, retellings) also measure reading as a process.

Before selecting a reading test, reading practitioners should have an in-depth understanding of the reading process, including knowledge of the various models of reading. Only after they have adopted a reading model that reflects their own definition of reading should they select a reading test. Practitioners should also define what is to be tested and the variables that might affect the students' test performance. Unless these factors are carefully considered, the appropriateness of the test selection will be questionable.

Our review of the literature and of the available tests has led us to draw several conclusions about current practice in testing reading at the college level. These conclusions—along with their implications for college reading programs and our recommendations for improvement—are described in the following pages. Table 1 provides a concise summary of these findings.

Conclusions

Based on our examination of available tests, we concur with the consensus of the reviewed literature: more and better reading tests are needed to evaluate the range of abilities and needs of college students. No one test is appropriate for use with all students in all postsecondary institutions. Better tests are needed at all levels of the achievement distribution, particularly at the neglected middle level. Most of the tests reviewed tend to focus on either the lowest ability students or the highest ability students, with little or nothing in between.

Most of the group reading tests reviewed were norm referenced with a less than adequate sample of postsecondary students to cover the diverse needs of junior/community colleges, postsecondary technical schools, colleges, and universities. Many of the tests used at the college level seem to have been conceived without adequate recognition of the diversity of postsecondary populations.

Vocabulary, comprehension, and reading rate are the skills most often tested by these standardized tests. None of them assess the extended types of reading required of most college students. Rather than assessing students with passages that resemble the materials they must read in their college textbooks, these tests rely on relatively short passages that resemble workbook exercises. Furthermore, most of the instruments seem to define and test reading as a set of discrete skills, none of which represents the reading skills and strategies more typical of and necessary for college courses.

Finally, we were dismayed by the tests' inadequate and often unavailable technical information. Many tests do not have the appropriate norming, reliability, validity, readability, and other technical information available in any of their test manuals. Other publishers provide this information only in documents that must be purchased separately.

Table 1

Reading Tests: Conclusions, Implications, Recommendations

Conclusions	Implications	Recommendations
No one test will meet the needs of all programs and all student populations.	Programs will need to utilize more than one assessment instrument to determine the reading needs of their differing populations.	College reading practitioners should be knowledgeable about the various appropriate screening and diagnostic assessments.
Few reading tests are normed on entering and undergraduate college students.	Most reading tests in use are inappropriate for many entering and undergraduate college students and may result in students being inappropriately placed in college reading courses. Most of the research on college reading has been conducted with tests that were not appropriately normed for the college population.	Colleges and universities should compile their own data and develop local norms. College reading programs should not rely on the outcomes of studies using tests that are inappropriately normed for the college population.
None of the standardized tests uses extended passages of the type college students are required to read in their textbooks.	Instruments in use do not test the type of reading typically required of college students.	Tests are needed with material that more accurately resembles college-type reading and assignment length.

Flippo, Hanes, and Cashen

Table 1 (Continued)
Reading Tests: Conclusions, Implications, Recommendations

Conclusions	Implications	Recommendations
Many tests reviewed defined and tested reading as a set of discrete skills, such as vocabulary, comprehension, and reading rate. Even those that noted the overall importance of comprehension often tested discrete skills.	Results of these tests provide little or no information concerning proficiency in necessary college reading requirements. Most of the research on college reading has been done with tests that are inappropriate for college reading requirements.	Tests for college students should be designed to evaluate appropriate college reading strategy requirements. College reading programs should not rely on outcomes of studies using tests that are inappropriate for college reading requirements.
Most standardized tests reviewed are survey instruments.	Few tests are available to diagnose individual college students' reading strengths and weaknesses.	Colleges should construct their own diagnostic assessments.
The technical information for most of the tests reviewed is inadequate and is not readily available in the test administration manuals.	Many test users never see or read the technical information.	Test publishers should include adequate technical information in the test manual.

Implications

Some of the implications of our general conclusions are obvious: college programs will need to find or develop several assessment instruments to evaluate their different populations. The instruments currently in use do not measure the types of reading required of most college students. Therefore, the results of these tests provide little information concerning students' abilities to handle the necessary college reading requirements.

No standardized group tests are available for diagnosing college students' strengths and weaknesses. The 1976 edition of the Stanford Diagnostic Reading Test (SDRT) provides some appropriate diagnostic information; however, that test has now been replaced by the 1984 edition which is not appropriate for the college population.

Most of the studies on college reading have been conducted with tests that researchers have indicated are inappropriate for the college population (Flippo, 1980a, 1980c, 1982a; Gordon & Flippo, 1983; Raygor & Flippo, 1981). Yet we often use these studies as a basis for making decisions or supporting recommendations in the field of college reading. The implication, of course, is that the validity of most of these studies should be questioned.

Finally, we suspect that because of budgetary or time constraints, many users of tests in college reading programs do not purchase or read the separately published technical information. Test users thus may be unaware of the norming, reliability, validity, and other technical information concerning these tests.

Recommendations

In light of the conclusions and implications of our review of the tests and the literature, we offer five recommendations for reading practitioners. First, college reading practitioners should use a variety of assessments on which to base their decisions. Each of these assessments should be appropriate to the students, the purpose of testing, and the tasks that are to be evaluated. To be able to determine such appropriateness, practitioners need to be better informed about the different types and uses of available reading tests (Goodwin, 1971; Gordon & Flippo, 1983; Landsman & Cranney, 1978; Lowe & Stefurak, 1970; Sweiger, 1972). Gordon and Flippo found that many college reading practitioners were not actively involved in research or professional associations, and only infrequently presented papers or attended conferences. This lack of involvement in, and awareness of, current developments in the field is a primary reason for the ill-informed decisions that are made about tests.

Our second recommendation is that college and university reading programs compile their own data and develop their own norms. The tests most available and most often used usually have inappropriate or inadequate norms for diverse college populations. We suggest that college reading practitioners take responsibility for developing local norms based on data collected over a period of 3 to 5 years.

In addition, practitioners need to be aware that many studies in the field of college reading used tests that were either inappropriate or inappropriately normed for the college population. They must consider this fact when utilizing the results of these studies. It may be that if the instrument or the norming is inappropriate, the study should not be considered at all.

Third, college reading professionals need to ensure that new tests are developed that more accurately reflect college-type reading in both content and length. To accomplish this task, they will need to work with test publishers, test development contractors, and other college faculty members. Publishers of reading tests might be more apt to develop appropriate instruments or revise existing ones if college reading professionals encouraged them by asking for new instruments, providing samples of what would be more appropriate, and choosing not to purchase the less appropriate tests currently available. Test publishers should be provided with prototypes of the materials and questions college students face in their introductory courses.

The impact on publishers would be greater if community colleges and universities in a given area or system joined efforts to work with publishers and contractors. The consortium should also contact test development contractors, such as Educational Testing Service, to discuss development of more appropriate screening and diagnostic instruments. (These companies specialize in developing tests specific to the needs of those contracting with them.) Once again, prototypes should be provided, and representatives from each postsecondary institution in the consortium should work with the contractor in developing the new instruments. Costs and expertise could be shared among participating institutions. This strategy would allow the development of tests that evaluated appropriate college reading requirements using appropriate content and length of materials. In addition, consortium members could provide an adequate supply of students for field testing and norming.

Our fourth recommendation is that professionals develop more informal, campus-specific diagnostic instruments for their populations. Several examples of this type of development were noted earlier. For instance, Smith and Jackson (1985) used students' retellings to make assessments. Other practitioners successfully used the cloze method and informal reading inventories for diagnostic evaluations. Perry (1959) used students' assignments to diagnose reading problems. Guthrie and Lissitz (1985) noted that the use of students' answers to questions, discussion, and written essays are all helpful diagnostic tools for instructional decision-making purposes.

We recommend that practitioners developing their own instruments concentrate on tests designed to diagnose the strengths and needs of students using appropriate college-related skills and strategies. Exams must present students with reading tasks that are accurate examples of the strategies we wish to test. We must also have enough accurate examples of each of the strategies and skills we wish to measure so we can determine which of them, if any, are causing problems for the students. Finally, we must test students' use of these different strategies and skills with the types of materials they are required to handle. For instance, students might have a problem summarizing a literary piece, but not a scientific experiment.

Our final recommendation is that test publishers provide adequate and pertinent technical information (norming, reliability, and validity data) in the manual for administering the test. This information should be presented in a clear and complete fashion and should be provided at no additional cost to those considering adopting a test. Although we feel that it is best to put all the information in one manual, when more than one manual is published for a test, the technical information should always be cross-referenced to make it usable. Once again, perhaps publishers would be more apt to act if a larger consortium united to make these reasonable demands.

Future Avenues of Research

It seems clear to us that some new research directions are needed in the area of college reading diagnosis. Although there have been attempts and suggestions to do something "different," only a few people in this field have really worked at, or discussed in depth, any alternative approaches to diagnosis and testing (e.g., Glaser, 1981; Guthrie & Lissitz, 1985; Johnston, 1983, 1984a; Peters, 1977; Raygor & Flippo, 1981; Simpson, 1982; Smith & Jackson, 1985; Valencia & Pearson, 1987).

Based on our analysis of the situation, we support the development of new tests designed to evaluate the reading tasks and strategies necessary for success in college. Such tests should utilize passages and require tasks and strategies comparable in difficulty and length to introductory-level college reading assignments. In essence, we think that decisions about students should be based on assessments and procedures appropriate to college reading and to each specific group of students to be evaluated. We see a need to reexamine totally the reading assessment of college students, including both formal and informal methods of assessment.

Many of our previous recommendations, if carried through, represent future directions for research and planning.

In addition, we see several other avenues for future research in this area.

1. We endorse the type of item success rate study used by Raygor and Flippo (1981) and the item analysis approach recommended by Wood (1989) as possible means of determining the appropriateness of any given test for an institution's different college populations. College reading practitioners should conduct studies like these in their own institutions before deciding on any test for their students.

2. The effects of time constraints on special populations of college students warrant continued study in the local setting. Investigations into the relative completion rates of minority, nontraditional, and developmental student groups may indicate that adjustments are needed in the time allocated to complete tests (Abraham, 1987; Kersteins, 1986a, 1986b, 1990). Practitioners should consider the test scoring technique used by Stetson (1982) to control for the possible situation of increased completion rates at the expense of test efficiency, particularly in pretest/posttest type studies evaluating individual student progress.

3. Research is needed to systematically investigate the actual reading needs of college students. To date, several studies have been conducted at different types of institutions to clarify the amount and type of reading required of undergraduate college students. Researchers in these studies asked both professors and their students exactly what reading was required for the students to succeed in their courses. Results of these studies have been reported by Orlando and colleagues at several professional meetings (1986, 1987, 1988, 1990), and Orlando et al. (1989) have published some of their results. More such studies, done

on a large-scale basis, could provide test developers with a more appropriate set of reading tasks and strategies than those evaluated by currently available tests.

4. Many decisions regarding the admittance, placement, instruction, and retention of college students have been made on the basis of studies that used tests researchers have called "inappropriate." New studies will be necessary to evaluate these decisions as well as the studies and tests used to reach them. If the tests were inappropriate, the results of the studies were probably invalid, and the decisions based on them are thrown into question. Some of the best research should come from the local setting. Practitioners are encouraged to promote research efforts at their home institutions and to document their findings to share at professional meetings and in publications. If the principles and methods of test selection discussed in this chapter are practiced, these investigations should make significant contributions.

5. Assessments should be developed to study students' schemata in a variety of college-related content areas. These assessments of stored information and knowledge would provide content instructors and reading professionals with valuable information. It should be pointed out that we would want items on these new instruments to be as passage independent as possible. In this way, as Johnston (1984a) and Simpson (1982) point out, we could assess prior knowledge.

6. Johnston (1983), Peters (1977), and Valencia and Pearson (1987) have suggested a more interactive approach to assessment. Interactive assessment models should be investigated and tested with the college population to determine the feasibility and benefits of this more time-consuming approach.

References and Suggested Readings

Abraham, A. (1987). *Report on college level remedial/developmental programs in SREB states.* Atlanta, GA: Southland Regional Education Board. (ED 280 369)

*Ahrendt, K.M. (1975). *Community college reading programs.* Newark, DE: International Reading Association.

Alexander, C.F. (1977). Adding to usefulness of standardized reading tests in college programs. *Journal of Reading, 20,* 288-291.

Anderson, C.A. (1971). Problems of individualization. In F.P. Greene (Ed.), *Reading: The right to participate* (pp. 211-214). Milwaukee, WI: National Reading Conference.

Anderson, C.A. (1973). A study of accountability in the community college reading program. In P.L. Nacke (Ed.), *Programs and practices for college reading* (Vol. 2, pp. 7-11). Boone, NC: National Reading Conference.

Anderson, I.H. (1937). Studies on the eye movements of good and poor readers. *Psychological Monographs, 48,* 21-35.

Anderson, R.C. (1972). How to construct achievement tests to assess comprehension. *Review of Educational Research, 42,* 145-170.

Anderson, R., Reynolds, R., Schallert, D., & Goetz, E. (1977). Frameworks for comprehending discourse. *American Educational Research Journal, 14,* 367-381.

Auslander, J., & Hill, F.E. (1928, 1968). *The winged horse.* New York: Doubleday.

Benson, J. (1981). A redefinition of content validity. *Educational and Psychological Measurement, 41,* 793-802.

Berg, P.C. (1973). Evaluating reading abilities. In W.H. MacGinitie (Ed.), *Assessment problems in reading* (pp.27-33). Newark, DE: International Reading Association.

*Blanton, W., Farr, R., & Tuinman, J.J. (Eds.). (1972). *Reading tests for the secondary grades: A review and evaluation.* Newark, DE: International Reading Association.

Bloesser, R.E. (1968). *Study skills project.* Cupertino, CA: Foothill Junior College District. (ED 022 437)

Bloom, M.E., Douglas, J., & Rudd, M. (1931). On the validity of silent reading tests. *Journal of Applied Psychology, 15,* 35-38.

Bloomers, P., & Lindquist, E.F. (1944). Rate of comprehension of reading: Its measurement and its relation to comprehension. *Journal of Educational Psychology, 15,* 449-473.

Bormuth, J.R. (1969). Development of readability analyses. (Final report, OEG-3-7-070052-0326). Washington, DC: U.S. Office of Education.

Bormuth, J.R. (1985). A response to "Is the Degrees of Reading Power test valid or invalid?" *Journal of Reading, 29,* 42-47.

Brensing, D.D. (1974). Improvement of the reading abilities of vocational students. *Dissertation Abstracts International, 35,* 4321-4322A. (University Microfilms No. 74-25, 593)

*Brown, F.G. (1983). *Principles of educational and psychological testing* (3rd ed.). New York: Holt, Rinehart & Winston.

*Brown, J.E., Bennett, J.M., & Hanna, G.S. (1980). The Nelson-Denny Reading Test (Forms E & F). Chicago, IL: Riverside.

Brown, J.E., Nelson, M.J., & Denny, E.C. (1973). The Nelson-Denny Reading Test (Forms C & D). Boston, MA: Houghton Mifflin.

Bruning, R. (1985). Review of Degrees of Reading Power. In J.V. Mitchell, Jr. (Ed.), *The ninth mental measurements yearbook* (pp. 443-444). Lincoln, NE: University of Nebraska Press.

Burgess, M.A. (1921). The measurement of silent reading. *Russell Sage Foundation Educational Monographs* (No. 143). New York: Department of Education.

Burkart, K.H. (1945). An analysis of reading abilities. *Journal of Educational Research, 38,* 430-439.

Burns, P.C., & Roe, B.D. (1985). *Informal Reading Inventory* (2nd ed.). Boston, MA: Houghton Mifflin.

Buswell, G.T. (1920). An experimental study of the eye-move span in reading. *Supplementary Educational Monographs* (No. 17, pp. 1-105).

Calfee, R. (1985). Review of Gates-MacGinitie Reading Tests. In J.V. Mitchell, Jr. (Ed.), *The ninth mental measurements yearbook* (pp. 593-595). Lincoln, NE: University of Nebraska Press.

California Achievement Test (CAT): Reading, E and F, Level 20. (1985). Monterey, CA: CTB/McGraw-Hill.

Carey, R.F., Harste, J.C., & Smith, S.L. (1981). Contextual constraints and discourse processes: A replication study. *Reading Research Quarterly, 16,* 201-212.

Carney, M., & Geis, L. (1981). Reading ability, academic performance, and college attrition. *Journal of College Student Personnel, 22*(1), 55-59.

Carsello, J. (1982, October). *Tests, workbooks, and books being used in college basic skills programs: The latest survey of college and university programs in the U.S.* Paper presented at the Twenty-Fifth Annual Conference of the North Central Reading Association, Flint, MI.

Cartwright, H.D. (1972). Individualization of instruction in a reading and study skills center with junior college and/or open door policy students. In F.P. Greene (Ed.), *College reading: Problems and programs of junior and senior colleges* (Vol. 2, pp. 118-122). Boone, NC: National Reading Conference.

Carver, R.P. (1975). Reading Progress Scale, college version. Kansas City, MO: Revrac.

Carver, R.P. (1985a). Is the Degrees of Reading Power test valid or invalid? *Journal of Reading, 29,* 34-41.

Carver, R.P. (1985b). Why is the Degrees of Reading Power test invalid? In J.A. Niles and R.V. Lalik (Eds.), *Issues in literacy: A research perspective.* (pp. 350-354). Rochester, NY: National Reading Conference.

Cashen, C.J. (1980). A study of the effect of the test environment on the reading comprehension, comprehending, and processing of text by junior high school readers. *Dissertation Abstracts International, 41,* 3503A.

Chall, J.S. (1958). *Readability: An appraisal and assessment.* Columbus, OH: Ohio State University.

Chester, R.D., Dulin, K.L., & Carvell, R. (1975). Mature readers' Nelson-Denny comprehension scores. In G.H. McNinch & W.P. Miller (Eds.), *Reading: Convention and inquiry* (pp. 227-234). Clemson, SC: National Reading Conference.

Cleland, D.L. (1965). A construct of comprehension. In J.A. Figurel (Ed.), *Reading and inquiry* (pp. 59-64). Newark, DE: International Reading Association.

Clymer, T. (1968). What is reading?: Some current concepts. In H.M. Robinson (Ed.), *Innovation and change in reading instruction,* Sixty-Seventh Yearbook of the National Society for the Study of Education (pp. 1-30). Chicago, IL: University of Chicago Press.

Coates, D.F. (1968). The enigma of the survey section of the Diagnostic Reading Test. In G.B. Schick & M.N. May (Eds.), *Multidisciplinary aspects of college adult reading* (pp. 70-78). Milwaukee, WI: National Reading Conference.

Cranney, A.G., & Larsen, J. (1972). Compensatory programs for specially admitted freshmen to the University of Florida, 1968-1971. In F.P. Greene (Ed.), *College reading: Problems and programs of junior and senior colleges* (Vol. 2, pp. 38-41). Boone, NC: National Reading Conference.

Creaser, J., Jacobs, M., Zaccarea, L., & Carsello, J. (1970). Effects of shortened time limits on the Nelson-Denny Reading Test. *Journal of Reading, 14,* 167-170.

Cronbach, L.J. (1949). *Essentials of psychological testing.* New York: Harper & Row.

Curtis, M.E., & Glaser, R. (1983). Reading theory and the assessment of reading achievement. *Journal of Educational Measurement, 20,* 133-147.

Dale, E., & Chall, J.S. (1948). A formula for predicting readability. *Educational Research Bulletin, 27,* 11-20.

Dale, E., & Eichholz, G. (1954-1969). *Children's knowledge of words, an interim report* (A Payne Fund Communication Project), Columbus, OH: Ohio State University, Bureau of Educational Research and Service.

Dale, E., & O'Rourke, J. (1976). *The living word vocabulary.* Chicago, IL: World Book-Childcraft.

Daneman, M. (1982). The measurement of reading comprehension: How not to trade construct validity for prediction power. *Intelligence, 6,* 331-345.

Daneman, M., Carpenter, P.A., & Just, M.A. (1982). Cognitive processes and reading skills. In B. Hutson (Ed.), *Advances in reading/languages research* (Vol. 1). Greenwich, CT: JAI Press.

Davis, B. (1944). Fundamental factors of comprehension in reading. *Psychometrika, 9,* 185-197.

Davis, B. (1947). A brief comment on Thurstone's notes on a reanalysis of Davis' reading tests. *Psychometrika, 11,* 249-255.

Davis, B. (1968). Research in comprehension in reading. *Reading Research Quarterly, 3,* 499-545.

Davis, F.B. (1978). Iowa Silent Reading Tests. In O.K. Buros (Ed.), *The eighth mental measurements yearbook* (pp. 1199-1201). Highland Park, NJ: Gryphon.

Davis, T., Kaiser, R., & Boone, T. (1987). *Speediness of the Academic Assessment Placement Program (AAPP) Reading Comprehension Test.* Nashville, TN: Tennessee State Board of Regents. (ED 299 264)

Degrees of Reading Power. (1983). New York: The College Board.

DeSanti, R. (1986). DeSanti Cloze Reading Inventory. Boston, MA: Allyn & Bacon.

Drabin-Partenio, I. & Maloney, W.H. (1982). A study of the background knowledge of three groups of college freshmen. *Journal of Reading, 25,* 430-434.

Erwin, T.D. (1981). The Nelson-Denny Reading Test as a predictor of college grades. *Reading Psychology, 2,* 158-164.

Eurich, A.C. (1930). The relation of speed of reading to comprehension. *School and Society, 32,* 404-406.

Evans, H., & Dubois, E. (1972). Community/junior college remedial programs: Reflections. *Journal of Reading, 16,* 38-45.

Farr, R. (1968). The convergent and discriminant validity of several upper level reading tests. In G.B. Schick & M.M. May (Eds.), *Multidisciplinary aspects of college adult reading* (pp. 181-191). Milwaukee, WI: National Reading Conference.

Farr, R. (1969). *Reading: What can be measured?* Newark, DE: International Reading Association.

Farr, R. (1972). Test reviews: Nelson-Denny Reading Test. In W. Blanton, R. Farr, & J.H. Tuinman (Eds.), *Reading tests for the secondary grades: A review and evaluation* (pp. 31-34). Newark, DE: International Reading Association.

Farr, R. (Coordinating Ed.). (1973). Iowa Silent Reading Tests (Levels 2 & 3). Cleveland, OH: Psychological Corporation.

*Farr, R., & Carey, R.F. (1986). *Reading: What can be measured?* (2nd ed.). Newark, DE: International Reading Association.

Feuers, S. (1969). The relationship between general reading skills and junior college academic achievement. *Dissertation Abstracts International, 30,* 3186A-3187A. (University Microfilms No. 70-2200)

Filby, N.N. (1978). Iowa Silent Reading Tests. In O.K. Buros (Ed.), *The eighth mental measurements yearbook* (pp. 1196-1197). Highland Park, NJ: Gryphon.

Flippo, R.F. (1980a). Comparison of college students' reading gains in a developmental reading program using general and specific levels of diagnosis. *Dissertation Abstracts International, 41,* 179-180A.

Flippo, R.F. (1980b, Winter). Diagnosis and prescription of college students in developmental reading programs: A review of the literature. *Reading Improvement, 17*(4), 278-285.

Flippo, R.F. (1980c). The need for comparison studies of college students' reading gains in developmental reading programs using general and specific levels of diagnosis. In M.L. Kamil & A.J. Moe (Eds.), *Perspectives on reading research and instruction.* Washington, DC: National Reading Conference. (ED 184 061)

Flippo, R.F. (1982a). Do we need differential diagnosis at the college level? Maybe. *Western College Reading Association Journal, 2*(2), 1-3.

Flippo, R.F. (1982b). Organizing for diagnostic instruction in a reading lab. *Reading Horizons, 22*(4), 288-291.

Florio, C.B. (1975). An assessment of the effectiveness of remedial reading courses at San Antonio College. *Dissertation Abstracts International, 36,* 2664A. (University Microfilms No. 75-24, 864)

Forsyth, R.A. (1978). Nelson-Denny Reading Test, Forms C and D. In O.K. Buros (Ed.), *The eighth mental measurements yearbook* (pp. 1207-1209). Highland Park, NJ: Gryphon.

Freedle, R.O., & Carroll, J.B. (1972). Language comprehension and the acquisition of knowledge: Reflections. In J.B. Carroll & R.O. Freedle (Eds.), *Language, comprehension, and the acquisition of knowledge* (pp. 361-368). New York: Wiley.

Freer, I.J. (1965). A study of the effect of a college reading program upon grade point average in Odessa College, Odessa, Texas. *Dissertation Abstracts International, 27,* 601A. (University Microfilms No. 66-6124)

Fry, E.B. (1977). Fry's Readability Graph: Clarifications, validity, and extension to level 17. *Journal of Reading, 21*(3), 242-252.

Gates, A.J. (1935). *The improvement of reading.* New York: Macmillan.

Gibson, E.J., & Levin, H. (1975). *The psychology of reading.* Cambridge, MA: MIT Press.

Glaser, R. (1981). The future of testing: A research agenda for cognitive psychology and psychometrics. *American Psychologist, 36*(9), 923-936.

Glazer, S.M., Searfoss, L.W., & Gentile, L.M. (Eds.). (1988). *Reexamining reading diagnosis: New trends and procedures.* Newark, DE: International Reading Association.

Goodman, K.S. (1968). *The psycholinguistic nature of the reading process.* Detroit, IL: Wayne State University Press.

Goodman, K.S. (1969). Analysis of oral reading miscues: Applied psycholinguistics. *Reading Research Quarterly, 5,* 9-30.

Goodman, K.S. (1976). Reading: A psycholinguistic guessing game. In H. Singer & R. Ruddell (Eds.), *Theoretical models and processes of reading* (2nd ed., pp. 497-508). Newark, DE: International Reading Association.

Goodwin, D.D. (1971). Measurement and evaluation in junior college reading programs. *Junior College Research Review, 6,* 1-3. (ED 053 714)

Gordon, B. (1983). A guide to postsecondary reading tests. *Reading World, 23,* 45-53.

*Gordon, B., & Flippo, R. (1983). An update on college reading improvement programs in the southeastern United States. *Journal of Reading, 27,* 155-163.

Gray, W.S. (1919). Principles of method in teaching reading as derived from scientific investigation. *Eighteenth yearbook of the National Society for the Study of Education.* Chicago, IL: National Society for the Study of Education.

*Guthrie, J.T., & Lissitz, R.W. (1985, Summer). A framework for assessment-based decision making in reading education. *Educational Measurement: Issues and Practice, 4,* 26-30.

Hakstian, A.R. (1978). Iowa Silent Reading Tests. In O.K. Buros (Ed.), *The eighth mental measurements yearbook* (pp. 1197-1199). Highland Park, NJ: Gryphon.

Hall, W.E., & Robinson, F.P. (1945). An analytical approach to the study of reading skills. *Journal of Educational Psychology, 36,* 429-442.

Hanna, G.S. (1985). Review of Degrees of Reading Power. In J.V. Mitchell, Jr. (Ed.), *The ninth mental measurements yearbook* (pp. 444-447). Lincoln, NE: University of Nebraska Press.

Holmes, J.A. (1962). Speed, comprehension, and power in reading. In E.P. Bliesmer & R.C. Staiger (Eds.), *Problems, programs, and projects in college-adult reading.* (pp. 6-14). Milwaukee, WI: National Reading Conference.

Holmes, J.A., & Singer, H. (1966). *The substrata factor theory.* Washington, DC: U.S. Government Printing Office.

Huey, E.B. (1908, 1968). *The psychology and pedagogy of reading.* Cambridge, MA: MIT Press.

Hunter, R., & Hoepfner, R. (1978). Iowa Silent Reading Tests. In O.K. Buros (Ed.), *The eighth mental measurements yearbook* (pp. 1200-1201). Highland Park, NJ: Gryphon.

Ironside, R.A. (1969, March). *Who assesses reading status and progress—tests, teachers, or students?* Paper presented at the Twelfth Annual Meeting of the College Reading Association, Boston, MA. (ED 031 374)

Janzen, J.L., & Johnson, E.F. (1970). The use of reading tests for entrance and placement testing in a community college. Calgary, Alberta: Mount Royal College. (ED 041 951)

Johns, J. (1981). Advanced Reading Inventory. Dubuque, IA: William C. Brown.

Johnson, R. (1972). Test reviews: Iowa Silent Reading Tests. In W. Blanton, R. Farr,& J.J. Tuinman (Eds.), *Reading tests for the secondary grades: A review and evaluation* (pp. 26-28). Newark, DE: International Reading Association.

*Johnston, P.H. (1983). *Reading comprehension assessment: A cognitive basis.* Newark, DE: International Reading Association.

*Johnston, P.H. (1984a). Prior knowledge and reading comprehension test bias. *Reading Research Quarterly, 14,* 219-239.

Johnston, P.H. (1984b, April). *A Vygotskian perspective on assessment in reading.* Paper presented at the annual meeting of the American Educational Research Association, New Orleans, LA.

Jongsma, E. (1972). Test reviews: California Achievement Tests: Reading. In W. Blanton, R. Farr, & J.J. Tuinman (Eds.), *Reading tests for the secondary grades: A review and evaluation* (pp. 9-11). Newark, DE: International Reading Association.

*Jongsma, K.S., & Jongsma, E.A. (1981, March). Test review: Commercial informal reading inventories. *The Reading Teacher, 34*(6), 697-705.

Karlsen, B., Madden, R., & Gardner, E.R. (1976). Stanford Diagnostic Reading Test, Blue Level. New York: Psychological Corporation.

Karlsen, B., Madden, R., & Gardner, E.R. (1984). Stanford Diagnostic Reading Test, Blue Level (3rd ed.). New York: Psychological Corporation.

Kasdon, L.M. (1975). Stanford Diagnostic Reading Test. In O.K. Buros (Ed.), *Reading tests and reviews, 2.* Highland Park, NJ: Gryphon.

Kelly, F.J. (1916). The Kansas Silent Reading Tests. *Journal of Educational Psychology, 7,* 63-80.

Kerstiens, G. (1986a). A testimonial on timed testing: Developmental students and reading comprehension tests. In M.P. Douglass (Ed.), *Fiftieth Yearbook of the Claremont Reading Conference* (pp. 261-267). Claremont, CA: Claremont Graduate School.

Kerstiens, G. (1986b, April). *Time-critical reading comprehension tests and developmental students.* Paper presented at the annual meeting of the American Educational Research Association, San Francisco, CA.

Kerstiens, G. (1990). A slow look at speeded reading comprehension tests. *Research in Developmental Education, 7*(3), 1-6.

Ketcham, H.E. (1960). Reading tests and college performance. In O.J. Causey (Ed.), *Research and evaluation in college reading* (pp. 63-66). Fort Worth, TX: Texas Christian University Press.

Kibby, M.W. (1981). Test review: The Degrees of Reading Power. *Journal of Reading, 24,* 416-427.

Kingston, A.J. (1955). Cautions regarding the standardized reading test. In O. Causey & A.J. Kingston (Eds.), *Evaluating college reading programs* (pp. 11-16). Fort Worth, TX: Texas Christian University Press.

Kingston, A.J. (1961). A conceptual model of reading comprehension. In E. Bliesmer & A.J. Kingston (Eds.), *Phases of college and adult reading*. Milwaukee, WI: National Reading Conference.

Kingston, A.J. (1965). Is reading what the reading tests test? In A.L. Thurston (Ed.), *The philosophical and sociological basis of reading* (pp. 108-109). Milwaukee, WI: National Reading Conference.

Kintsch, W.F. (1974). *The representation of meaning in memory.* Hillsdale, NJ: Erlbaum.

Kintsch, W., & Vipond, D. (1979). Reading comprehension and readability in educational practice and psychological theory. In L.G. Nilsson (Ed.), *Perspectives on memory research.* Hillsdale, NJ: Erlbaum.

Landsman, M.B., & Cranney, A.G. (1978). Training and activities of Florida community college reading teachers. *Florida Reading Quarterly, 14,* 17-22.

Langsam, R.S. (1941). A factorial analysis of reading ability. *Journal of Experimental Education, 10,* 57-63.

Lennon, R.T. (1962). What can be measured? *The Reading Teacher, 15,* 326-337.

Lowe A.J., & Stefurak, D.W. (1970). The college reading improvement programs of Georgia: 1969-1970. In G.B. Schick & M.M. May (Eds.), *Reading: Process and pedagogy* (Vol. 2, pp. 118-124). Milwaukee, WI: National Reading Conference.

MacGinitie, W.H. (1978). Gates-MacGinitie Reading Tests, Level F (2nd ed.). Boston, MA: Houghton Mifflin.

Malak, J.F., & Hageman, J.N. (1985). Using verbal SAT scores to predict Nelson scores for reading placements. *Journal of Reading, 28,* 301-304.

Maxwell, M. (1981). *Improving student learning skills.* San Francisco, CA: Jossey-Bass.

*McWilliams, L., & Rakes, T.A. (1979). *Content inventories: English, social studies, science.* Dubuque, IA: Kendall/Hunt.

Monroe, W.S. (1918). Monroe's Standardized Silent Reading Tests. *Journal of Educational Psychology, 9,* 303-312.

Nelson, M.J., Denny, E.C., & Brown, J.I. (1960). Nelson-Denny Reading Test (Forms A & B). Boston, MA: Houghton Mifflin.

Nist, S. (1983). Comprehending comprehension assessment. *Georgia Journal of Reading, 9*(1), 11-14.

Noble, J. (1986, Summer). Estimating reading skill from ACT assessment scores. *College and University, 61,*(4), 310-317.

Nurnberg, M., & Rosenblum, M. (1949). *How to build a better vocabulary.* Englewod Cliffs, NJ: Prentice Hall.

Orlando, V.P., Caverly, D.C., Flippo, R.F., & Mullen, J. (1987, May). *Reading demands of college students in history and psychology classes.* Paper presented at the Thirty-Second Annual Convention of the International Reading Association, Anaheim, CA.

Orlando, V.P., Caverly, D.C., Flippo, R.F., & Mullen, J. (1988). *Reading and studying in college: A follow-up.* Paper presented at the Thirty-Eighth Annual Meeting of the National Reading Conference, Tucson, AZ.

Orlando, V.P., Caverly, D.C., Mullen, J., & Flippo, R.F. (1986, December). *Text demands in college classes: An investigation.* Paper presented at the Thirty-Sixth Annual Meeting of the National Reading Conference, Austin, TX.

Orlando, V.P., Caverly, D.C., Swetnam, L., & Flippo, R.F. (1989). Text demands in college classes: An investigation. *Forum for Reading, 21*(1), 43-48.

Orlando, V.P., Flippo, R.F., & Caverly, D.C. (1990, May). *Meeting text demands in college classes.* Paper presented at the Thirty-Fifth Annual Convention of the International Reading Association, Atlanta, GA.

Pardy, M. (1977). A comparative study of the effects of the use or misuse of sustained silent reading on reading skill proficiency and self-concepts of college students engaged in a traditional diagnostic prescriptive program. *Dissertation Abstracts International, 38,* 5957A. (University Microfilms No. 7802921)

Perkins, D. (1984). Assessment of the use of the Nelson-Denny Reading Test. *Forum for Reading, 15*(2), 64-69.

*Perry, W.G., Jr. (1959). Students' use and misuse of reading skills: A report to the Harvard faculty. *Harvard Educational Review, 29,* 193-200.

Peters, C.W. (1977). Diagnosis of reading problems. In W. Otto, N. Peters, & C.W. Peters (Eds.) *Reading problems: A multidisciplinary perspective* (pp. 151-188). Reading, MA: Addison Wesley.

Phillips, G.O. (1969). The relative effectiveness of three instructional approaches upon the reading, study habits and attitudes, and academic performance of disadvantaged black college freshmen. *Dissertation Abstracts International, 31,* 1084A. (University Microfilms No. 70-15, 460)

*Pikulski, J.J., & Shanahan, T. (Eds.). (1982). *Approaches to the informal evaluation of reading.* Newark, DE: International Reading Association.

Popham, W.J. (1975). *Educational evaluation.* Englewood Cliffs, NJ: Prentice Hall.

Rankin, E.F., & Helm, P. (1986). The validity of cloze tests in relation to a psycholinguistic conceptualization of reading comprehension. *Forum for Reading, 17*(2), 46-59.

Raygor, A.L. (1978). Nelson-Denny Reading Test, Forms C and D. In O.K. Buros (Ed.), *The eighth mental measurements yearbook* (pp. 1209-1211). Highland Park, NJ: Gryphon.

Raygor, A.L. (1979). Raygor Readability Estimator. Rehoboth, MA: Twin Oaks.

Raygor, A.L. (1980). Minnesota Readability Assessment. Rehoboth, MA: Twin Oaks.

*Raygor, A.L., & Flippo, R.F. (1981). Varieties of comprehension measures: A comparison of intercorrelations among several reading tests. In G. McNinch (Ed.), *Comprehension: Process and product.* Athens, GA: American Reading Forum. (ED 198 485)

Readence, J.E., & Moore, D.W. (1983). Why questions? A historical perspective on standardized reading comprehension tests. *Journal of Reading, 26,* 306-313.

Rice, H.D. (1971). A study to determine the effectiveness of a developmental reading program in a community college setting. *Dissertation Abstracts International, 32,* 5573A-5574A. (University Microfilms No. 72-10)

Robinson, F.P., & Hall, P. (1941). Studies of higher-level reading abilities. *Journal of Educational Psychology, 32,* 241-251.

Robinson, F.P. & McCollom, F.H. (1934). Reading rate and comprehension accuracy as determinants of reading test scores. *Journal of Educational Psychology, 25,* 154-157.

Robinson, H.M. (1966). The major aspects of reading. In H.A. Robinson (Ed.), *Reading: Seventy-five years of progress* (Supplementary Educational Monograph No. 96). Chicago, IL: University of Chicago Press.

Ross, E.P., & Roe, B.D. (1986). *The case for basic skills in programs in higher education.* Bloomington, IN: Phi Delta Kappa Educational Foundation.

Rumelhardt, D., Lindsay, P., & Norman, D. (1972). A process model for long-term memory. In E. Tulving & W. Donaldson (Eds.), *Organization and memory.* New York: Academic.

Rupley, W.H. (1985). Review of Gates-MacGinitie Reading Tests. In J.V. Mitchell, Jr. (Ed.), *The ninth mental measurements yearbook* (pp. 595-597). Lincoln, NE: University of Nebraska Press.

Sadden, L.J., & Reid, J. (1984). The cloze procedure as a reading test. *Journal of Developmental Education, 9*(2), 30-31.

Schank, R.C. (1972). Conceptual dependency: A theory of natural language understanding. *Cognitive Psychology, 3,* 552-631.

Schoenberg, B.M. (1969). The development and evaluation of a program for the teaching of reading in junior college. *Dissertation Abstracts International, 30,* 2861A-2862A. (University Microfilms No. 69-21)

Schreiner, R. (Ed.). (1979). *Reading tests and teachers: A practical guide.* Newark, DE: International Reading Association.

Schreiner, R.L., Hieronymus, A., & Forsyth, A. (1969). Differential measurement of reading abilities at the elementary school level. *Reading Research Quarterly, 5,* 84-99.

Seashore, R.H., Stockford, L.B.O., & Swartz, B.K. (1937). A correlation analysis of factors in speed of reading tests. *School and Society, 46,* 1180.

Shank, S. (1930). Student responses in the measurement of reading comprehension. *Journal of Educational Research, 22,* 119-129.

*Simpson, M. (1982). A diagnostic model for use with college students. *Journal of Reading, 26,* 137-143.

Smith, F. (1973). *Psycholinguistics and reading.* Orlando, FL: Holt, Rinehart & Winston.

Smith, F. (1978). *Understanding reading: A psycholinguistic analysis of reading and learning to read* (2nd ed.). Orlando, FL: Holt, Rinehart & Winston.

*Smith, S.P., & Jackson J.H. (1985). Assessing reading/learning skills with written retellings. *The Reading Teacher, 28*(7), 622-630.

Spache, G. (1962). What is comprehension? In E. Bliesmer & R. Staiger (Eds.), *Problems, programs, and projects in college-adult reading.* Milwaukee, WI: National Reading Conference.

Spearritt, D.(1972). Identification of subskills of reading comprehension by maximum likelihood factors. *Reading Research Quarterly, 8,* 92-111.

Squire, J.R. (1987). Introduction: A special issue on the state of assessment in reading. *The Reading Teacher, 40*(8), 724-725.

Starch, D. (1915). The measurement of efficiency in reading. *Journal of Educational Psychology, 6,* 1-24.

Stephens, E.C., Weaver, D.R., Ross, G.A., & Emond, S.B. (1986, Fall/Winter). The cloze procedure as predictor of undergraduate achievement in introductory courses. *Forum for Reading, 18*(1), 32-36.

Stetson, E.G. (1982). Reading tests don't cheat, do they? *Journal of Reading, 25,* 634-639.

Stewart, E.W. (1970). Reading improvement program for college students. In G.B. Schick & M.M. May (Eds.), *Reading: Process and pedagogy* (pp. 202-207). Milwaukee, WI: National Reading Conference.

Sullivan, L.L. (1980). In K.V. Laurdisen (Ed.), *Examining the scope of learning centers: New directions for college learning assistance.* San Francisco, CA: Jossey-Bass.

Swanson, D.E. (1937). Common elements in silent and oral reading. *Psychological Monographs, 48,* 36-50.

Sweiger, J.D. (1972). Designs and organizational structure of junior and community college reading programs across the country. In F.P. Greene (Ed.), *College reading: Problems and programs of junior and senior colleges* (pp. 1-7). Boone, NC: National Reading Conference.

Taschow, H.G. (1968). A comparative study of a corrective reading program and its effects on two freshman reading groups at Central Oregon Community College. *Dissertation Abstracts International, 29,* 2160A. (University Microfilms No. 69-464)

Taylor, E., Frackenpohl, H., & White, C.E. (1969). *A revised core vocabulary: A basic vocabulary for grades 9-13* (Research and Information Bulletin No. 5, revised). Huntington, NY: McGraw-Hill.

Thorndike, E.L. (1914). The measurement of ability in reading. *Teachers College Record, 15,* 207-277.

Thurstone, L.L. (1946). Note on reanalysis of Davis' reading tests. *Psychometrika, 11,* 185-188.

Tiegs, E.W., & Clark, W.W. (1970). *California Achievement Test,* Level 5. Monterey, CA: CTB/McGraw-Hill.

Tierney, R.J. (1985a). Review of Nelson-Denny Reading Test, Forms E and F. In J.V. Mitchell, Jr. (Ed.), *The ninth mental measurements yearbook* (pp. 1035-1037). Lincoln, NE: University of Nebraska Press.

Tierney, R.J. (1985b). Review of Stanford Diagnostic Reading Test, Blue Level, 1976 edition. In J.V. Mitchell, Jr. (Ed.), *The ninth mental measurements yearbook* (pp. 1463-1464). Lincoln, NE: University of Nebraska Press.

Tinker, M.A. (1932). The relation of speed to comprehension in reading. *School and Society, 36,* 158-160.

Tinker, M.A. (1945). Rate of work in reading performance as measured in standardized tests. *Journal of Educational Psychology, 36,* 217-228.

Tittle, C., & Kay, P. (1971). *Selecting tests for an open admissions population.* Paper presented at the annual meeting of the American Educational Research Association, New York. (ED 048 359)

Traxler, A.E. (1941). *Problems of measurement in reading.* Paper presented at the American Council on Education's invitational conference on testing problems, New York.

Triggs, F.O. (1952). *Diagnostic reading tests: A history of their construction and validation.* New York: Committee on Diagnostic Tests.

Valencia, S., & Pearson, P.D. (1987). Reading assessment: Time for a change. *The Reading Teacher, 40*(8), 726-732.

Van Meter, B.J. (1988). A survey of the uses of the Nelson-Denny Reading Test in the community/junior colleges of Maryland. *Reading: Issues and Practices, 5,* 78-84.

Van Meter, B.J., & Herrman, B.A. (1986-1987, Winter). Use and misuse of the Nelson-Denny Reading Test. *Community College Review, 14*(3), 25-30.

Van Roekel, B.H. (1978). Stanford Diagnostic Reading Test. In O.K. Buros (Ed.), *The eighth mental measurements yearbook* (pp. 1298-1300), Highland Park, NJ: Gryphon.

Wark, D.M., & Flippo, R.F. (1991). Preparing for and taking tests. In R.F. Flippo & D.C. Caverly, (Eds.), *Teaching reading and study strategies at the college level.* Newark, DE: International Reading Association.

Webb, M.W. (1983). A scale for evaluating standardized reading tests, with results for Nelson-Denny, Iowa, and Stanford. *Journal of Reading, 26,* 424-429.

Winograd, T. (1972). Understanding natural language. *Cognitive Psychology, 3,* 1-191.

Wolf, W., King, M., & Huck, G. (1968). Teaching critical reading to elementary school children. *Reading Research Quarterly, 3,* 435-498.

Wood, K. (1988). Standardized reading tests and the postsecondary curriculum. *Journal of Reading, 32,* 224-230.

Wood, K. (1989). Reading tests and reading assessment. *Journal of Developmental Education, 13*(2), 14-19.

Wright, G.L. (1973). An experimental study comparing the differential effectiveness of three developmental reading treatments upon the rate, vocabulary, and comprehension skills of white and black college students. *Dissertation Abstracts International, 34,* 5811A. (University Microfilms No. 74 6257)

Ysseldyke, J.E. (1985a). Review of the Nelson-Denny Reading Test, Forms E and F. In J.V. Mitchell, Jr. (Ed.), *The ninth mental measurements yearbook* (p. 1037). Lincoln, NE: University of Nebraska Press.

Ysseldyke, J.E. (1985b). Review of Stanford Diagnostic Reading Test, Blue Level, 1976 edition. In J.V. Mitchell, Jr. (Ed.), *The ninth mental measurements yearbook* (pp. 1464-1465). Lincoln, NE: The University of Nebraska Press.

Appendix to Chapter 4:
Commercially Available Tests Reviewed
Rona F. Flippo and Carol J. Cashen

California Achievement Test (CAT), Level 5, 1970 Edition

Test/Authors

California Achievement Test (CAT): Reading Level 5, 1970 Edition
Tiegs and Clark (1970)

Type of Test

Survey, formal, norm-referenced, standardized, group

Use(s) of Test

Screening:
- to measure students' achievement in reading, with emphasis on content and objectives in the basic curricular area of reading
- to measure students' knowledge of reference information

Skills/Strategies Tested

1. Vocabulary
2. Reading comprehension:
   - knowledge of reference information
   - comprehension and reading in science, social studies, mathematics, and general reading

Note: For all tests reviewed, the following applies: The readability of passages was determined by use of the Fry Readability Graph (1977) and/or the Raygor Readability Estimate (1979), except where otherwise noted; testing time does not include time for passing out materials, giving directions, or rest periods.

Population Recommended by Reviewers

While Level 5 was designed for use with high school students, it can be used as a global screening test for entering college freshmen.

Overall Theory of Reading

The CAT is designed to measure the skill with which the student performs in curricular tasks basic to learning progress. To this end, it measures both comprehension of content material and level of performance in using the tool of reading in progressively more difficult situations. The publishers suggest that comprehension can be subdivided into discrete skills: the manual discusses testing skills such as drawing inferences, recalling facts, and identifying main ideas.

Readability/Source of Passages

The CAT consists of five reading passages. The publisher suggests they are typical of material found in students' science, social science, mathematics, and general reading texts. The text becomes progressively more difficult.

Format/Test Parts

The test consists of two parts: vocabulary and reading comprehension. The vocabulary section contains 40 items, each consisting of a stem word in minimal context (e.g., "*divorced* from truth") and a list of four alternatives. The comprehension section contains two parts. The first part consists of 6 items designed to measure students' knowledge of reference information (e.g., glossary, appendix). Each item has a list of four alternatives. The second part consists of reading passages that are progressively more difficult. Each passage is followed by a number of incomplete statements with a choice of four alternatives for each. A total of 39 items test relationships, inferences, recall of facts, and identification of the main idea.

Testing Time

Vocabulary: 10 minutes; Reading comprehension: 40 minutes. (The manual suggests a total of 58 minutes for administration, including directions.)

Forms Available

Two equivalent and parallel forms, A and B.

Levels Available

Five levels for grades 1.5 to 12.9. Level 5 is appropriate for grades 9.0 to 12.9.

Types of Scores Available

Raw scores, grade equivalents, Achievement Development Scale Score, percentiles, stanines

Norm Groups

Norming information is described for all levels of the CAT (grades 1 through 12); there is no subset to describe the high school population sampled. The manual states that 203,684 students in grades 1 through 12 from public and Catholic schools in 36 states were sampled. Tests were administered between February and April of 1970. When selecting the sample population, the following demographics were considered: geographic region, school district size, and community type (e.g., urban, suburban, or rural).

Appendix

Date Published or Last Revised

1970

Reliability

The publishers offer a 104-page technical report on validity, national standardization, and reliability. The manual contains a *brief* review excerpted from the report. Reliability was determined by three methods; consistency was determined through use of the Kuder-Richardson Formula 20.

Validity

The only form of validity examined is content validity. Included in that review are selection of content, writing of items, tryout of items, selection of items, and preparation of the standardized edition. Selection of content was based on an analysis of (1) reading texts recommended and approved by agencies at the state level, and (2) recommended curricular objectives and courses of study in states representing all sections of the country. Vocabulary items were selected from broad general areas rather than specific subject areas. Words are included from one grade below to two or more grades above the middle grade of the test level. Comprehension includes reading selections typical of those found in social studies, science, and mathematics. Items are sequenced within the test according to increasing difficulty to allow early success and provide motivation to continue.

Scoring Options

Machine scoring:
- Compu Scan #2561 (Scored on NCS optical scanner)
- IBM 1230 (Scored by IBM optical scanning equipment)
- Digitek #5961 (Scored by optical scanning equipment)

Hand scoring:
- IBM 1230 (hand-scoring stencils available from publisher)
- Scoreze #567

Publisher

CTB/McGraw-Hill, 2500 Garden Road, Del Monte Research Park, Monterey, CA 93940

Recommended Other Reviews

Jongsma (1972), Smith (1978)

Weaknesses

1. The test was not designed for college students. No scores are provided for them, not even extrapolated ones.
2. While the publishers claim the vocabulary section lists words "in context," the minimal text provides few contextual clues.
3. While the test does measure some reference skills, the skills tested are extremely basic for college students.

Strengths

1. Passages used in the reading comprehension section resemble text students are required to read in school.
2. The test can be administered in 1 hour.

3. The test measures students' reading ability in differing subject areas. The results might prove helpful in selecting introductory college-level courses.
4. The technical report is extensive and well written.

California Achievement Test (CAT), Levels 19 and 20, 1985 Edition

Test/Authors

California Achievement Test (CAT): Reading E and F, Levels 19 and 20, 1985 Edition

Type of Test

Survey, formal, standardized, norm-referenced, criterion-referenced

Use(s) of Test

Initial screening. The test is designed to measure achievement of basic reading skills commonly found in state and district curricula.

Skills/Strategies

1. Vocabulary
2. Reading comprehension

Population Recommended by Reviewers

While Levels 19 and 20 were designed to measure the achievement of senior high school students, they can be used as a screening instrument for entering college students. Level 19, designed for Grades 8.6 to 11.2, might be more appropriate for vocational/technical school students. Level 20, designed for Grades 10.6 to 12.9, should be used with entering 4-year college students.

Overall Theory of Reading

The paramount aim is to provide valid measurement of academic basic skills in reading, which include vocabulary development and comprehension. The publishers list the following measurable skills: vocabulary (which is subdivided into five categories), literal comprehension, inferential comprehension (three categories), and critical comprehension (two categories).

Readability/Source of Passages

Vocabulary level is carefully controlled to ensure that words selected are appropriate to each test level. This was partially accomplished by reference to Dale and O'Rourke (1976). The Dale-Chall formula (1948) and the Fry formula (1977) were applied to control readability. Readability levels are available in the Class Management Guide.

Format/Test Parts

The test consists of two parts: vocabulary and comprehension. The vocabulary section contains 55 items. For measuring knowledge of synonyms, antonyms, and homonyms, each word is presented in minimal context (e.g., drastic *termination*), with a choice of four answers. For affixes, a set of prefixes and suffixes is presented along with a choice of four answers. For words in context, 9 items each present a sentence with one word omitted, with four alternatives from which to choose. Also, a paragraph is presented in cloze format with six words omitted. Four alternatives are offered for each option. The comprehension section consists of 10 reading solutions designed to measure literal, inferential, and critical comprehension. The section includes 55 items, each with four answers. The readings include narratives, poetry, book and movie reviews, and textbook style copy. The section tests recall of facts, character analysis, understanding of central thought and interpretation of events, forms of writing, and figurative language.

Testing Time

Vocabulary: 30 minutes. Reading Comprehension: 50 minutes (plus 7 minutes of instructional time).

Forms Available

Two equivalent and parallel forms (E and F)

Levels Available

Forms are available for kindergarten through high school. Level 19: grades 8.6-11.2. Level 20: grades 10.6-12.9.

Types of Scores Available

Scale scores, grade equivalents, normed curve equivalents, percentiles, stanines, objective performance objectives

Norm Groups

Level 19 was normed on more than 47,000 ninth and tenth graders, while Level 20 was normed on almost 36,000 eleventh and twelfth graders. Students from public and private schools were tested in the fall and spring of 1984/85. First-level stratification included four geographic regions (New England and Mideast, Great Lakes and Plains, Southeast, and Southwest and West). Second-level stratification was based on community type—urban, suburban, or rural.

Date Published or Last Revised

1985

Reliability

CTB/McGraw Hill published an extensive technical report in 1987. The reliability of CAT E and F is described by several kinds of data. Internal consistency was measured by the Kuder-Richardson formula 20. Short-interval repeated testing reliabilities for CAT E and F were collected in May 1986. Interlevel articulation studies were done in 1985. Results are interpreted through 38 pages of tables in the technical report.

Validity

To provide a valid measurement of students' skills in reading, comprehensive reviews were made of state and district curriculum guides, textbook series, instructional

Commercially Available Tests Reviewed

programs, and norm-referenced and criterion-referenced assessment instruments. CAT E and F is designed to measure students' understanding of broad concepts rather than their understanding of content specific to any particular instructional program. Specifications for item development were designed to ensure comprehensive coverage of skills implicit in category objectives. Reading vocabulary items measure categorization, synonyms and antonyms, multimeaning words, affixes, and words in context. Reading comprehension items measure skills in understanding sentence meaning, passage details and analysis, character analysis, central thought, and interpretation of events. In passages similar to reading materials that students encounter in secondary grades, general and critical comprehension skills are given increased emphasis.

Scoring Options

Machine-scoring:
• Compu Scan
Hand-scoring:
• Scoreze
• Compu Scan with hand-scoring stencils

Cost

Test Review Kit (Grades 7-12): $17.35
Reusable test books (35): $21.70 (each package includes an Examiner's Manual with a scoring key)
Answer sheets:
• machine scored
     Compu Scan $ 7.65
• hand scored
     Scoreze (25) $10.10
     Stencils (3) $18.60
Locator test (35): $13.30 (includes directions and answer sheets)

Publisher

CTB/McGraw-Hill, 2500 Garden Road, Del Monte Research Park, Monterey, CA 93940

Recommended Other Reviews

None available

Weaknesses

1. The test was not designed for use with college students. No scores are provided for them, not even extrapolated ones.
2. Reliability and validity studies are not yet available.
3. The comprehension section does not resemble college-level reading material. The graphics included suggest junior high school reading books.

Strengths

1. The standardization process was conducted to allow virtually all students to attempt all items. Thus, the problem of speed should not be a factor in this test.
2. A Locator Test consisting of 20 vocabulary items is available to provide a reliable way to match students with appropriate test levels.

Degrees of Reading Power (DRP), 1983

Test/Author
Degrees of Reading Power (DRP), 1983

Type of Test
Survey, formal, standardized, criterion-referenced

Use(s) of Test
1. To evaluate the current level of students' achievement in reading
2. To determine the most difficult prose a student can use with instructional assistance and as an independent reader
3. To measure growth in the ability to read with comprehension
4. To indicate the extent of compensatory or remedial help, if any, a student may need in order to achieve various personal as well as school-determined expectations or goals

Skills/Strategies Tested
Reading comprehension

Population Recommended by Reviewers
The CP form is suggested for 4-year colleges and universities. The PA/PB form, designed for high school students, may be a better choice for 2-year colleges and vo-tech institutions.

Overall Theory of Reading
The DRP measures a student's ability to derive meaning from connected prose text. The text is written at different levels of difficulty or readability. The purpose of the DRP is to measure the end result of reading instruction, rather than to measure subskills. For students to answer questions correctly, they must read and comprehend the text pertaining to those items.

Readability/Sources of Passages
The readability of passages is measured with a scale ranging from 0 to 100 DRP units, rather than in grade equivalencies. In practice, commonly encountered English text runs from about 30 DRP units at the easy end of the scale to about 85 DRP units at the difficult end. Bormuth's (1969) mean cloze formula and a set of standardized procedures are used to derive DRP units. The test consists of a series of nonfiction prose passages on topics randomly selected from the *Encyclopaedia Britannica*. The passages are presented in order of increasing difficulty. The number of passages in a test varies by level: E3, suggested for 4-year colleges and universities, contains 9 passages, while F3, suggested for 2-year colleges and vo-tech institutions, contains 11 passages. Ten 12-passage DRP forms, each ranging in difficulty from easiest possible prose to that found in professional journals, were composed following the requirements of an equating or a calibrating design. Every form shared test passages with three other forms. Each pair of overlapping forms has four passages in common.

Format/Test Parts

The DRP is a modified cloze test. Each passage is a prose selection of progressive difficulty. Test items are created by the deletion of seven words in each passage. The student selects the most appropriate word from the five options provided for each blank. E3 has 63 items, and F3 has 72 items. The test incorporates the following characteristics:

1. The test passage must be read and understood for students to respond correctly. That is, the sentences containing the blanks will make sense with each of the options when read in isolation. However, when the surrounding text is taken into account, only one response is plausible.
2. Regardless of the difficulty of the passage, all response options are common words.
3. Item difficulty is linked to text difficulty.

Testing Time

Untimed. Reports from colleges (both 2- and 4-year) using the DRP indicate that the majority of those tested complete the test in approximately 1 hour. (Note: Students are urged to stop when the test no longer is comprehensible; guessing is not encouraged.)

Forms Available

Two equivalent and parallel forms for each level

Levels Available

E3 and F3

Types of Scores Available

Raw scores, reading levels (independent, instructional, frustration), percentiles, stanines, normal curve equivalents (normalized standard scores with a mean of 50 and a standard deviation of 21.06)

Norm Groups

A sample of 34,000 fourth through twelfth graders representing national demographics took the test. Ethnicity information was provided by the teachers, economic level by the administrators based on participation in school lunch programs. Students in grades 4 through 10 were randomly assigned one test form in November and a second overlapping one in May. Eleventh and twelfth graders took two test forms, one in November, the other in May.

Date Published or Last Revised

1983; revised 1989

Reliability

No studies by publisher

Validity

The publisher suggests that because of the design of the test (i.e., the student who comprehends the prose ought to be able to answer items correctly), the DRP is unambiguously a measure of ability to read with comprehension. By definition, this is the central validity issue of a reading test.

Scoring Options

Hand scoring: scoring stencils (available from publisher).
Machine scoring: DRP/NCS answer sheets purchased from publisher and returned for scoring.

Cost

Test booklets (35): $49.40
  (10 percent discount for more than 40 sets)
Scoring stencils: $8.30
Teacher's Manual: $17.95
Scoring and reporting (per student): $1.40

Publisher

DRP Services, Touchstone Applied Science Associates, Sields Lane, Brewster, NY 10509

Recommended Other Reviews

Bormuth (1985), Bruning (1985), Carver (1985a, 1985b), Hanna (1985), Kibby (1981)

Weaknesses

The scores for college students are all extrapolated.

Strengths

1. A real attempt has been made to develop a state-of-the-art, nonthreatening reading test. The test relieves two major anxieties students face in most testing situations by being untimed and encouraging students to stop when they can no longer comprehend the text.
2. Independent and instructional reading levels are provided.
3. An attempt has been made to assess the readability level of textbooks. While the process requires a microcomputer, the large amount of text that is reviewed by the program may produce more reliable results.
4. The publisher suggests that the students' reading level (in DRP units) can be matched to the textbook readability (also in DRP units). There is currently some debate over this claim (see Bormuth, 1985; Carver, 1985a, 1985b).

The test publisher views reading as a holistic process not divisible into discrete subskills. This can be either a strength or a weakness depending on one's personal theory of reading.

Gates-MacGinitie Reading Tests, Level F (2nd Edition), 1978

Test/Authors

Gates-MacGinitie Reading Tests Level F (2nd edition)
MacGinitie (1978)

Type of Test

Survey, formal, standardized, norm-referenced

Use(s) of Test

1. Initial screening
2. To assess progress and make changes as appropriate

Skills/Strategies Tested

1. Vocabulary
2. Reading comprehension

Population Recommended by Reviewers

Neither the author nor the publisher of the test in any way represents it as an instrument suggested for postsecondary school students. In fact, the manual states that norms for students continuing beyond high school grades have not been done and that an extension of the norm tables would not be appropriate or comparable. However, given the careful test development procedure used for this instrument and the limited number of appropriate tests available, this test could be a possible screening alternative for conditionally admitted, lower ability community/junior college students. Community/junior colleges using this test should, however, refrain from using the norm tables for twelfth grade students as anything more than an indication of possible reading ability problems or adequacies, and should instead develop their own local college norms. We stress that this test is suggested as a possibility only because so few appropriate screening instruments are available for this population. This test will not give an indication of ability to handle college-type textual material, and will provide only an indication of very basic reading ability.

Overall Theory of Reading

Comprehension is the main concern in evaluating reading achievement. Since research indicates that it is not possible to validly measure the various components of reading comprehension, the Gates-MacGinitie produces only a single comprehension score, which provides an indication of students' ability to handle the semantic implications of syntax and the logical relationship of ideas. Since students' comprehension can be limited by problems with decoding or understanding the components of words, a vocabulary score is also provided. The author indicates that this general level of reading achievement should be added to other information about students and used as a basis for selecting students for further individual diagnosis and prescription, for evaluating the effectiveness of instruction, and for other evaluation and reporting purposes. The author has a clinical perspective of reading.

Readability/Source of Passages

The comprehension test passages are prose selections taken from various published content area materials and are written in standard English. These passages include narrative-descriptive, social sciences, natural sciences, and humanities materials. Readability of sampled passages ranged from the eleventh to sixteenth grade levels, with an average of fourteenth grade level. The vocabulary test words were chosen to represent a balance of nouns, verbs, adjectives, and adverbs, selected as important words of general usefulness.

Format/Test Parts

The vocabulary test has 45 items. It uses words in isolation, each followed by five single word choices. The student is to select the word that most nearly matches the test word in meaning. The comprehension test has 43 items, with passages of varying lengths (all are fairly short), followed by completion-type questions with four possible short alternatives, requiring an explicit or implicit understanding of information in the passage.

Testing Time

Vocabulary: 20 minutes; Comprehension: 35 minutes

Forms Available

Two equated forms (1 and 2)

Levels Available

One level (Level F) is available for the grades 10-12 population; this may be adaptable for some college populations.

Types of Scores Available

Percentile ranks, normal curve equivalent scores, stanines, grade equivalents, extended scale scores

Norm Groups

Norms for Level F were obtained in October 1976 for grade 10 and in May 1977 for grades 10, 11, and 12. Approximately 15,700 students from grades 10-12 were tested. They represented four geographic regions, various school sizes, different family incomes and education, and minority populations. Approximately 2,400 of these students were in grade 12; 3,300 were in grade 11; and the remainder were in grade 10.

Date Published or Last Revised

Second edition, 1978 (first edition published in 1965)

Reliability

Kuder-Richardson Formula 20 reliability coefficients were computed. These ranged from .90 to .92 for vocabulary, and from .89 to .91 for comprehension. Alternate-form reliability coefficients, computed only for the tenth grade population, range from .81 to .90.

Validity

Very little validity information is provided in the test manuals. Construct validity studies were done on several levels of the Gates-MacGinitie, but not with Level F. The test does appear to have face validity in that it was carefully developed to test the general vocabulary and comprehension abilities that it purports to test, using words and passages selected to be representative samples for grades 10-12. However, the readability levels of the passages used in the test are not reported anywhere in the test manuals. Data from the standardization indicate that more than 95 percent of the students taking the test were able to complete it. This indicates that the test should be appropriate for sampling the reading of even the lowest ability students.

Scoring Options

Hand scoring:
- hand-scorable answer sheet test booklets that include answer keys
- MRC answer sheets (MRC Scoring Mask available from publisher)

Self-scoring: self-scorable answer sheets

Machine scoring: MRC answers sheets (answer sheets are sent to the publisher's scoring service); complete instructions are included with the MRC answer sheet materials.

Cost

Teacher's Manual: $3.54
Technical Summary: $9.51
Hand scorable answer sheet/test booklets (package of 35, including one teacher's manual and one answer key):

    Form 1 $15.75
    Form 2 $15.75

MRC answer sheets:
    Pkg. of 25 $ 9.84
    Pkg. of 100 $ 22.89
    Pkg. of 500 $105.15

Self-scorable answer sheets:
    Pkg. of 35 $ 18.27
    Pkg. of 250 $ 78.78

MRC scoring masks: $3.63 each (same key can be used for Forms 1 and 2)

Publisher

Houghton Mifflin

Within the continental United States, send orders to: College Order Department, Houghton Mifflin Company, Wayside Road, Burlington, MA 01803

Outside the continental United States, send orders to: The Riverside Publishing Company, International Sales, Houghton Mifflin, One Beacon Street, Boston, MA 02108

Recommended Other Reviews

Calfee (1985), Rupley (1985)

Weaknesses

1. The Gates-MacGinitie, Level F, was not designed to be used with college students.
2. The vocabulary test uses words in isolation rather than in context, which would have been more appropriate for college students.
3. The passages on the comprehension test are very short. We would prefer much longer selections more representative of the length of materials for entering college students.
4. The sentences in many of the comprehension test paragraphs are extremely long. In some cases, sentences are so long that the paragraph consists of only two sentences. This caused the readability of the paragraphs to be fairly high, according to traditional readability formulas (an average of 14th grade level), for a test designed for high school students.
5. No readability information is provided for the comprehension paragraphs in either of the test manuals. Users interested in readability would have to do their own readability estimates.

6. Although it gives partial reliability and validity data, the Teacher's Manual does not contain the complete technical information. To get the additional information, test users must also consult the Technical Manual, which is sold separately.
7. The test validity information provided in both manuals is weak and very limited.
8. Although a large number of students were used in the standardization, only a relatively small percentage of them were used to norm Level F, and the majority of those students were tenth graders, rather than twelfth graders.

Strengths

1. Overall test development and norming procedures were done with care, indicating potential for a quality instrument that measures what it has been designed to measure, and no more. The procedures used to develop this test provide us with a sense of the integrity of this instrument.
2. The comprehension test evaluates explicit and implicit comprehension from passages selected from a variety of basic content areas.
3. The publisher provides quite a bit of information in the Teacher's Manual, which is free with the purchase of a package of tests. We have examined few tests that provide this much information in their teacher's manuals, although, as noted under "Weaknesses," some important information is lacking.

Iowa Silent Reading Tests (ISRT), *Level 2, 1973 Edition*

Test/Authors

Iowa Silent Reading Tests (ISRT): Level 2, 1973 Edition
Farr (1973)

Type of Test

Survey, formal, standardized, norm-referenced

Use(s) of Test

Initial screening:
- to identify below-average readers
- to counsel students about their educational plans
Diagnosis:
- to determine students' functional reading levels (independent and instructional)
- to plan instruction in the various reading skills, such as vocabulary, comprehension, work-study skills, and efficient reading
- to identify students' ability to use the dictionary and the library, including knowledge of reference materials
- to measure students' ability to skim and scan for specific information
- to survey students' reading interests

Skills/Strategies Tested

1. Vocabulary: Measures depth, breadth, and precision of students' applied word knowledge.

2. Reading comprehension: Measures students' comprehension of literal detail, reasoning ability, ability to evaluate what is read, and short-term recall.
3. Directed reading: Measures students' work-study skills, including ability to use reference materials and to skim and scan.
4. Reading efficiency: Measures students' rate of reading with comprehension when material is easy.

Population Recommended by Reviewers

Level 2 is recommended as a screening test for community colleges and vocational/technical institutions. The directed reading section may also be used with lower level readers enrolled in 4-year institutions.

Overall Theory of Reading

Silent reading is a multifaceted ability requiring skill in several areas, including vocabulary, reading comprehension, use of reference materials, skimming and scanning for specific information, and reading with comprehension at a reasonable speed.

Readability/Source of Passage

Words in the vocabulary section have been selected to represent general reading vocabulary. This is a change from the earlier edition of the ISRT, in which the vocabulary words were selected as significant words in four high school subjects. Reading passages for the comprehension section were selected from a variety of sources of the type students are required to read; none was adapted from a textbook or other classroom material. Passages vary from 100 to 300 words. Difficulty as determined by the Dale-Chall Readability Formula (1948) ranges from seventh to twelfth grades, with the majority of the passages at ninth/tenth grades.

Format/Test Parts

The test consists of four parts: vocabulary, reading comprehension, directed reading, and reading efficiency. The vocabulary section contains 50 items arranged in cycles of five. The first cycle begins with the easiest item and proceeds to four progressively more difficult ones; the second cycle begins with the second easiest item, and similarly increases in difficulty. This pattern, which continues through the test, is an attempt to prevent the student from becoming discouraged or from attempting only items at the beginning of the test. For each question, a single word stimulus is followed by four single-word synonym choices. These choices each form a cluster related by association but not by meaning, which requires the student to make fine discriminations among the words. All options are the same part of speech as the stimulus and are of approximately the same length. The reading comprehension section is made up of 50 items. Part A (38 items) requires the student to answer questions based on six short passages. Part B (12 items) tests short-term recall of a longer passage by requiring answers to an essay without looking back at it. Each of the 50 items has four answer choices. Directed reading contains 44 items. Part A is made up of 24 items, each with four possible answers. Item format is either an incomplete sentence or a question. Part B has 20 items. Reading efficiency is a speeded test containing six short, easy reading passages. The 40 items the student must complete utilize a modified cloze procedure.

Testing Time

Vocabulary: 15 minutes; Reading comprehension: Part A 26 minutes, Part B 13 minutes; Directed reading: Part A 13 minutes, Part B 13 minutes; Reading efficiency: 4 minutes. The publishers note that total testing time, including directions and distribution/collection of materials, is approximately 2 hours and 16 minutes.

Forms Available
Two equivalent and parallel forms, E and F

Levels Available
Level 2 was designed for grades 9 through 14.

Types of Scores Available
Raw scores, standard scores, percentiles, stanines, Reading Efficiency Index (measures accuracy and speed)

Norm Groups
A standardization sample was selected to be representative of the secondary public school population based on geographic location, size of school district, and socioeconomic index. Level 2 standardization tested all participating students in grades 9 through 12. No data are given on the size of the sample; however, the geographic distribution of the sample closely parallels that of the total U.S. public school enrollment.

Date Published or Last Revised
First published in 1927, the ISRT was revised in 1943 and in 1972.

Reliability
The Kuder-Richardson reliability coefficients for 2-year junior colleges are:
- Form E—Vocabulary, .92, reading comprehension, .90, and reading power, .95.
- Form F—Vocabulary, .93, reading comprehension, .89, reading power, .95, and directed reading, .87.

Validity
The validity of the ISRT-Level 2 can be evaluated by examining the test content and analyzing its relationship to the abilities on which successful reading depends. A brief description of the editor's theory of reading is provided in the column headed "Overall Theory of Reading."

Scoring Options
Machine scoring:
- MRC Answer Documents (scored by Measurement Research Center)
- IBM 1230 and Digitek/OpScan (scored by Harcourt Brace Jovanovich Scoring Service or locally)
- NCS Answer Folders (available from National Computer Systems or local scoring agencies)

Hand scoring: All above answer documents can also be scored by hand with the appropriate answer key. Stencil keys are available for IBM 1230, Digitek/OpScan, or Hand Scorable answer documents. To hand score NCS or MRC answer documents, use the list of correct responses provided in the Manual of Directions.

Cost
Test booklets (35):	$24.00
Answer sheets:	
• hand scored (35)	$ 9.50
• Machine scored	
MRC (100)	$42.00

Answer Key: $ 9.50
Guide: $12.00
Manual of Directions: $ 3.50

Publisher

Psychological Corporation, 7500 Old Oak Boulevard, Cleveland, OH 44130

Recommended Other Reviews

Davis (1978), Filby (1978), Hakstian (1978), Hunter and Hoepfner (1978), Johnson (1972), Webb (1983)

Weaknesses

1. Level 2 was normed on high school students planning to attend a postsecondary institution.
2. The test cannot be administered in a traditional class period.

Strengths

1. While the test is primarily a screening instrument, it does provide some viable diagnostic options.
2. Level 2 measures some study skills a student needs to succeed in college, including use of reference materials and skimming and scanning.
3. The Manual of Directions is well written and easy to follow.
4. The Guide for Interpretation and Use provides extensive information for the practitioner in a well-written style.

Iowa Silent Reading Tests (ISRT),
Level 3, 1973 Edition

Test/Authors

Iowa Silent Reading Tests (ISRT): Level 3, 1973 Edition
Farr (1973)

Type of Test

Survey, formal, standardized, norm-referenced

Use of Test

Initial screening:
- to identify below-average readers
- to counsel students about their educational plans
Diagnosis:
- to determine students' functional reading levels (independent and instructional)
- to plan instruction in various reading skills, such as vocabulary, comprehension, and efficient reading

Skills/Strategies Tested

1. Vocabulary: Measures depth, breadth, and precision of students' applied word knowledge.

2. Reading comprehension: Measures students' ability to understand, reason, and evaluate.
3. Reading efficiency: Measures students' rate of reading with comprehension when material is easy.

Population Recommended by Reviewers

Level 3 tests were designed to provide discrimination among students who are good readers. Therefore, Level 3 can be used as a screening test for average entering college freshmen, for students contemplating graduate study, and for professional people. For college students who have demonstrated reading difficulties, Level 2 (reviewed earlier) should be used. Those with severe reading problems might profit from taking the Level 1 tests.

Overall Theory of Reading

Silent reading is a multifaceted, complex behavior requiring skill in several areas, including vocabulary, reading comprehension, and reading efficiency (rate plus comprehension). Good readers must be able to evaluate written material, make inferences, draw conclusions, and sense an author's mood and tone. The acquisition of reading skills is merely a means to an end; therefore, the application of these skills is stressed.

Readability/Sources of Passages

Since the vocabulary section is designed to measure knowledge of words encountered in everyday reading, only words of a general nature were selected. Sources for stimulus words were Taylor, Frackenpohl, and White (1969), Dale and Eichholz (1954-1969) and Nurnberg and Rosenblum (1949). Passages for the reading comprehension section were selected from adult materials of the types advanced students are required to read; none was adapted from a textbook or other classroom material. Sources for selections are listed in the Manual of Directions. Subject matter includes social science, natural science, and literature for both Forms E and F. Form F also has a mathematics selection. The literature passages are written in a style that makes use of various literary devices found in poetry. Readability for the passages ranges from grades 9 to 15 on Form E and 7 to 15 on Form F based on the Dale-Chall Formula (1948). The vocabulary level of the clozures and the distractors does not exceed grade 12.

Format/Test Parts

The test consists of three parts: vocabulary, reading comprehension, and reading efficiency. The vocabulary section contains 50 items arranged in cycles of five. The first cycle begins with the easiest item and proceeds to four progressively more difficult ones; the second cycle begins with the second easiest item, and similarly increases in difficulty. This pattern, which continues through the test, is an attempt to prevent the student from becoming discouraged or from attempting only items at the beginning of the test. For each question, a single word stimulus is followed by four single-word synonym choices. These choices each form a cluster related by association but not by meaning, which requires the student to make fine discriminations among the words. All options are the same part of speech as the stimulus and are of approximately the same length. The reading comprehension section includes five single passages, each approximately 300 words in length, and two parallel passages presenting different viewpoints on the same subject. Each selection is followed by questions or incomplete sentences, with four answer choices. This section has 50 items. Reading efficiency is a speeded test that contains six short, easy reading passages. The 40 items the student must complete utilize a modified cloze format.

Commercially Available Tests Reviewed   189

Testing Time

Vocabulary: 15 minutes; Reading comprehension: 37 minutes; Reading efficiency: 4 minutes

Forms Available

Two equivalent and parallel forms (E and F)

Levels Available

Level 3 is for academically accelerated high school students in grades 10 through 12, for college students, and for professional groups.

Types of Scores Available

Raw scores, standard scores, percentiles, stanines, Reading Efficiency Index (measures accuracy and speed)

Norm Group

While some preliminary research was carried out using college freshmen in the development of the reading comprehension section, no college students were included in the national standardization samples. These samples were selected on the basis of geographic location, size of school district, and a socioeconomic index based on median family income and median years of schooling of adults in the community. Testing took place between April 17 and May 5, 1972. The test was administered in 15 school districts to students in grades 10, 11, and 12. Norms for college preparatory students for each grade are reported in the Manual of Directions, including norms for grade 12 students planning to attend a 2-year or 4-year college. Performance data for students pursuing other courses of study are available from the publisher. Because the standardization sample represents students planning to attend a college or university, the editors recommend that colleges/universities develop local norms for placement purposes.

Date Published or Last Revised

1972

Reliability

Alternate-forms reliability was tested with students in grade 11. Approximately 200 students were administered both Form E and Form F of Level 3 within a 3-week period.

Alternate-forms reliability coefficients are:

Vocabulary	.86
Reading Comprehension	.79
Reading Power	.90
Reading Efficiency	.73

Kuder-Richardson reliability coefficients for 4-year college or university students are:

	Form E	Form F
Vocabulary	.91	.90
Reading Comprehension	.90	.89
Reading Power	.94	.94

Additional data on college preparatory students and 2-year junior college students are reported in the Level 3 Manual of Directions.

Validity

The validity of the ISRT, Level 3, can be evaluated by examining the test content and analyzing its relationship to the abilities on which successful reading depends. A brief description of the editors' theory of reading is provided in the column headed "Overall Theory of Reading."

Scoring Options

Machine scoring:
- MRC Answer Documents (scored by Measurement Research Center)
- IBM 1230 and Digitek/OpScan (scored by Harcourt Brace Jovanovich Scoring Service or locally)
- NCS Answer Folders (available from National Computer Systems or local scoring agencies)

Hand scoring: All above answer documents can also be scored by hand with the appropriate answer key. Stencil keys are available for IBM 1230, Digitek/OpScan, or Hand Scorable answer documents. To hand score NCS or MRC answer documents, use the list of correct responses provided in the Manual of Directions.

Cost

Test booklets (35):	$24.00
Answer sheets:	
• hand scored (35)	$ 9.50
• machine scored	
MRC (100)	$25.00
Scoring keys:	$ 7.50
Guide:	$12.00
Manual of Directions:	$ 3.50

Publisher

The Psychological Corporation, 555 Academic Court, San Antonio, TX 78204

Recommended Other Reviews

Davis (1978), Filby (1978), Hakstian (1978), Hunter and Hoepfner (1978), Johnson (1972)

Weaknesses

1. Level 3 does not include measurement of students' work-study skills (e.g., ability to use reference material, ability to skim and scan). The editors assume these skills have been mastered in high school. Instructors interested in measuring those skills must use Level 2.
2. Level 3 was normed on eleventh and twelfth grade students planning to attend a postsecondary institution.
3. The testing time slightly exceeds the normal college class period.
4. While the test material for the reading comprehension sections was selected from material adults are required to read, no material from actual college textbooks was used.

Strengths

1. The Manual of Directions is well written and easy to follow.

2. The Guide for Interpretation and Use provides extensive information for the practitioner in a well-written style. A full chapter in the guide is devoted to the use of the ISRT for instructional purposes at the college level.
3. The reading efficiency test checks reading rate and includes reading comprehension.
4. In addition to the vocabulary test section, vocabulary in context is measured within the reading comprehension test.
5. An optional reading survey is available to assess students' reading interests.

Minnesota Reading Assessment (MRA), 1980

Test/Authors
Minnesota Reading Assessment (MRA)
Raygor (1980)

Type of Test
Survey, formal, standardized, norm-referenced

Use(s) of Test
Initial screening

Skills/Strategies Tested
1. Reading and retention
2. Vocabulary
3. Paragraph comprehension

Population Recommended by Reviewers
This test could adequately be used as a screening instrument to identify students with suspected weak reading abilities in a community/junior college, technical, or other postsecondary school setting. Because of the low item difficulty, this test should be used only for those students in the lower half of the achievement distribution or those students who have marginal or less than adequate entrance prerequisites.

Overall Theory of Reading
The author of the MRA views reading ability as a composite of skill in comprehension, vocabulary, and rate with comprehension.

Readability/Source of Passages
Passages include material drawn from postsecondary textbooks with an emphasis on easy social studies, technical, and business skill materials, rather than on the more traditional content of college-level textbooks. Passages are at about the sixth grade level for the rate and retention part. The paragraph comprehension part ranges from seventh grade to college level, with an average of ninth-tenth grade.

Format/Test Parts
The reading rate and retention test (20 items) has a three-page (double columned) article followed by multiple choice and completion-type questions, each with four

alternatives. The reading rate in words per minute is based on a 3-minute timed reading of the article. The retention score is based on comprehension of the timed reading. The vocabulary test (50 items) uses words in isolation followed by four short definition-type alternatives or synonyms for the word. The paragraph comprehension test (20 items) gives passages followed by completion questions with four possible alternatives.

Testing Time

Reading rate and retention: 15 minutes; Vocabulary: 10 minutes; Paragraph comprehension: 15 minutes

Forms Available

Two parallel forms (A and B)

Levels Available

One level is available for the postsecondary population.

Types of Scores Available

Percentile ranks

Norm Groups

Four groups were used in the establishment of the norm tables: (1) students from nine vocationally oriented postsecondary schools in Minnesota and one in Utah; (2) students from seven community colleges in Minnesota, one in California, and one in South Carolina; (3) students from two universities or 4-year colleges in Minnesota and one in Louisiana; and (4) hearing impaired students from six community colleges, technical schools, and universities from six different sections of the country. The exact number of students for each norm group is not provided. It appears that the norming was done in 1980.

Date Published or Last Revised

The MRA was published in 1980.

Reliability

An internal reliability study was done with 95 students: 51 took Form A and 44 took Form B. Reliability estimates resulting from that study are: Cronbach's Alpha (.917, .934); Horst (.924, .941); Kuder-Richardson 20 (.917, .934); and Kuder-Richardson 21 (.900, .920) for Forms A and B respectively. A study of interform reliability was conducted on a sample of 24 students. The Interform Pearson Product-Moment correlations relating Form A to Form B are as follows: rate, .76; retention, .53; vocabulary, .83; paragraph comprehension, .57; and total score, .82.

Validity

The test has content validity in that it surveys the basic reading abilities needed to read material in many postsecondary technical schools and community colleges, with materials taken or developed from texts used in those institutions. The test was designed for this population of students. It has face validity to the extent that it is used to assess the type of student for whom it was designed. Several criterion-related validity studies were done using the Nelson-Denny Reading Test (Forms C and D), the Stanford Diagnostic Reading Test (Forms A and B), and the McGraw-Hill Basic Skills Reading Test. The results indicated reasonable correlations for the various test parts.

Scoring Options

Self-scoring: The self-scoring answer sheet available from Kendall/Hunt allows students to score their own tests.

Hand scoring: Hand-scoring answer sheets are available from Kendall/Hunt. Each package of answer sheets includes a stencil answer key.

Cost

Examiner's Manual: free on request

Test booklets (25):
  Form A $15.00
  Form B $15.00

Self-scoring answer sheets (25):
  Form A $12.00
  Form B $12.00

Hand-score answer sheets (pkg. of 25 including stencil answer key):
  Form A $10.00
  Form B $10.00

Publisher

The MRA was originally published by Twin Oaks Publishing. The test is now available from: Kendall/Hunt, Order Department, 2460 Kerper Boulevard, Dubuque, IA 52001

Recommended Other Reviews

Raygor and Flippo (1981)

Weaknesses

1. The vocabulary part tests the definitions of words in isolation.
2. The norm data, except for the data on the hearing impaired group, was mostly gathered in Minnesota. There is a need for norms with a more representative geographical perspective. Also, information regarding the number of students in the norm groups is not provided.
3. Although normative data is provided for the hearing impaired group, no evidence, information, or directions are provided regarding administration of this test with that population.
4. Because the number of students used in the reliability studies was extremely small, the reliability of this instrument is questionable.
5. Kendall/Hunt, which has acquired this test and plans to reprint it when the present inventory is depleted, has not indicated whether it will renorm the test.

Strengths

1. This test was specifically designed for use with the technical and community college student population.
2. It discriminates among the low-ability students of this population to assess who needs remedial-level assistance.
3. This test has content validity for this population. Additionally, the criterion-related validity of this test is well documented. Other than the norming and reliability concerns indicated under "Weaknesses," this test is potentially valid for the population intended.
4. Total testing time is only 40 minutes, so the test could be given during one class period.

5. Rate score is based on a 3-minute timed reading of a long but easy article, and the comprehension of this timed reading is taken into consideration when the rate and retention score is calculated.
6. Self-score answer sheets are available so students can score their own tests.
7. The publisher provides administration and technical information free of charge in one concise document. Free keys for hand scoring the test are also provided.

Nelson-Denny Reading Test, Forms C and D, 1973

Test/Authors
The Nelson-Denny Reading Test, Forms C and D
Brown, Nelson, and Denny (1973)

Type of Test
Survey, formal, standardized, norm-referenced

Use(s) of Test
Primary use: Initial screening
• to identify students who may need special help in reading
• to identify superior students who might profit from placement in advanced/accelerated classes
Secondary uses:
• predicting success in college courses
• diagnosing strengths and weaknesses in vocabulary, reading comprehension, and reading rate

Skills/Strategies Tested
1. Vocabulary
2. Comprehension
3. Reading rate

Population Recommended by Reviewers
This test could be used effectively with average entering college students for screening purposes. Due to the difficulty of the reading comprehension passages, students reading more than 2 years below their grade level could become frustrated. The test could also be used for preprofessional and pregraduate students in community reading efficiency courses. For maximum effectiveness, local norms should be developed.

Overall Theory of Reading
The Nelson-Denny is an evaluation of reading ability as measured by vocabulary development, reading comprehension, and reading rate.

Readability/Sources of Passages
The first passage is the longest and the easiest, probably because it is used to measure reading rate. It is an excerpt from *The Winged Horse* by Auslander and Hill (1928, 1968). Remaining passages are taken from *Scholastic* magazine or textbooks covering the humanities, science, social science, and business.

Format/Test Parts

The vocabulary section gives 100 words in minimum context (e.g., *to desist* is to ...). The comprehension section has eight passages followed by multiple choice questions with five alternatives. The first passage has eight questions; the rest have four each for a total of 36 questions. For rate, the students read for 1 minute from the first passage of the comprehension section and then mark the point they've reached when time is called.

Testing Time

Regular administration
   Vocabulary: 10 minutes; Comprehension: 20 minutes; Rate: 1 minute*

Cut-time administration (for efficient reading classes and those with a preponderance of upperclassmen)
   Vocabulary: 7.5 minutes; Comprehension: 15 minutes; Rate: 1 minute*

*Included in comprehension time

Forms Available

Two equivalent and parallel forms (C and D). See note under Nelson-Denny, Forms E and F

Levels Available

One level is available for grade nine through college.

Types of Scores Available

Standard scores, percentile ranks, grade equivalents

Norm Groups

The test was normed on both high school and college students. A total of 3,558 college students were sampled, 1,210 from 6 2-year institutions and 2,348 from 11 4-year colleges. The sample is not stratified by geographic location or size of institution. The results are not presented as a representative sample of the national college population. The publisher suggests that the appropriateness of the sample will have to be judged by each individual user.

Date Published or Last Revised

The test was first published in 1973 and revised in 1976.

Reliability

The split-halves reliability coefficients were obtained by computing Pearson product-moment correlations and were corrected with the Spearman-Brown formula. College freshmen in the sample numbered 1,942. The reliability coefficients for vocabulary was .96, for reading comprehension, .83, and for total score, .95. Although a study was conducted to determine reliability by the equivalent forms method, no college students were included in that sample. For high school seniors (185 out of the total sample of 1,213), the reliability coefficient for vocabulary was .97, for reading comprehension, .84, and for total score, .95.

Validity

The concurrent validity of Forms C and D was demonstrated in a study with 282 upstate New York twelfth graders. Results showed correlations ranging from .70 for the SAT/Nelson-Denny Comprehension subtest to .84 for the PSAT/Nelson-Denny total score.

Appendix

Scoring Options

Hand scoring: Answer keys are provided in the manual.
Self-scoring: Answer sheets are available from publisher.
Machine scoring: MRC answer cards can be purchased from and returned to publisher for scoring; IBM 1230 or Digitek answer sheets can also be used (obtain scoring key from publisher).

Cost

Test booklets (35):	$25.83
Examiner's Manual:	$ 6.18
MRC answer cards (100):	$15.06
Self-marking answer sheets:	
pkg. of 35	$25.83
pkg. of 250	$98.37

Publisher

Riverside Publishing Company, 8420 Bryn Mawr Avenue, Suite 1000, Chicago, IL 60631

Recommended Other Reviews

Erwin (1981), Farr (1972), Forsyth (1978), Gordon (1983), Nist (1983), Perkins (1984), Raygor (1978), Webb (1983)

Weaknesses

1. When used as a screening instrument with underprepared readers, the test can be frustrating—partly because the comprehension passages are quite difficult and partly because of time constraints.
2. The reading rate test allows only 1 minute to measure reading rate and does not check comprehension.

Strengths

1. The instrument may be a valid measure of the reading efficiency of students in advanced college reading courses or in speed/efficient reading courses. It might also be used effectively to measure the reading ability of students preparing for graduate study. For these student populations, cut-time administration should be used.
2. The reading passages represent fairly typical text reading for college students; however, except for the first selection, passages are brief and thus do little to measure extended reading.
3. The test can be administered in a typical college class period.

Nelson-Denny Reading Test, Forms E and F, 1980

Test/Authors

Nelson-Denny Reading Test, Forms E and F
Brown, Bennett, & Hanna (1980)

Type of Test

Survey, formal, standardized, norm-referenced

Use(s) of Test

Primary use: Initial screening
- to identify students who may need special help in reading
- to identify superior students who could profit from placement in advanced/accelerated classes

Secondary uses:
- predicting success in college courses
- diagnosing strengths and weaknesses in vocabulary, reading comprehension, and reading rate

Skills/Strategies Tested

1. Vocabulary
2. Comprehension
3. Reading rate

Population Recommended by Reviewers

This test could be used effectively with average entering college students for screening purposes. Due to the difficulty of the reading comprehension passages, students reading more than 2 years below their grade level could become frustrated. The test could also be used for preprofessional and pregraduate students and for students in community reading efficiency courses. For maximum effectiveness, local norms should be developed.

Overall Theory of Reading

The authors list reading comprehension, vocabulary development, and reading rate as the three most important skills in the reading process, noting that they are related, interdependent functions.

Readability/Sources of Passages

The first passage is the longest and the easiest, probably because it is used for measuring rate. The passage is an excerpt from *The Winged Horse* by Auslander and Hill (1928, 1968). Two of the other reading selections are written at high school level grades 9-10), and five are at the college level (three at 13th and two at 17th). Remaining passages are taken from *Scholastic* magazine or textbooks covering the humanities, social science, and science.

Format/Test Parts

The vocabulary section gives 100 words in minimum context (e.g., to *presume* ...). The comprehension section has eight passages followed by multiple choice questions with five alternatives. The first passage has eight questions; the rest have four each for a total of 36 questions. For rate, the students read from the first passage of the comprehension section for 1 minute and then mark the point they've reached when time is called.

Testing Time

Regular administration
   Vocabulary: 15 minutes; Comprehension: 20 minutes; Rate; 1 minute*

Cut-time administration (for speed reading classes, efficient reading classes, and classes with a preponderance of junior/senior students)
   Vocabulary: 11 minutes; Comprehension; 15 minutes; Rate: 1 minute*

* Included in comprehension time

Forms Available

Two equivalent and parallel forms (E and F). The C/D and E/F forms are not all parallel and equivalent, and should not be used interchangeably. Each set of forms should be used as a separate test. (Forms C and D can be used as pre/posttests, as can E and F. However, C and F for example, cannot be used as pre/posttests, as they are neither equivalent nor parallel.)

Levels Available

One level is available for grade nine through college.

Types of Scores Available

Standard scores, stanines, percentile ranks, rate equivalents

Norm Groups

Three samples were selected: one from the high school population, one from the 2-year college population, and one from the 4-year college/university population. For the college samples, 6,000 students from 41 2-year institutions and 5,000 students from 32 4-year colleges/universities were sampled in November 1979. For both, two criteria were used to select a representative group: geographic regions and size of institution. The largest percentage of college students come from the far west, followed by the midwest; the sample's largest group was from the southwest, followed by the southeast. The largest percentage of college students come from schools with more than 5,000 students; the sample's largest group for 2-year colleges was from schools with 1,200 to 5,000 students, and for 4-year institutions from schools with more than 5,000 students. Racial and ethnic characteristics were not part of the sampling basis.

Date Published or Last Revised

This new form of the Nelson-Denny was tested in 1979 and published in 1980. Earlier versions were the Nelson-Denny Forms A/B and C/D.

Reliability

The method selected to assess reliability was the administration of two different forms of the test on separate occasions (alternate-form reliability). In all of the sampling, examiners had half of the examinees take Form E while the other half took Form F. Two weeks later, each examinee took the other form. The publisher's results shows the median reliability coefficient for vocabulary to be .92, for comprehension, .77, and for the total score, .91. The median for reading rate was .69.

Validity

The only form of validity measured by the publisher was context dependence, using the model proposed by Hanna and Oaster (1979). In this study, a sample of 225 college sophomores from two 4-year institutions varying in region and size took part. Half of the examinees took Form E with the reading passages present and next took Form F with its passages absent. The other half took Form E with its passages absent followed by Form F with its passages present. Results are presented in two scores. The Context Dependence Index (CDI) measures the degree to which correct item responses are influenced by the context. It should be positive and significant. The Context Independence Index (CII) measures the degree to which examinees can answer the items through previous knowledge or application of logic. It is an undesirable characteristic and should ideally be zero or negative. For the sampling population, the CDI was .29 for Form E and .44 for Form F. The CII was .09 for Form E and .03 for Form F.

Scoring Options

Hand scoring: Answer keys are provided in the manual. Use MRC answer sheets and make a stencil key for scoring.
Self-scoring: Answer sheets are available from the publisher.
Machine scoring: Use the NCS 7010 answer sheets and set up an institutional scoring system. (Any sheet that is compatible with machine scoring may be used in place of the NCS 7010.)

Cost

Test booklets (35):	$22.17
Examiner's Manual:	$ 5.13
MRC answer sheets:	
pkg. of 35:	$15.12
pkg. of 100:	$27.69
Self-marking answer sheets:	
pkg. of 35 (incl. manual)	$22.08
pkg. of 250 (not incl. manual)	$86.94

Publisher

Riverside Publishing Company, 8420 Bryn Mawr Road, Suite 1000, Chicago, IL 60631

Recommended Other Reviews

Farr (1972), Gordon (1983), Tierney (1985a), Ysseldyke (1985a)

Weaknesses

1. Although time has been allotted to the vocabulary test, the manual states that fewer than one in five students will complete this section unless they are in the last 2 years of college. Thus, time constraints still appear to be a problem.
2. The rate section remains a problem. Only 1 minute is allowed for testing reading rate, and no comprehension check is involved.
3. The difficulty level of the reading passages is still a problem for underprepared students.

Strengths

1. The instrument may be a valid measure of the reading efficiency of students in advanced college reading courses or in speed/efficient reading courses. It might also be used effectively to measure the reading ability of students preparing for graduate study. For these student populations, cut-time administration should be used.
2. A strong attempt was made to norm the revised test on entering college students. The publisher tested 11,000 entering college students. Few other reading survey tests have been normed on a college population; most rely on high school seniors.
3. The test can be administered in a typical college class period.
4. The passages in the reading comprehension section are an attempt to test students' ability to read typical textbook material. However, due to the brevity of all passages except the first, extended reading cannot be measured.

Reading Progress Scale, College Version, 1975

Test/Authors

Reading Progress Scale, College Version
Carver (1975)

Type of Test

Survey, informal, criterion-referenced

Use(s) of Test

Initial screening

Skills/Strategies Tested

Decoding meaning of sentences within passages

Population Recommended by Reviewers

This test could be used to quickly screen junior/community college freshmen and sophomores to determine who should be further assessed for possible placement in remedial reading courses. The test is most useful for detecting students with very low reading abilities.

Overall Theory of Reading

The author views reading as the ability to comprehend written material. In the test manual, he clearly states that this test has been designed to measure the ability to decode the meaning of words in passages of designated levels of readability, not the ability to draw inferences or other higher order comprehension abilities.

Readability/Source of Passages

Passages are approximately 100 words long and are from social studies/civics content materials for Form 2C and from meteorology and geology content materials for Form 5C. Each form has four passages, one representative of grades 1-3, one of grades 4-6, one of grades 7-9, and one of grades 10-12. The passages have equal cloze difficulty score increments. Readability was determined by use of a cloze procedure (Bormuth, 1969).

Format/Test Parts

The test has four numbered cloze passages with two alternatives for each blank. Passages are arranged by level of difficulty, from one (the easiest) to four (the most difficult). Each passage has 29 items. The student completes as many passages as possible within the time allowed.

Testing Time

Seven minutes

Forms Available

Two forms (2C and 5C)

Levels Available

One level is available for the college population.

Types of Scores Available

Pass/fail reading level scores (18 correct out of the possible 20 for each passage indicates passing for that particular readability level)

Norm Groups

Approximately 1,800 first-year students from Lansing Community College (Michigan) were tested in the fall of 1975 to determine success rates.

Date Published or Last Revised

Forms 2 and 5 were published in 1971. In 1975, Forms 2 and 5 were modified by Lansing Community College and published for use as a college screening test. Later that year they were published by Revrac as Forms 2C and 5C.

Reliability

In 1977-1978, Lansing Community College administered both forms of the test to 98 students; 71.4 percent scored at the same reading level on both forms, and 20.4 percent scored one level different on one form than on the other. Only 8.2 percent received scores that differed by more than one level. Thus, with this group of college students, the test provided a fairly reliable reading level score.

Validity

A predictive validity study was done with approximately 3,000 students at Lansing Community College by determining the probability that students would obtain a certain cumulative grade point average (GPA) if they scored at certain reading ability levels on the test. The study found that students who score low on the test were more likely to have low GPAs than either average or high GPAs; students who scored high on the test were more likely to have high GPAs than either average or low GPAs.

Scoring Options

Self-scoring can be done by students on the self-scoring answer sheets.
Hand scoring is also possible; the instructor simply uses the same self-scoring answer sheets.

Cost

Manual: free
Form 2C (pkg. of 100): $30.00
Form 5C (pkg. of 100): $30.00
(Tests include self-scoring answer sheets)

Publisher

Revrac Publications, 207 West 116th Street, Kansas City, MO 64114

Recommended Other Reviews

No other reviews critiqued by authors.

Weaknesses

1. The tryouts, reliability, and validity studies for the college version were all conducted with students at Lansing Community College. The test is reliable and valid only to the extent that other student populations are similar to the one at Lansing Community College during 1975-1978.
2. The test uses very broad range generalizations of reading ability grade levels.
3. All of the emphasis is on understanding materials written at questionable reading ability levels, rather than on more appropriate college-level reading comprehension needs, such as application of content presented.

Strengths

1. The college forms of the test were developed for use with students in community colleges.
2. The test is quick to administer, allowing the possibility of giving the test while new students register for classes.
3. The test is designed for self-scoring and provides immediate feedback with simple explanations of the results.
4. The focus is on reading paragraphs rather than on discrete subskills of reading.

Stanford Diagnostic Reading Test (SDRT), Blue Level, 1976 Edition

Test/Authors

Stanford Diagnostic Reading Test (SDRT), Blue Level, 1976 Edition
Karlsen, Madden, and Gardner (1976)

Type of Test

Diagnostic, formal, norm-referenced, standardized

Use(s) of Test

1. Initial diagnostic assessment
2. To assess individual progress and make changes as appropriate

Skills/Strategies Tested

1. Literal comprehension
2. Inferential comprehension
3. Word meaning
4. Word parts
5. Phonetic analysis
6. Structural analysis
7. Scanning and skimming
8. Fast reading

Population Recommended by Reviewers

This test could be used to get a more diagnostic view of each student's reading abilities and inabilities before assigning underprepared students to college reading improvement programs. It is particularly discriminating for freshmen and sophomores in the lower achieving groups in community/junior colleges and in lower division university programs.

Overall Theory of Reading

The test authors view reading as a developmental process with four major components: decoding, vocabulary, comprehension, and rate. They acknowledge that comprehension should be the ultimate goal of the reading process but note that considerable instructional emphasis must be placed on the development of efficient reading habits. They advocate the clinical approach to diagnosis, using many sources of information taken at different times and under different conditions, including informal classroom observations.

Readability/Source of Passages

Passages include material drawn from the natural and social sciences, human interest stories, fiction, poetry, and biography written at ninth to thirteenth grade readability levels, with an average of eleventh grade readability.

Format/Test Parts

Comprehension—Passages are followed by multiple choice questions with four alternatives. (60 items)

Word meaning—30 items, each requiring completion of one definition-type sentence.

Word parts—Words in isolation with a word part underlined and a choice of four alternatives for the meaning of the part. (30 items)

Phonetic analysis—30 words in isolation with a sound underlined and a choice of three alternative words, one of which has the same sound.

Structural analysis—Four sound units are presented in isolation with directions that it is possible that three of them blended together will make a word. The student must indicate which of the four choices must be eliminated or indicate the choice of "no word." (24 items)

Scanning and skimming (32 items)—Part A (scanning): Students read a one-sentence question followed by four alternatives and then scan a full-page content-related article (with subheadings) to select the correct phrase or word to answer the question. Part B (skimming): Students are timed as they skim another full-page article. Following the time allowed (2 minutes), they must answer 16 general and specific questions about the article. There are four short answer alternatives following each one-sentence question.

Fast reading—A multiple choice cloze format (maze) is used. Students read easy content material for 2 minutes, and as they read they select the correct alternative from the three choices given. (30 items)

Testing Time

Reading comprehension: 35 minutes; Word meaning: 12 minutes; Word parts: 12 minutes; Phonetic analysis: 12 minutes; Structural analysis: 9 minutes; Scanning and skimming: Scanning (Part A), 6 minutes, Skimming (Part B), 8 minutes; Fast Reading: 2 minutes

(Total testing time is 96 minutes)

Forms Available

Two parallel forms (A and B)

Levels Available

One level is available for the college population: Blue Level (formerly published as the SDRT Level III in 1974).

Types of Scores Available

Progress indicators, scaled scores, percentile ranks, stanines, grade equivalents

Norm Groups

Approximately 2,500 first-year students from 11 colleges in six communities were tested in January 1973. They were selected to be representative of the national junior/community college population at that time in terms of geographic location, city size, diversity of student body, and curriculum. Students took either Form A or Form B. In order to obtain comparable data for the two forms, Form A of the Stanford Test of Academic Skills (TASK) was also administered to all students. The scores of the samples were matched on the basis of their TASK score distributions by eliminating cases (N = 539 for Form A SDRT Blue Level).

Date Published or Last Revised

The SDRT Level III was published in 1974. In 1976, the name was changed to the SDRT Blue Level, but no changes were made to the test.

Reliability

For the 539 college freshman subjects, the Kuder-Richardson Formula 21 was used to estimate the internal consistency of items for all subtests and combinations of subtests except for scanning and skimming and fast reading (the formula is not appropriate for estimating the reliability of timed tests). The reliability for overall reading comprehension was .92 for Forms A and B; for overall vocabulary (word meaning and word parts), .89 for Forms A and B; and for overall decoding (phonetic and structural analysis), .93 for Form A and .94 for Form B. Alternate-form reliability estimates were obtained for the fast reading and scanning and skimming subtests for samples in grades 9 and 11 only. The reliability for grade 11 was .79 for fast reading and .80 for scanning and skimming.

Validity

The test has content validity in that it measures objectives stated in the test manual. However, individual colleges must determine how valid these objectives are for their own purposes and program philosophy. If reading is seen as decoding words using phonics and structural analysis skills, knowledge of very basic vocabulary, comprehension of fairly short reading selections, and rate of reading and finding information in relatively easy material, then face validity is high. A criterion-related validity study was done with the Stanford TASK. The results indicated reasonable intercorrelations for the reading subtests.

Scoring Options

Hand scoring: Use MRC answer folders and purchase stencil keys from the publisher.

Machine scoring: Use MRC answer folders and send the test folders to the Measurement Research Center (Iowa City, IA) for scoring. Complete instructions are included with the MCR answer folder materials.

Cost

Manual for Administering and Interpreting: $6.00
Test booklets (35):
    Form A $30.00
    Form B $30.00
MRC answer folders (35):
    Form A $18.00
    Form B $18.00
Key for hand scoring:
    Form A $ 8.00
    Form B $ 8.00
Handbook of Instructional Techniques and Material: $10.00

Publisher

The Psychological Corporation, 555 Academic Court, San Antonio, TX 78204

Recommended Other Reviews

Kasdon (1975), Raygor and Flippo (1981), Tierney (1985b), Van Roekel (1978), Webb (1983), Ysseldyke (1985b)

Weaknesses

1. Two of the subtests (phonetic analysis and structural analysis) have little relevance to the tasks involved in most college-level reading. These subtests are not recommended. Furthermore, the test does not measure the higher order decoding skills that are more appropriate for the college level (such as use of context, punctuation, and sentence structure).
2. The vocabulary word parts subtest uses words in isolation. We would prefer a measure using words in a whole sentence or paragraph.
3. When administered in its entirety, this test is more representative of a skills-based theory of reading than of a holistic approach. This may be either a strength or a weakness depending on one's view of reading.
4. This edition of the SDRT has been superceded by the third edition (also reviewed here). Therefore, the tests and related materials will be available only while supplies last.

Strengths

1. The 1976 SDRT has been normed and standardized for use with the freshman college population.
2. The scanning and skimming, fast reading, and literal and inferential comprehension subtests are excellent for the college-level population recommended.
3. The Manual for Administering and Interpreting is well done; it provides essential information and makes some excellent points. We have seen few tests with manuals that are this complete and comprehensive, containing all of the important norming, reliability, validity, and other technical data necessary to use the test appropriately.
4. The publisher also has a Handbook of Instructional Techniques and Materials, which can be purchased separately (although it may or may not be appropriate for college students).

Stanford Diagnostic Reading Test (SDRT), Blue Level, 1984 Edition

Test/Authors
Stanford Diagnostic Reading Test (SDRT), Blue Level, 1984 Edition
Karlsen, Madden, and Gardner (1984)

Type of Test
Diagnostic, formal, norm-referenced, standardized

Use(s) of Test
1. Initial diagnostic assessment
2. To assess individual progress and make changes as appropriate

Skills/Strategies Tested
1. Literal comprehension
2. Inferential comprehension
3. Vocabulary
4. Word parts
5. Phonetic analysis
6. Structural analysis
7. Scanning and skimming
8. Fast reading

In addition, item clusters from the literal and inferential comprehension subtests have been grouped to give an indication of:
• textual reading comprehension
• functional reading comprehension
• recreational reading comprehension

Population Recommended by Reviewers
This test could be used to get a more diagnostic view of each student's reading abilities and inabilities before assigning underprepared students to reading improvement programs. However, this test is recommended only for freshmen in the lower achieving groups in community/junior colleges and in lower division university special admittance programs. The test would probably not discriminate for the more academically able college students; in fact, the authors/publisher have not included college students at all in this new edition.

Overall Theory of Reading
The test authors view reading as a developmental process with four major components: decoding, vocabulary, comprehension, and rate. They acknowledge that comprehension should be the ultimate goal of the reading process but note that considerable instructional emphasis must be placed on the development of efficient reading habits. They advocate the clinical approach to diagnosis, using many sources of information taken at different times and under different conditions, including informal classroom observations.

Readability/Source of Passages
Passages include material drawn from the natural and social sciences, human interest stories, fiction, poetry, and biography written at the ninth to thirteenth grade readability

levels, with an average of eleventh grade readability. For this edition, passages have been added that include functional reading materials.

Format/Test Parts

Comprehension—Passages are followed by multiple choice questions with four alternatives. (60 items)

Vocabulary—30 items, each requiring completion of one definition-type sentence.

Word parts—Words in isolation with a word part underlined and a choice of four alternatives for the meaning of the part. (30 items)

Phonetic analysis—Words in isolation with a sound underlined and a choice of three alternative words, one of which has the same sound. (30 items)

Structural analysis—Four choices of syllabication for a word in isolation. (30 items)

Scanning and skimming (32 items)—Part A (scanning): Students read a one-sentence question followed by four alternatives and then scan a full-page content-related article (with subheadings) to select the correct phrase or word to answer the question. Part B (skimming): Students are timed as they skim another full-page article. Following the time allowed (3 minutes), they must answer 16 general and specific questions about the article. There are four short answer alternatives following each one-sentence question.

Fast reading—A multiple choice cloze format (maze) is used. Students read easy content material for 3 minutes, and as they read they select the correct alternative from the three choices given. (30 items)

Testing Time

Reading comprehension: 40 minutes; Vocabulary: 15 minutes; Word parts: 15 minutes; Phonetic analysis: 12 minutes; Scanning and skimming: Scanning (Part A): 8 minutes; Skimming (Part B): 11 minutes; Fast reading: 3 minutes

(Total testing time is 116 minutes)

Forms Available

Two parallel forms (G and H)

Levels Available

One level is available for the college population: Level Blue

Types of Scores Available

Progress indicators, stanines, percentile ranks, scaled scores, normal curve equivalents, grade equivalents

Norm Groups

No college students were used in the norming of this edition of this test. The norming population is restricted to students in grades 8-12, and norming was done in the fall of 1983 and spring of 1984.

Date Published or Last Revised

The third edition was published in 1984. This edition differs significantly from the 1976 edition (also reviewed here).

Reliability

For the approximately 980 subjects in grade 12, the Kuder-Richardson Formula 20 was used to estimate the internal consistency of all SDRT subtest scores, except for scanning and skimming and fast reading (the formula is not appropriate for estimating the reliability of timed tests). The reliability of overall reading comprehension was .92 and .91 for Forms G and H, respectively; of overall vocabulary (vocabulary and word parts), .89 for Forms G and H; of overall decoding (phonetics and structural analysis), .91 for Forms G and H. No internal consistency reliability studies were done for freshman college students. Alternate-form reliability estimates were obtained for the fast reading and scanning and skimming subtests for 216 students in grade 10 only. The reliability was .60 for fast reading and .66 for scanning and skimming.

Validity

The test has content validity in that it measures the objectives stated in the test manual. However, users must determine how valid these objectives are for their purposes, populations, and programs. A correlation study was done for 856 ninth grade students, correlating their scores on the SDRT, Blue Level, Form G and scores on comparable subtests of the Stanford Achievement Test, Advanced, Form E. The correlation was .74 for reading comprehension and .64 for vocabulary. No validity studies were done with older students.

Scoring Options

Hand scoring: Use MRC answer folders and purchase stencil keys from the publisher; also, you may use hand-scorable answer documents or MRC Machine Scorable Answer Documents and purchase the appropriate keys from the publisher.
Machine scoring: Use MRC answer folders and send the test folders to the Measurement Research Center (Iowa City, IA) for scoring. Complete instructions are included with the MRC answer folder materials.

Cost

Directions for Administering: $2.00

Manual for Interpreting; $6.00

Norms Booklet: $3.50

Test Booklets (35):
    Form G $30.00
    Form H $30.00

Hand-scorable answer documents (35);
    Form G $11.00
    Form H $11.00

MRC machine-scorable answer documents (35):
    Form G $18.00
    Form H $18.00

Key for hand-scoring answer documents:
    Form G $ 8.50
    Form H $ 8.50

Key for MRC machine-scorable answer documents:
    Form G $ 8.00
    Form H $ 8.00

Handbook of Instructional Techniques and Materials: $10.00

Publisher

The Psychological Corporation, 555 Academic Court, San Antonio, TX 78204

Recommended Other Reviews

No other reviews critiqued by authors.

Weaknesses

1. The 1984 SDRT has not been normed or standardized for use with the college freshman population.
2. Validity data and reliability data cannot be generalized to the lower ability college freshman population.
3. The phonetic analysis subtest has little relevance to the tasks involved in most college-level reading and is not recommended. The structural analysis subtest has been improved over the one used in the 1976 edition; however, although syllabication is a somewhat more appropriate skill for college students, the test still does not measure many important college content-related word analysis skills.
4. The vocabulary word parts subtest uses words in isolation. We would prefer a measure using words in a whole sentence or paragraph.
5. When administered in its entirety, this test is more representative of a skills-based theory of reading than of a holistic approach. This may be either a strength or a weakness depending on your view of reading.
6. The passages used for the comprehension subtest have been made too simple for the needs of most of the college population. The passages are significantly shorter than those used in the 1976 edition, and focus more on functional reading than on content reading.
7. The directions for administering, the norms data, and the information for interpreting the test and technical information have all been published separately for this edition. At best, this causes inconvenience for the user, and at worst it keeps users from receiving the appropriate and necessary information.

Strengths

1. The scanning and skimming and the fast reading subtests are excellent for the college level population recommended. The time for these tests has been lengthened in this edition, which should strengthen the diagnostic information these subtests yield.
2. The comprehension subtest provides item clusters to yield diagnostic information regarding a student's literal and inferential comprehension and their textual, functional, and recreational reading comprehension.
   (However, note our concern about the appropriateness of this subtest for the recommended college population under the "Weaknesses" column. Also, note that there are no norms available for the recommended college population.)
3. The publisher also has a Handbook of Instructional Techniques that can be purchased separately (although it may or may not be appropriate for the college population).

Author Index

Note: "Mc" is alphabetized as "Mac." A "t" following a page number indicates that the reference may be found in a table.

Abraham, A., 119, 162, 164
Adams, S.M., 54, 65
Adler, M.J., 2, 24
Ahrendt, K.M., 136, 164
Akst, J., 90, 115
Alexander, C.F., 135, 147, 164
Anderson, C.A., 131, 132, 164
Anderson, I.H., 129, 164
Anderson, O.S., 56, 65
Anderson, R.C., 19, 24, 131, 164
Anderson, S., 70, 72, 73, 82, 115
Applebee, A.N., 2, 18, 20, 24, 26
Arons, A.B., 1, 24
Atwell, M., 14, 24
Aulls, M., 14, 24
Auslander, J., 164, 195, 198
Bacon, L., 65
Baker, G.A., 42, 47, 50, 53, 54, 68
Balajthy, E., 54, 65
Baldwin, R., 116
Ball, D , 70, 72, 73, 82, 115
Baron, J.B., 26
Bartholomae, D., 17, 25
Beal, P.E., 51, 55, 65
Bear, R., 30
de Beaugrande, R., 3, 25
Behrens, H., 96, 115
Belenky, M.F., 6, 22, 25
Bengis, L., 65
Bennett, J.M., 145, 164, 197
Benson, J., 134, 164
Berg, P.C., 128, 164
Beyer, B., 18, 25
Birnbaum, J.C., 12, 25
Blair, T.R., 55, 68
Blanc, R.A., 52, 62, 65, 67
Blanton, W., 138, 164, 166, 168
Bleich, D., 19, 20, 25
Bliesmer, E.P., 168, 169, 171
Bliss, L., 112, 115
Bloesser, R.E., 132, 164
Bloom, M.E., 121, 164
Bloomers, P., 122, 164
Boone, T., 149, 166
Borich, G., 91, 94, 98, 100, 115
Bormuth, J.R., 134, 164, 181
Boylan, H.R., 30, 34, 38, 45, 49, 58t, 60, 65, 66, 80, 101, 115, 116
Brandt, R., 26
Brensing, D., 132, 164
Brier, E., 30, 66
Broderick, B., 11, 15
Brown, F.G., 141, 142, 143, 144, 164
Brown, J.E., 145, 164, 169, 195, 197
Brown, S., 101, 117
Browning, N.F., 10, 25

Brozo, W.G., 38, 68, 112, 116
Bruner, J.S., 22, 23, 25
Bruning, R., 164, 181
Bullock, T., 52, 66
Burgess, B.A., 62, 66
Burgess, M.A., 121, 164
Burkart, K.H., 128, 164
Burke, C., 20, 25
Burns, P.C., 153, 165
Buros, O.K., 166, 167, 168, 170, 172
Buswell, G.T., 129, 165
Butkowski, I., 112, 116
Cahalan, M., 42, 66
Calfee, R., 165, 184
Campbell, D., 83, 86, 87, 89, 98, 116
Carey, R.F., 122, 131, 134, 136, 137, 138, 165, 166
Carney, M., 119, 165
Carpenter, K., 56, 66
Carpenter, P.A., 134, 166
Carroll, J.B., 129, 167
Carsello, J., 133, 165
Carter, H.L.J., 32, 66
Cartwright, H.D., 132, 165
Carvell, R., 136, 165
Carver, R.P., 134, 152, 154, 165, 181, 201
Cashen, C.J., 45, 66, 129, 165
Castelli, C., 39, 63, 66
Causey, O.S., 66, 67, 169
Caverly, D.C., 11, 25, 169, 170, 172
Center, S., 30
Chall, J.S., 134, 165, 166, 176, 186, 189
Chand, S., 45 , 67, 99, 116
Chester, R.D., 136, 165
Chisson, B.S., 48, 66
Christ, F.L., 39, 66, 115, 116
Christiansen, L., 4, 25
Clark, F.E., 55, 68
Clark, W.W., 172, 173
Cleland, D.L., 128, 165
Clement, J., 24
Clifford, G.J., 3, 25
Clinchy, B.M., 25
Clowes, D.A., 64, 66, 72, 87, 104, 116
Clymer, C., 46, 55, 66
Clymer, T., 128, 165
Coates, D.F., 135, 165
Cook, T., 98, 116
Cousins, B., 104, 116
Crafton, L., 13, 25
Cranney, A.G., 34, 62, 66, 133, 135, 159, 165, 169
Creaser, J., 133, 165
Cronbach, L.J., 70, 77, 82, 102, 116, 127, 165
Cross, K.P., 45, 66, 77, 113, 116
Culler, J., 3, 25
Curtis, C. , 112, 116
Curtis, M.E., 129, 165

Dahl, K., 14, 15, 25
Dale, E., 134, 166, 176, 186, 189
Daneman, M., 133, 134, 166
Davis, B., 128, 166
Davis, F.B., 166, 188, 191
Davis, T., 149, 166
DeBuhr, L.E., 52, 65
Dempsey, J., 51, 52, 55, 66
Denny, E.C., 164, 169, 195
DeSanti, R., 153, 166
Devirian, M., 33, 42, 68
Dillard, M.L., 50, 66
Donaldson, W., 171
Donovan, R.A., 57, 58t, 66
Douglas, J., 121, 164
Douglass, M.P., 168
Drabin-Partenio, I., 131, 166
Dressel, P., 91, 116
Dubois, E., 135, 166
Dulin, K.L., 136, 165
Eichholz, G., 166, 189
Eisenstein, E., 3, 25
Eller, W., 66, 67
Elliott, M.K., 51, 67
Emond, S.B., 171
Enright, G.D., 30, 31, 33, 42, 66, 67, 68
Erwin, T.D., 168, 197
Eurich, A.C., 121, 166
Evans, C.S., 18, 25
Evans, H., 135, 166
Fairbanks, M.M., 40, 51, 67
Farr, R., 122, 128, 134, 135, 136, 137, 138, 164, 166, 168, 185, 197, 200
Farris, E., 42, 66
Feuers, S., 132, 166
Figurel, J.A., 165
Filby, N.N., 166, 188, 191
Fischer, K.M., 23, 27
Fish, S., 3, 25
Fitz-Gibbon, C., 79, 116
Flippo, R.F., 42, 67, 123, 126, 127, 132, 133, 135, 137, 145, 148, 158, 159, 161, 162, 166, 167, 169, 170, 172, 206
Florio, C.B., 132, 167
Foley, W., 117
Forsyth, R.A., 128, 167, 171, 197
Frackenpohl, H., 172, 189
Freedle, R.O., 129, 167
Freeley, J., 99, 100, 116
Freeman, E., 70, 73, 88, 107, 117
Freer, I.J., 132, 167
Freire, P., 4, 23, 24, 25, 27
Fry, E.B., 146, 167, 176
Gabriel, D., 47, 67
Gardner, E.R., 168, 203, 207
Gates, A.J., 128, 167
Gawkoski, R.S., 47, 67
Gebhard, A., 10, 25
Geis, L., 119, 167
Gentile , L.M., 152, 154, 167
Gephard, W., 117

Gibbs, G., 21, 22, 25
Gibson, E., 129, 167
Glaser, R., 129, 130, 161, 165, 167
Glass, G., 101, 116
Glazer, S.M., 152, 154, 167
Goetz, E., 164
Gold, B.K., 56, 67
Goldberger, N.R., 25
Goodlad, J., 2, 25
Goodman, K.S., 13, 25, 129, 167
Goodman, Y., 13, 25
Goodwin, D.D., 132, 133, 159, 167
Gordon, B., 42, 67, 133, 135, 158, 159, 167, 197, 200
Grant, M.K., 57, 58t, 67
Gray, W.S., 121, 128, 167
Green, T., 52, 69
Greene, F.P., 164, 165, 172
Guba, E., 117
Guthrie, J.T., 95, 117, 124, 125, 130, 137, 160, 161, 167
Haburton, E., 99, 112, 116
Hageman, J.N., 119, 169
Hakstian, A.R., 167, 188, 191
Hall, P., 122, 128, 170
Hall, W.E., 168
Haller, E., 93, 116
Hamberg, S., 50, 67
Hamilton-Wieler, S., 24, 25
Hammond, R., 117
Hanna, G.S., 145, 164, 168, 181, 197
Hansen, J., 14, 27
Hardt, U., 24, 25
Harste, J.C., 20, 25, 131, 165
Harter, J., 52, 66
Hasby, P., 54, 65
Havelock, E.A., 19, 25
Hawkers, T., 19, 25
Hayman, R.L., 65
Hecht, M., 90, 115
Heerman, C.E., 67
Helm, P.K., 45, 67, 152, 170
Hepworth, D., 38, 67
Herrman, B.A., 136, 172
Hieronymous, A., 128, 171
Hill, F.E., 164, 195, 198
Hirsch, E.D., Jr., 2, 6, 7, 25, 26
Hoeber, D.R., 57, 58t, 67
Hoepfner, R., 168, 188, 191
Holmes, J.A., 128, 168
Huck, G., 128, 172
Huey, E.B., 129, 168
Hughes, C., 26
Hull, G., 17, 26
Hunt, R., 16, 26
Hunter, R., 168, 188, 191
Hutson, B., 166
Illych, I., 5, 26
Ironside, R.A., 132, 135, 168
Jackson, J.H., 20, 26, 120, 130, 154, 160, 161, 171
Jacob, C.T., Jr., 67
Jacobs, M., 165
Janzen, J.L., 135, 168
Jernigan, L., 56, 67

Johns, J., 168
Johnson, D., 39, 63, 66
Johnson, E.F., 135, 152, 168, 175
Johnson, I.T., 67
Johnson, R., 168, 188, 191
John-Stein, V., 19, 26
Johnston, P.H., 130, 131, 145, 161, 163, 168
Jones, B.F., 26
Jones, E., 48, 67
Jongsma, E.A., 153, 168
Jongsma, K.S., 153, 168
Kaiser, R., 149, 166
Kamil, M.L., 89, 116, 167
Karlsen, B., 168, 203, 207
Kasdon, L.M., 168, 206
Kay, P., 135, 172
Keimig, R., 10 4, 116
Kelly, F.J., 121, 168
Kennedy, M.L., 10, 11, 26
Kerstiens, G., 30, 31, 67, 118, 135, 148, 162, 168, 169
Ketcham, H.E., 135,169
Kibby, M.W., 169, 181
Kincaide, K.M., 54, 67
King, M., 128, 172
Kingston, A.J., 122, 127, 128, 135, 169
Kintsch, W.F., 129, 134, 169
Kleine, P.F., 67
Koeller, S., 18, 26
Kozol, J., 3, 6, 7, 26
Kucer, S.B., 15, 26
Kuhn, T.S., 7, 26
Kulik, C.C., 28, 61, 62, 67, 108, 116
Kulik, J.A., 28, 61, 62, 67, 108, 116
Lalik, R.V., 165
Land, F., 93, 94, 116
Landsman, M.B., 133, 159, 169
Landward, S., 38, 67
Langer, J.A., 13, 18, 19, 20, 26
Langsam, R.S., 122, 169
Lanier, D., 48, 66
Larsen, J.J., 62 , 66, 135, 165
Laurdisen, K.V., 171
Laurillard, D., 23, 26
Lays, M., 12, 27
Leithwood, K., 104, 116
Lenning, O.T., 65, 67
Lennon, R.T., 128, 169
Levin, H., 129, 167 a2
Levin, M., 1 01, 116 2
Levitz, R., 111, 117
Lindquist, E.F., 122, 164
Lindsay, P., 129, 171
Lissitz, R.W., 124, 125, 130, 137, 160, 161, 167
Lochead, J., 24
Lowe, A.J., 133, 159, 169
McCollom, F.H., 121, 170
McConkey, D., 101, 117
McDonald, R.T., 47, 67
Macedo, D., 4, 23, 25
MacGinitie, W.H., 164, 169, 181
McGinley, W., 19, 26

McHugh, F., 56, 67
McKinley, N., 53, 67
McMurtie, R.S., 40, 67
McNinch, G.H., 68, 165, 170
McWilliams, L., 152, 169
Madden, D.C., 52, 66, 67
Madden, R., 168, 203, 207
Majer, K., 89, 117
Malak, J.F., 119, 169
Maloney, W.H., 131, 166
Maring, G.H., 98, 117
Marshall, J.D., 9, 26
Martin, D.C., 52, 62, 65
Marzano, R., 7, 26
Maxey, J., 47, 6 7
Maxwell, M., 30, 31, 40, 48, 58t, 60, 62, 67, 80, 86, 87, 90, 106, 112, 117, 131-132, 169
May, M.M., 165, 166, 169, 171
Meister, G., 101, 116
Merriam, H., 117
Mikulecky, L., 54, 65
Miller, W.D., 68, 165
Mitchell, J.V., Jr., 164, 165, 168, 171, 172, 173
Mitchell, K., 20, 25
Moe, A.J., 167
Monroe, W.S., 121, 169
Moore, D.W., 120, 170
Moore, R., 83, 86, 89, 94, 95, 117
Moorman, G., 110, 117
Morante, E.A., 62, 68
Morgan, A., 21, 22, 25
Morris, L., 79, 116
Moses, K., 56, 67
Mouly, C., 97, 112, 117
Moxley, R., 14, 26
Mueller, R., 112, 115
Mullen, J., 169, 170
Muscatine, C., 6
Myers, C., 89, 117
Nacke, P.L., 67, 164
Nayman, R.L., 66
Nelson, M.J., 164, 169, 195
Niles, J.A., 165
Nilsson, L.G., 169
Nist, S., 169, 197
Noble, J., 119, 136, 169
Norman, D., 129, 171
Nurnberg, M., 169, 189
Obler, S.S., 62, 68
Olgivy, J., 7, 27
Ong, W.J., 19, 26
Orasanu, J., 27
Orlando, V.P., 162, 169, 170
O'Rourke, J., 166, 176
Otto, W., 170
Pardy, M., 135, 170
Patton, M., 81, 117
Patton, M.J., 37, 68
Paul, R., 5, 6, 7, 26
Pearson, P.D., 13, 19, 24, 27, 116, 130, 163, 172
Perkins, D., 170, 197
Perry, W.G., Jr., 2, 5, 6, 21, 26, 32, 68, 130, 160, 170
Peters, C.W., 140, 141, 142, 143, 163, 170

Peters, N., 170
Petersen, B.T., 25, 27
Peterson, P., 64, 68
Phillips, G.O., 135, 170
Piaget, J., 21
Pikulski, J.J., 153, 154, 170
Pitts, S.K., 10, 26
Pollock, J.E., 38, 68
Popham, W.J., 116, 131, 170
Presseisen, B., 26
Provus, M., 86, 88, 91, 117
Pugh, S., 15, 27, 40, 68
Rakes, T.A., 152, 169
Randlett, A.L., 62, 68
Rankin, E.F., 152, 170
Rankin, S., 26
Rauch, M., 52, 68
Raygor, A.L., 37, 68, 135, 136, 146, 148, 158, 161, 162, 170, 176, 192, 197, 206
Readance, J.E., 116, 120, 170
Reagan, S., 14, 26
Reed, K.X., 48, 68
Reedy, V., 39, 68
Reid, J., 152, 171
Reynolds, R., 164
Rice, H.D., 132, 170
Riegel, K., 21, 27
Robinson, F.P., 111, 117, 121, 122, 128, 168, 170
Robinson, H.A., 170
Robinson, H.M., 128, 165, 170
Robyak, J.E., 37, 68
Roe, B.D., 118, 119, 153, 165, 170
Rosen, S.S., 46, 68
Rosenblum, M., 169, 189
Ross, E.P., 118, 119, 170
Ross, G.A., 171
Rossi, H., 70, 73, 88, 109, 117
Roueche, J.E., 32, 33, 38, 42, 43, 45, 47, 49, 50, 53, 57, 58t, 67, 68
Roueche, S.D., 34, 42, 44, 47, 48, 49, 50, 53, 58t, 60, 67, 68
Rubin, A., 14, 27
Rubin, R., 50, 67
Rudd, M., 121, 164
Ruddell, R., 167
Rumelhardt, D., 129, 171
Rupley, W.H., 55, 68, 171, 184
Ryan, E.B., 23, 27
Sadden, L.J., 152, 171
Salvatori, M., 17, 27
Sanacore, J., 10, 27
Sawyer, R., 47, 67
Schallert, D., 164
Schank, R.C., 129, 171
Schick, G.B., 165, 166, 169, 171
Schmelzer, R., 38, 68
Schoenberg, B.M., 132, 171
Schreiner, R.L., 128, 135, 171
Schulman, S., 56, 68
Schwalb, B.J., 28, 61, 62, 67, 108, 116
Schwartz, P., 7, 27
Scriven, M., 95, 117
Searfoss, L.W., 152, 154, 167

Seashore, R.H., 121, 171
Shanahan, T., 153, 154, 170
Shank, S., 121, 171
Shanklin, N., 16, 27
Shaw, P., 32, 48, 68
Shea, M.A., 98, 117
Shor, L., 24, 27
Siegel, M., 19, 27
Silverman, S., 102, 117
Simpson, M.L., 33, 68, 131, 145, 161, 163, 171
Singer, H., 128, 16 7, 168
Smith, F., 129, 171, 175
Smith, G.D., 32, 33, 42, 68, 69
Smith, K., 101, 117
Smith, L.J., 32, 56, 65
Smith, S.L., 131, 165
Smith, S.P., 15, 27, 120, 130, 152, 154, 160, 161, 171
Snow, J.J., 32, 33, 38, 43, 45, 49, 57, 58t, 68
Somers, R.L., 64, 69
Spache, G., 128, 171
Spann, M., 77, 117
Spaulding, N.V., 55 , 69
Spearritt, D., 128, 171
Spivey, N., 100, 117
Squire, J.R., 17, 27, 130, 171
Staiger, R.C., 168, 171
Stake, R., 78, 79, 86, 91, 95, 117
Stanley, J.C , 83, 86, 87, 89, 116
Starch, D., 121, 171
Starks, G., 62, 69
Stefurak, D.W., 133, 159, 169
Stephens, E.C., 154, 171
Sternberg, R., 26
Sternglass, M., 15, 27
Stetson, E.G., 149, 162, 171
Stewart, E.W., 132, 171
Stockford, L.B.O., 121, 171
Stotsky, S., 9, 11, 27
Stufflebeam, D., 82, 86, 87, 88, 89, 92, 117
Suen, H., 100, 117
Sugimoto, R., 69
Suhor, C., 26
Sullivan, L.L., 34, 43, 69, 118, 171
Swanson, D.E., 129, 171
Swartz, B.K., 121, 171
Sweiger, J.D., 133, 159, 171
Swetnam, L., 170
Taschow, H.G., 132, 172
Taule, J.M., 25
Taylor, E., 172, 189
Taylor, L., 21, 22, 25
Thomas, K., 110, 117
Thompson, C., 77, 117
Thorndike, E.L., 121, 172
Thurston, A.L., 169
Thurstone, L.L., 129, 172
Tiegs, E.W., 172, 173
Tierney, R.J., 12, 13, 18, 19, 26, 27, 172, 200, 206
Tinker, M.A., 122, 172
Tittle, C.K., 135, 172
Tomlinson, B., 51, 52, 55, 66, 69
Townsend, B.S., 40, 69

Traxler, A.E., 129, 172
Triggs, F.O., 31, 53, 69, 122, 172
Trosky, O., 13, 27
Tucker, J., 62, 69
Tuinman, J.J., 138, 164, 166, 168
Valencia, S., 130, 161, 163, 172
van Doren, C., 2, 24
Van Meter, B.J., 133, 136, 172
Van Roekel, B.H., 172, 206
Vipond, D., 134, 169
Walker, C., 42, 44, 46, 69
Walvekar, C., 80, 81-82, 86, 116, 117
Wark, D.M., 145, 172
Warner, D.A., 98, 117
Waterhouse, L.H., 23, 27
Weaver, D.R., 171
Webb, M.W., 135, 172, 188, 197, 206
Wehrle, P., 99, 100, 116
Wepner, S., 99, 100, 116
White, C.E., 172, 189
White, W.F., 39, 69
White, W.G., 30, 66
Wilkinson, B.L., 38, 68
Willow, D., 112, 116,
Winograd, T., 129, 172
Wittrock, M.C., 19, 27
Wolf, W., 128, 172
Wolfe, R.F., 52, 53, 69, 100, 117
Wood, C., 13, 27
Wood, K , 119, 120, 147, 162, 173
Woods, J.C., 47, 69
Woodward, V., 20, 25
Worting, A., 18, 27
Wright, D.A., 34, 42, 69
Wright, G.L., 132, 173
Ysseldyke, J.E., 173, 200, 206
Zaccarea, L., 165

Author Index

Subject Index

Note: "Mc" is alphabetized as "Mac." A "t" following a page number indicates that the reference may be found in a table.

ACADEMIC LITERACY: cognitive view, 9; cultural literacy, 5-7; definitions, 2-4; knowledge theories, relation to, 8; processes, language/thinking connections, 22-24; research trends, 12, 16-18; studies, 8-9. *See also* Macrological studies; Micrological studies; Writing

ADMINISTRATIVE ORGANIZATION: learning assistance programs, 38-39, 41-45

ADVANCED READING INVENTORY (1981), 153

AMERICAN COLLEGE TESTING PROGRAM (ACT), 47, 48, 99, 119

BURNS/ROE INFORMAL READING INVENTORY (1985), 153

CALIFORNIA ACHIEVEMENT TEST (CAT), LEVEL 5 (1970 EDITION), 173-176

CALIFORNIA ACHIEVEMENT TEST (CAT), LEVELS 19 & 20 (1985 EDITION), 176-178

COLLEGE READING TESTS: origins of, 120-122; purposes, 119-120; research, need for, 161-163; selection options, 122-127; types, 122-124. *See also* Commercial reading tests; (Individual test titles); Test reviews

COMMERCIAL READING TESTS: evaluation criteria, 138-139; item analysis, 147-148; local norms,149-150; norms, evaluation of, 139-140; readability levels, 146; reliability, 140-141; reviews, 173-210; scaled scores, 150-151; selection criteria, 146-147; time limits, effects of, 148-149; validity, 141-146. *See also* College reading tests; (individual test titles); Test reviews

COOPERATIVE ENGLISH TESTS—READING (1960), 138

COUNSELING SERVICES: learning assistance programs, 36-38

CRITICAL THINKING SKILLS: literacy, relation to, 4-7; micrological versus macrological, 5; underpreparation of entering undergraduates, 1-2. *See also* Knowledge

CULTURAL LITERACY. *See* Academic literacy

DAVIS READING TEST (1961), 138

DEGREES OF READING POWER (DRP) (1983), 134, 145, 179-181

DESANTI CLOZE READING INVENTORY (1986), 153

DEVELOPMENTAL EDUCATION: learning assistance programs, 45-46

DIAGNOSTIC READING TESTS (1947), 133, 138

ETHNOGRAPHIC EVALUATION, 95-96, 112-113

EVALUATION, PROGRAM: criteria, 106-107; guidelines, 102-106; ingredients for program success, 61-62; purposes, 70-71; roles, 72-78; types, 78-82. *See also* Formative evaluation; Qualitative evaluation; Quantitative evaluation; Studies, evaluation; Summative evaluation; Theoretical models, evaluation

FACULTY/STAFF ACADEMIC BACKGROUND: influence on learning assistance programs, 35

FINANCIAL PRESSURES: impact on program evaluation, 75-78

FORMATIVE EVALUATION, 64, 78-80

FUNDING: influence on learning assistance programs, 35

GATES-MACGINITIE READING TESTS, LEVEL F (2ND EDITION), 181-185

GOAL ATTAINMENT SCALING, 100-101

GOVERNMENT AGENCIES: pressure for program evaluation, 73-74

GOVERNMENT POLICIES AND STATUTES: influence on learning assistance programs, 35-36

HIGHER EDUCATION INSTITUTIONS: learning assistance programs and, 36

INDIVIDUALIZED INSTRUCTION: learning assistance programs, 53-55

INFORMAL READING ASSESSMENT, 151-154

INFORMAL READING INVENTORIES (IRIs), 152-154

INSTITUTIONAL POLICY/PHILOSOPHY: influence on learning assistance programs, 35

IOWA SILENT READING TESTS (ISRT), LEVEL 2 (1973 EDITION), 185-188

IOWA SILENT READING TESTS (ISRT), LEVEL 3 (1973 EDITION), 188-192

KNOWLEDGE: views of, 7-8

LEARNING ASSISTANCE PROGRAMS: administration, 41-42; administrative structure, place within, 42-45; admission criteria, 46-49; categories, 29; characteristics, influences on, 34-36; developmental education, emphases, 45-46; faculty development impact, 65; history, 28-32; instructional methods, 53-56; needs, student, 32-33; number and distribution of, 33-34; organizational patterns, 49-53; services offered, 50-53; structures, 36-40; success, ingredients for, 56-57, 58t-59t, 60-62. *See also* Program evaluation

LITERACY. *See* Academic literacy

MCGRAW-HILL BASIC SKILLS READING TEST (1970), 138

MACROLOGICAL STUDIES: learner-constructed knowledge, 21-22; literacy as inquiry, 18-20

MANAGEMENT BY OBJECTIVES, 101

MICROLOGICAL STUDIES: language processes, linking, 13-16; reading/writing connection, 9-12

MINNESOTA READING ASSESSMENT (MRA) (1980), 192-195

NELSON-DENNY READING TEST, 47, 48, 50, 54, 133-136

NELSON-DENNY READING TEST, FORMS A & B (1960), 138

NELSON-DENNY READING TEST, FORMS C & D (1973), 195-197

NELSON-DENNY READING TEST, FORMS E & F (1980), 197-200

NELSON-DENNY READING TEST, EXAMINER'S MANUAL, 145

OUTREACH PROGRAMS: learning assistance programs, 53

PLACEMENT, STUDENT: testing for, 47; voluntary, 48

QUALITATIVE EVALUATION, 80-82

QUANTITATIVE EVALUATION, 80-82

READING ASSESSMENT: grade equivalent scores, 133-134; needs of college students, 130-131; norm-referenced versus criterion-referenced tests, 131-132; product versus process approach, 128-130; technical problems, 134-135; tests, lack of, 135-136; tests, misuse of, 132-133. *See also* Informal reading assessment

READING PROGRAMS. *See* Learning assistance programs

READING PROGRESS SCALE, COLLEGE VERSION (1975), 145, 201-203

READING TESTS: *See* College reading tests

SCHOLASTIC APTITUDE TEST (SAT), 47, 48, 53, 119

SEQUENTIAL TESTS OF EDUCATIONAL PROGRESS: READING (1969), 138

SMALL GROUP INSTRUCTION: learning assistance programs, 55
STANDARDIZED READING TESTS. *See* Commercial reading tests
STANFORD DIAGNOSTIC READING TEST (SDRT), BLUE LEVEL (1976 EDITION), 203-206
STANFORD DIAGNOSTIC READING TEST (SDRT), BLUE LEVEL (1984 EDITION), 207-210
STUDIES, EVALUATION: experimental research, 96-98; nonexperimental, 100-102; quasiexperimental, 84t, 89-91
STUDY SKILLS PROGRAMS. *See* Learning assistance programs
SUMMATIVE EVALUATION, 64, 78-80

TESTING: *See* College reading tests
TEST REVIEWS: conclusions, 155, 156t-157t, 158; implications, 156t-157t, 158; recommendations, 156t-157t; 158-161
THEORETICAL MODELS, EVALUATION: congruency comparison, 85t, 91- 93; cost effectiveness, 85t, 93-94, 101; experimental, 84t, 87-89; goal free/responsive, 85t, 94-96, 102; professional judgment, 83, 84t, 86-87; quasiexperimental, 84t, 89-91
TUTORING: learning assistance programs, 55-56
WRITING: effect on reading, 9-12, 16; integration with reading, 16-18

Subject Index